D1551597

The Christians Who Became Jews

SYNKRISIS

Comparative Approaches to Early Christianity in Greco-Roman Culture

SERIES EDITORS

Dale B. Martin (Yale University) and L. L. Welborn (Fordham University)

Synkrisis is a project that invites scholars of early Christianity and the Greco-Roman world to collaborate toward the goal of rigorous comparison. Each volume in the series provides immersion in an aspect of Greco-Roman culture, so as to make possible a comparison of the controlling logics that emerge from the discourses of Greco-Roman and early Christian writers. In contrast to older "history of religions" approaches, which looked for similarities between religions in order to posit relations of influence and dependency, Synkrisis embraces a fuller conception of the complexities of culture, viewing Greco-Roman religions and early Christianity as members of a comparative class. The differential comparisons promoted by Synkrisis may serve to refine and correct the theoretical and historical models employed by scholars who seek to understand and interpret the Greco-Roman world. With its allusion to the rhetorical exercises of the Greco-Roman world, the series title recognizes that the comparative enterprise is a construction of the scholar's mind and serves the scholar's theoretical interests.

EDITORIAL BOARD

Loveday Alexander (Sheffield University)
John Bodel (Brown University)
Kimberly Bowes (University of Pennsylvania)
Daniel Boyarin (University of California, Berkeley)
Fritz Graf (Ohio State University)
Ronald F. Hock (University of Southern California)
Hans-Josef Klauck (University of Chicago)
Angela Standhartinger (Marburg University)
Stanley K. Stowers (Brown University)

The Christians
Who Became Jews

*Acts of the Apostles and
Ethnicity in the Roman City*

Christopher Stroup

Yale

UNIVERSITY PRESS

New Haven & London

Published with assistance from the foundation established in memory of
Amasa Stone Mather of the Class of 1907, Yale College.

Copyright © 2020 by Yale University.
All rights reserved.
This book may not be reproduced, in whole or in part, including illustrations, in any
form (beyond that copying permitted by Sections 107 and 108 of the U.S. Copyright Law
and except by reviewers for the public press), without written permission from
the publishers.

Yale University Press books may be purchased in quantity for educational, business, or
promotional use. For information, please e-mail sales.press@yale.edu (U.S. office) or
sales@yaleup.co.uk (U.K. office).

Set in Monotype Bulmer type by Westchester Publishing Services.
Printed in the United States of America.

Library of Congress Control Number: 2019947773
ISBN 978-0-300-24789-3 (hardcover : alk. paper)

A catalogue record for this book is available from the British Library.

This paper meets the requirements of ANSI/NISO Z39.48-1992 (Permanence of Paper).

10 9 8 7 6 5 4 3 2 1

For Amy

Contents

Preface

THE CITY OF APHRODISIAS IN CARIA, located in modern-day Turkey, holds a distinctive place in descriptions of the expansion and consolidation of Roman influence in Asia Minor. Archeological evidence suggests that just as Rome was solidifying its power in the region, the city began redefining its own identity in terms of Rome. By a stroke of good luck, the city became an early supporter of the Roman armies before it was clear that they would prevail as the dominant force in the region. This early support along with some other important connections put the city on favorable terms with Rome for generations to come. As with all political, religious, and social relationships, however, Aphrodisias was under constant threat of the disruption of its desirable status quo. Emperors changed, regional powers shifted, and other cities made claims on the city's privileged place in the imperial hierarchy.

Sometime during the second or third century CE, the leaders of Aphrodisias responded to these pressures by approving the inscription of a collection of documents on the city's theater wall. With documents spanning more than two hundred years, the monumental inscription charted the city's relatively recent history emphasizing the city's connection to Rome and the Roman emperors. Some of the documents are short letters to Aphrodisian leaders while others are correspondences between emperors and their generals or the leaders of other cities, but each document in its own way presents a curated history of Aphrodisias and the city's privileged place in the Roman hierarchy. At the top of this archive wall, in large letters, a phrase that seems to capture the archive's intent is inscribed: ΑΓΑΘΗ ΤΥΧΗ, "good luck."

The Aphrodisians seemed intent on creating their own good luck by retelling their city's story in Roman terms. Taken as an archive, the inscriptions tell us that Aphrodisias was not only the city of the great goddess

Aphrodite but also a city protected by Augustus, that Rome was protecting Aphrodisias from its enemies near and far, and that the emperors would come to the rescue if anyone willed the city harm. By placing the archive in the public theater space, Aphrodisias found a means of locating itself within the greater order of the Roman Empire. The city's place was literally inscribed in its cultural center. By resurrecting and publicly displaying these documents, some of which were hundreds of years old, Aphrodisias found a way to intertwine its own history with Rome's. This had the power not only to shape the story of the relationship between Aphrodisias and Rome, but also to retell how the two cities could be perceived and conceived of relating. By inscribing an archive of the city's history with Rome in a public space, Aphrodisias was able to build its identity around the space it shared or desired to share with Rome. In a sense, this allowed Aphrodisias to exist on the same map as Rome. Through the selection and arrangement of inscribed documents, Aphrodisians crafted how their city's citizens understood and interpreted their history and their place in the Roman world. As a central place of public gathering and entertainment, the theater was an ideal location for the dissemination of civic knowledge and ideology. The archive was more than a repository of historical obscurities. It provided Aphrodisians with a way to construct their reality in political, religious, and ethnic terms.

The archive wall was not the only place that Aphrodisians retold the story of their connection with Rome, as we shall see later in this book. And Aphrodisias was not alone in this impulse. Material evidence from the ancient world is filled with similar identity negotiations that leverage the power of gods, people, and places and in the end have the power to make innovative changes to identity, especially with the arrival of Greek culture in the fifth and fourth centuries BCE and the Roman armies in the second and first centuries BCE. The central thrust of this book is that a close examination of such material evidence and the identity negotiations that take place through physical objects can provide us with new ways of looking at familiar literary documents from the ancient world, especially the documents that have come to be collected in the Christian Bible. The author of the Acts of the Apostles, like the Aphrodisian elites who approved the archive wall inscriptions, had to situate his new group, the Christians, within Roman, religious, and civic hierarchies. While the Aphrodisians could look to a past connection with Rome, the author of Acts was faced with the difficult challenge of telling the story of a new association in a time when Romans looked suspiciously on new and foreign religious movements. Like the Aphrodisians, the author leverages the power of gods, ancestry, and locations to legitimate Christian identity, and I argue that in the telling of his history, Christians became Jews. That is the story of this book.

As with most meaningful endeavors, this book would be a shadow of its current form without the numerous people who invested their time and energy in me and my work. It began as a dissertation under the supervision of Jennifer Wright Knust and James C. Walters at Boston University. Jenny supervised the completion of this dissertation, ushering me through a significant final revision with her incisive, supportive, and timely feedback. Her interest in my project and thoughtful questions strengthened every aspect of this book. James opened my eyes to the importance of material evidence and helped me see ancient Christian texts in a new way. I am grateful for the direction that he provided during this book's various phases through his supervision, perceptive feedback, and guidance.

Many others at Boston University and beyond also have provided feedback at various points during this book's development. Jonathan Klawans commented on drafts of multiple chapters, contributed greatly to the current shape of the project, and offered sound advice on numerous occasions. Paula Fredriksen, whose influence is apparent throughout this project, commented on drafts of multiple chapters and spent many hours discussing ancient Christian views of Jews and Judaism with me. Denise Kimber Buell generously served as an external reader for the dissertation defense.

Many others have read or heard portions of this book at various stages. I thank in particular Loveday Alexander, Harold Attridge, Eric Barreto, John Collins, Nate DesRosiers, Eldon J. Epp, David Frankfurter, Steve Friesen, Dale Martin, Tessa Rajak, Dan Schowalter, Steve Walton, Larry Wills, Adela Yarbro Collins, and the late François Bovon. It was in François's doctoral seminar on Acts that I stumbled upon the initial research that eventually developed into this book. His characteristically kind encouragement and gentle guidance saved me from many pitfalls at the initial stage of research.

I have been fortunate to present my work and receive feedback through presentations in the Book of Acts, Speech and Rhetoric, and Archaeology of Religion sections of the Society of Biblical Literature; the New England and Eastern Canada region of the SBL; and the Theoretical Roman Archeology Conference (TRAC). I am also grateful for the insightful comments provided by the external reviewers; Heather Gold, Susan Laity, and Jessie Dolch of Yale University Press; Larry Welborn, co-editor of the Synkrisis series; Caitlin Lubinski, who helped edit multiple chapters; and Zachary Smith, who also compiled the indexes.

Many colleagues and friends have been my dialogue partners and an enormous source of joy throughout the various stages of this book. I thank in particular Jason Adams, Chris Allison, Jonathan Bailes, Mark Booker, Alan Briggs, Michael Cover, Andrew Davis, David Decosimo, Michal Beth Dinkler, David Eastman, Linford Fisher, Justus Ghormley, Meghan Henning, Andrew Henry, Chris Hoklotubbe, Jason Hood, Dave Horner, Ryan Knowles, Jonathan Koefed, Charith Peris, Matt Sigler, Courtney Wilson VanVeller, Sam Wood, and Terry Yin.

Many of the revisions for this book were completed while I served as assistant editor of *New Testament Abstracts* and assistant research professor of New Testament at the Boston College School of Theology and Ministry. I thank John Baldovin, Dick Clifford, Andrew Davis, Angela Harkins, Chris Matthews, and Tom Stegman for their continued encouragement and support of me and my teaching, research, and writing.

Last and most important, I thank my family for the unconditional support they continue to provide. My parents, Steve and Ginger, and in-laws, Bill and Mary Lee Moritz, have been a constant source of encouragement, wisdom, and perfectly timed support. Thank you for believing in me long before the outcome of this journey was clear. My brothers, Mark and Paul; brothers-in-law, Josh and Kevin; and sisters-in-law, Joni, Sarah, Ashley, and Erin, continue to inspire me in so many ways. Thank you. My children, Micah, Livia, and Calvin, are a source of joy and a welcome reminder that there is so much more to life beyond the walls of my office. Amy, my best friend and the love of my life, never ceases to amaze me with her strength, wisdom, and compassion, especially when I was in the depths of writing, editing, and revising. It is to her that I dedicate this book.

Note on Abbreviations

IN THE TEXT AND NOTES I USE the abbreviations for journal titles and primary sources in *The SBL Handbook of Style* (2nd ed.; Atlanta: SBL, 2014). All other journal titles are given in full. References to the Greek text of the New Testament follow *Novum Testamentum Graece* (28th ed., Nestle-Aland), and references to the Septuagint follow Alfred Rahlfs, *Septuaginta* (Stuttgart: Deutsche Bibelgesellschaft, 1979), unless noted otherwise. All English translations are mine unless noted.

The Christians Who Became Jews

Jews and Christians in the Polis

SPREADING OUT FROM THE SHORES OF the Mediterranean
Sea, the cities of the Roman Empire were filled with gods and the citizens
who honored them with festivals, processions, buildings, and benefactions. The followers of Jesus—later called Christians—lived and moved in
these cities, navigating avenues lined with statues honoring various deities, organizing their days and months around the feast days that struc-
tured civic calendars, and wandering past (and through) the many temples
and shrines that populated the busy urban landscape.[1] The importance of
this urban context should not be overlooked: civic, ethnic, and religious
identities were intertwined with these visible, material, and practical signs
of communal life, wherever one was placed within the city's bustling topography. Connections between life in the city and daily religious practices were therefore fundamental to the development of Christian identity.
A primary focus on literary sources by recent scholars has tended to mask
this broader religious, cultural, and civic setting by not taking into account the possible impacts of materiality on authors. This has left the impression that categories like "Christian," "Jew," and "pagan" were
recognizably bounded groups, fixed identities known to those who held
them and also visible to outsiders.[2] In reality, identities were highly contested and negotiable. They were enacted by writers with distinctive rhetorical goals who operated within this broader culture of civic-religious
engagement.

In this book, I compare the literary construction of Jewish and Christian identity in Acts of the Apostles with the material construction of various ethnic and civic identities by inhabitants of Roman-era cities. From this

comparison, I argue that the writer of Acts, like others living within urban Roman environments, negotiated ethnic similarities and differences in light of preconceptions about god(s), ancestry and tradition, and geography. The author of Acts, I contend, uses a connection between gods, people, and place to strategically represent Jewish identity as hybrid in order to identify all Jesus followers, both Jews and non-Jews, as Jewish.[3] At the same time, the writer creates an internal distinction between Jesus followers and other Jews, which privileges "Christians" as the members of an ideal, unified Jewish community and contrasts them with what are identified as factious, local Jewish "associations," a term that I use strategically in place of "synagogues" to identify local Jewish communities.[4]

With this book, I seek to intervene in the all-too-common scholarly reception of first- and second-century Christian identity as nonethnic.[5] On one hand, I argue that Acts attempts to identify all Jesus followers as Jews in order to place them in the hierarchical, god-infused urban landscape. Jesus followers are now a type of urban Jew. On the other hand, I contend that the author of Acts endeavors to differentiate his Jesus-following Jews from other Jews in cities. The followers of Jesus do not make up just another Jewish community; rather, being a Jesus follower is a better way of being Jewish, the author claims. This double deployment of Jewishness by Luke pushes against interpretations that view Acts as anti-Jewish rather than intra-Jewish, while at that same time instilling an incipient supersessionist impulse in the author's description of Christian origins. Ancient and modern Christians have deployed such an impulse in anti-Jewish ways on numerous occasions.[6] An examination of the long and tragic history of anti-Jewish interpretations of Acts is beyond the scope of this book, but it is my hope that juxtaposing the representation of Jewish and Christian identity in Acts with material remains from contemporaneous environments will highlight the centrality of claims about ethnic identity for both early Christians and inhabitants of first- and second-century cities. Such ethnic claims not only shaped contemporaneous contexts but also have had a lasting impact on overt and hidden racial and racist theories that litter Western history and are still perpetuated today.

I offer three contributions to the study of Acts and in turn the study of ancient Christianity more broadly. First, I bring the study of Acts into conversation with recent contributions to the study of Roman-era civic religious activity, with a particular focus on material evidence. Scholars have long noted that the narrative of Acts revolves around urban centers, but much more can be said both about the ways that the veneration of civic and ancestral gods classified populations and about how the writer of Acts worked within these classificatory systems to define the contours of "Jew" and "Christian."[7] Second, I demonstrate that Acts identifies Jews in multiple, complex ways throughout the book rather than as a unified stereotyped entity of "the Jews." These representations of Jewish identity are not tangential to the larger narrative program of the writer of Acts; as I argue, they are significant for understanding the way that Acts frames Christian identity. Finally, using Paul's interactions with Jewish communities in three cities as an example, I demonstrate that Acts arranges Paul's movements through Roman civic landscapes in ways that privilege Christians as a unified and legitimate embodiment of Jewishness within the *polis*—the idealized urban and cultural centers of the Roman era.[8] What I offer in this book, therefore, is a recontextualization of the interpretation of Acts and Jewish identity within larger Roman-era discourses that configured the relations between gods and humans along ancestral and civic lines.[9]

Religious, Ethnic, and Civic Identity

In recent decades, scholars of ancient Christianity have noted the importance of ethnicity and ethnic rhetoric to the formation of ancient Christian identity.[10] As a continuation of that scholarship, I argue that Acts represents Jewish identity as hybrid and multiple in order to situate the earliest Christians within the Greco-Roman city as members of an ideal Jewish community, which was both ancestral and accepted in the city. To the author of Acts, becoming a Christian changed the ethnicity of non-Jews, similar to the way that proselytes underwent an ethnic change when they adopted particular Jewish practices and became Jews.[11] This argument develops out of two theoretical assumptions. First, ethnicity and civic identity are flexible categories that are rhetorically and practically constructed in strategic ways.[12] Second, what scholars commonly call "religion" was central to the maintenance of ethnic and civic identity in the world of early Christianity.

Sociologists and anthropologists—along with many archeologists, classicists, ancient historians, and scholars of Hellenistic Judaism and ancient Christianity—now view ethnicity as socially constructed rather than as given or essential. Sociologist Rogers Brubaker calls ethnicity "relational, processual, dynamic, eventful, and disaggregated" rather than primordial or unchanging.[13] Anthropologist Richard Jenkins defines ethnicity as a "collective identification that is socially constructed in the articulation of purported cultural similarity and difference."[14] Classicist Jonathan Hall comments, "Ethnic identity is not a 'natural' fact of life; it is something that needs to be actively proclaimed, reclaimed and disclaimed through discursive channels."[15] Shaye Cohen, scholar of ancient Judaism, agrees with sociologists who say that "ethnic or national identity is imagined; it exists because certain persons want it to exist and believe it exists."[16] Scholar of ancient Christianity Denise Buell observes, "changes in how races and ethnicities are defined over time indicates that they are in fact social creations and not eternal realities."[17] Ethnic identities, including Greek, Roman, and Jewish identities, are socially constructed.

Yet modern scholars also differ in their understanding of how ethnic identities are socially constructed. Some, like Anthony D. Smith, have focused on common features in articulating ethnic differences, such as commonalities in names, ancestry myths, shared culture, links to a homeland, and a sense of solidarity.[18] According to this view, ethnicities are constructed in relation to the putative "core" of a given people group. Other scholars, notably Fredrik Barth, have emphasized the role that differences between groups and group boundaries play when determining ethnic identity.[19] From this perspective, ethnicities are fashioned in relation to outsiders who serve as the backdrop against which insiders can recognize and perform their own cultural difference.

Others have paid close attention to how discourses of ethnicity "rely upon the notion of fixity or primordiality even while they are always under negotiation and flux."[20] This viewpoint posits ethnicities that are continually formed and re-formed through appeals to a fixed "core" and to set boundaries, yet they remain flexible in practice and in representation.[21] They are continually negotiated and renegotiated by both insiders and outsiders in a given context. As postcolonial theorists have long noted, however, the putative "core" and supposed boundaries of ethnic identifications change as rhetorical situations change.[22] Thus authors use ethnic rhetoric to define and defend where boundaries lie and what constitutes the "core" of a given group. Viewing ethnicities as both flexible and rhetorically fixed in specific situations provides a means of analyzing ethnic identifications that moves beyond discussion of various definitions of the "core" and boundaries of a given people group to an examination of how ethnic identity is used in a given rhetorical situation.

ETHNIC REASONING AND THE RHETORIC OF IDENTITY

Denise Buell has proposed one helpful way to navigate this complex topic in her book on ancient Christian self-definition *Why This New Race? Ethnic Reasoning in Early Christianity*.[23] Buell observes that ancient Christians regularly identified themselves in ways similar to ethnic groups. This contradicts the still pervasive scholarly view that ancient Christian identity was a religious identity that somehow transcended ethnic categorization.[24] The Christian use of ethnic language raises an important question: If ancient Christians used language typically associated with ethnic groups, how can Christians (as relative newcomers) compare with people groups like the Jews that had existed for generations? Buell's concept of "ethnic reasoning" helps answer this question.

"Ethnic reasoning" refers to the rhetoric of peoplehood that ancients used to communicate and persuade others about identity. Moreover, it describes the varying ways that ancients used the rhetoric of peoplehood to assert and negotiate identity in specific rhetorical situations.[25] Though Buell focuses her attention on the use of ethnic reasoning by ancient Christians, the concept extends to discussions of other populations that scholars do not usually identify as associated with an ethnic category, such as

Romans or Corinthians, and to the ways they also used the rhetoric of ethnicity to make claims about their identities.[26] Ancients employed what
Buell calls ethnic reasoning to assert what scholars now classify as ethnic,
religious, civic, and cultural identities.

Ethnic reasoning thus provides a way to read evidence and compare
ethnic rhetoric that extends beyond "ethnic groups" to include religious,
civic, and ethnic designations. An examination of ethnic reasoning also invites a careful account of how people groups use other populations rhetorically to maintain their own identities. For example, Greeks and Romans
famously portrayed other ethnic groups as uncivilized "barbarians" in order to support their imperial expansions.[27] These "barbarians" then used
education and culture to claim to be Greeks or Romans and to distinguish
themselves from their fellow "barbarians."[28] Likewise, ancient Christians
could distinguish themselves from Jews while at the same time claiming
the Jewish God, Jewish history, and the Jewish scriptures as their own.[29]
Jews also used ethnic rhetoric in the way that they asserted multiple ethnic identities. Jews in Alexandria, for example, could claim to be simultaneously Alexandrians and Jews, while other inhabitants of the city could
assert that Jews were not Alexandrians but were in fact outcasts like the despised Egyptians.[30] Reading each of these situations as a form of ethnic
reasoning provides a means of moving between discrete modern categories
like ethnicity, religion, civic identity, and cultural identity in ways that take
into account the hybrid ethnic rhetoric already inscribed in ancient texts
and material remains.

"RELIGION" AND THE PRODUCTION OF ETHNIC AND CIVIC IDENTITY

Inhabitants of Roman-era cities enacted ethnic and civic identities in part
through religious activity, and attention to the ways that first- and second-
century inhabitants of Roman cities used religious, ethnic, and civic identity demonstrates the inextricable connection between categories that
scholars regularly treat as separate. Affiliation with a particular god or cult
was one important means of asserting and maintaining identity, and the

veneration of a god or gods created and established commonalities that allowed ancients to define populations in both ethnic and civic terms. In the words of Arthur Darby Nock, "The gods of a people were one of its attributes" and "a city honoured certain deities to whom it looked for the satisfaction of its need."[31]

In antiquity, religious activities were not only used in the maintenance of ethnic and civic identities, but they were central to their production. Buell writes, "By the first century C.E., religion was well established as a public discourse that was especially useful for asserting, contesting, and transforming ethnoracial as well as civic identities across the Mediterranean basin. How and who one worshipped could indicate or create one's ethnoracial and/or civic membership, even as it was viewed as a product of that membership." She highlights four ways that religious identity was useful for the production of ethnic and civic identity in the ancient world: "(1) to mark differences between groups, helping to produce a collective civic or ethnoracial identity—especially under conditions of colonialism and diaspora; (2) to enable ethnoracial transformations; (3) to establish connections between otherwise distinctive groups; and (4) to assert and regulate differences within groups." She goes on to state, "While these functions cannot always be neatly distinguished and are often intertwined in a given text, it is useful to note how religion gets defined in ways that make it suitable for both asserting fixity and enacting and negotiating ethnoracial fluidity."[32]

Buell's claim is useful for analysis of Acts in a number of ways. For example, in Acts 7, the author presents a speech of the disciple Stephen that recounts a selective Jewish history and shifts from the first person ("we"/"our") to the second ("you"/"your") at a particularly prominent point. The sudden change from "our ancestors" (πατέρες ἡμῶν) to "your ancestors" (παρέρες ὑμῶν) constructs and regulates a difference among Jews. "Our ancestors" support the Holy Spirit and the prophets, while "your ancestors" always (ἀεί) oppose the former and persecute the latter (7:51–52). This contrast does not mark a difference in ethnic identity—all of those discussed are still Jews. Rather, it uses specific aspects of Jewish religiosity, the work of the Holy Spirit and the role of the prophets, to make an internal distinction among Jews.[33] Moreover, what at the beginning of the speech was a shared, fixed identity has become in the context of the speech a divided identity.[34] As this brief example shows, paying attention to how religious activities function in the production of ethnic identity by focusing on the use of ethnic reasoning offers a helpful way of examining Jewish identity in Acts. The theoretical frame of ethnic reasoning allows a comparison between the negotiation of Jewish identity in Acts with similar negotiations of identities that were occurring in cities across the Roman world. In the Roman world civic elites used religious ideology to negotiate civic identity by moving between claims of ethnic fixity and ethnic fluidity in ways similar to the writer of Acts.[35]

In this book I assert that ethnic and civic identities are constructed rather than unchanging and that they are central to who makes up the "core" of an ethnic group and where boundaries of that ethnic group are located. Paying attention to the specific ways that different situations represent these identities as fixed, fluid, and/or hybrid highlights the construction of ethnicity and civic identity and illuminates a given writer's specific rhetorical strategies. Buell's concept of ethnic reasoning is helpful for investigating evidence that uses ethnic language to negotiate what moderns would consider nonethnic identities, like religious or civic identities. Rather than existing as a discrete category, what is commonly called "religion" played a significant role in the negotiation of ethnicity and civic identity in the ancient world. Careful attention to the way religious ideology was used in the production of these identities is needed in the reexamination of many well-worn topics in the study of the New Testament and ancient Christianity, like Jewish and Christian identities in Acts.[36]

Reading Acts and Reading the City

The place of composition and the location of the intended audience of Acts are unknown.[37] Nonetheless, it is probable that it was written in the context of a *polis*. Cities and civic life play an important role in the development of the narrative generally, and as I argue in chapter 4, Acts constructs Jewish and Christian identity according to recognizable civic norms and practices.[38] Moreover, the author of Acts, like most ancient Christians, likely lived in one of the god-filled cities of the Roman Empire. This means that his (the writer was most likely male) religious world would have been shaped by religious activity in the city.[39] Thus, my analysis of Acts emphasizes a comparison with material evidence from Roman-era cities. It "reads" Acts and material remains together in order to better understand the historical, social, and cultural contexts from which the representations of Jews in Acts arose. By reading Acts alongside material remains, I am able to better examine how Acts is similar to and differs from its surrounding urban context in its use of ethnic reasoning.[40]

Many scholars have employed archeological evidence in their interpretation of Acts.[41] Much of this work, however, has sought either to validate the historicity of Acts or to shed some insight on specific details of the text. For example, Acts depicts a disturbance in Ephesus that developed because of Paul's preaching (19:23–41). According to the writer, members of the local guild of silversmiths became frustrated with the decline in sales of their statues of Artemis because people were persuaded by Paul's claim that "things made with hands are not gods" (οὐκ εἰσὶν θεοὶ οἱ διὰ χειρῶν γινόμενοι) (19:26), and a disturbance arose. As a result, a riotous mob rushed to the city theater (19:29). Alexander, a local Jew, tried to speak to the crowd, but his words were drowned out by the shouts of the gathered mass: "Great is Artemis of the Ephesians!" (μεγάλη ἡ Ἄρτεμις Ἐφεσίων) (19:34). A city clerk (γραμματεύς) finally calmed the assembly and reassured them that Paul's claims did not threaten the glory of Artemis (19:35–41). Nothing could diminish the glory of the great goddess.[42]

This vivid narrative has provided commentators with ample opportunity to discuss archeological evidence like the historical theater in Ephesus, even if their primary interest is in the Acts story.[43] Paul Trebilco, for example, writes: "The theatre in Ephesus was built into the western slope of Mt. Pion, and was 154m in width with an auditorium 38m in height. The seating capacity was perhaps 20,000. The theatre was constructed in the first half of the third century B.C., enlarged under Claudius (41–54 A.D.), other changes were made under Nero (54–68 A.D.), and Trajan (98–117 A.D.), so the riot may well have occurred while the theatre was undergoing alterations."[44] Trebilco accurately describes the city's historical theater.[45] Such descriptions provide a plausible historical context for the specific story of Paul in Ephesus; and if Richard Pervo's suggestion that Acts was written in Ephesus or its environs is correct, the author of Acts certainly would have known this theater well.[46] Connecting a scene described in Acts with the archeological remains in Ephesus is helpful for introducing modern readers to the *realia* of the ancient world; however, such descriptions do not provide comparative material for analysis of the rhetoric of Acts. Archeology serves as a support rather than as a guide for interpretation.[47]

I approach the relationship between Acts and archeology differently. I take both literary and archeological evidence as representational and strategic. Thus, I do not aim to present archeology as a privileged site of the "real" that can be employed to verify a literary account; instead, I view material like both the story of Paul in Ephesus and the theater in Ephesus as strategic presentations shaped by the intentions of specific individuals in specific social and cultural contexts.

Rather than describing the archeological features of a monument mentioned in Acts, such as the theater of Ephesus, I examine material evidence and argue that material remains and texts (like Acts) share a similar complex of ideas, strategies, and practices that were used to navigate claims of peoplehood. Unlike some other interpretive studies that engage archeology, reading Acts and material remains together does not imply that the author directly interacted with, or even knew of, the archeological material discussed. Adopting the approach developed by Laura Nasrallah, I draw literary and material evidence together so that "we can overhear and glimpse the discursive world in which literature, images, and architecture were produced, and among which both Christians and non-Christians formulated their arguments."[48] The writer's discursive world is the same as that of the producers of material culture, and both engaged and interacted with their larger social, cultural, and discursive contexts.

Therefore, in order to better appreciate and understand the construction of Jewish identity in Acts, I compare how religious and ethnic rhetoric are employed in the negotiation of Jewish identity in Acts with how religious and ethnic rhetoric are used in the negotiation of civic identity in material remains. I do this while reading both texts and material evidence as representational artifacts. The concept of ethnic reasoning provides a way to explore how ancient inhabitants of Roman-era cities used religious activities and imagery to construct ethnic and civic identities; it also provides a theoretical justification for this methodological decision to regard archeology and literary works as products that can be read side by side. They participate in the same ethnic discourse.

Of course, I am selective in my use of material evidence in this book. I focus on two examples from the vast amount of material evidence available that are particularly illuminating when comparing the ways that ethnic identity is delimited in Acts and in the context of Greek cities in Asia Minor: the Sebasteion (imperial temple complex) in Aphrodisias of Caria, and the Salutaris Foundation inscription from Ephesus. These two pieces of evidence are valuable for my work for a number of reasons. First, as I argue in subsequent chapters, both the temple complex and the inscription employ each of Buell's four observed uses of religious activity in ethnic reasoning. They (1) mark difference and produce a collective civic identity, (2) negotiate ethnic change, (3) form connections between previously distinct groups, and (4) establish and manage differences between groups.[49] Second, both pieces of evidence were created within a generation or two of the composition of Acts, assuming a late-first-century/early-second-century CE date for Acts.[50] Third, both pieces of evidence are from the Greek East, in particular the Roman province of Asia. This geographical parameter is useful because a number of scholars point to Asia as a likely location for the composition of Acts, thus narrowing the discursive overlap.[51]

By comparing literary and material remains in this way, I am able to analyze the ways that Jewish identity in Acts is culturally informed in order to delineate the author's contributions to both Jewish identity and Christian identity. As subsequent chapters demonstrate, a comparison of Acts with the Sebasteion and Salutaris Foundation inscription provides a new contextual framework for understanding the negotiation of religious, ethnic, and civic identities in Acts and the formation of Christian identity.

Jews and Non-Jews

Before diving into such a comparison, I need to address a looming issue important for the study of Acts. In recent years, some scholars of Acts have begun using the term "Judean" rather than "Jew" to translate the Greek term Ἰουδαῖος (*Ioudaios*).[52] This reflects a lively scholarly debate that has arisen around the translation of the term among scholars of Hellenistic Judaism and ancient Christianity.[53] Scholars proposing that "Judean" is a better alternative to "Jew" claim that Ἰουδαῖος was a geographic and ethnic term; therefore, "Judean" preserves the connection between geography and ethnicity better than "Jew," which is a religious term anachronistically applied to what was in fact an ethnic, geographical, and political designation, as well as a religious one.[54]

Those who defend "Jew" as a better translation, however, contend that the term is both an ethnic and a religious word that best reflects the range of meaning of Ἰουδαῖος. This was a religious term, they insist, and the category can contain ethnic as well as political overtones.[55] The distinction between the two English terms hinges on the separation between religion and ethnicity that is common in much modern scholarship but was unknown in antiquity. As Caroline Johnson Hodge observes, "the debates about translating [Ἰουδαῖος] illustrate just how entrenched the religion/ethnicity dichotomy is in our thinking."[56] Thus, the problem rests not in translation but in the modern categories of religion and ethnicity, which separate religious activities from political activities and ethnic identity from cultural identity. Acknowledging that both "Judean" and "Jew" have specific weaknesses, I use the terms "Jew" and "Jewish" throughout.[57]

Related to this decision, I use the term "non-Jews" to identify those whom ancient Greek-speaking Jews usually termed ἔθνη (*ethnē*). Simply put, ἔθνη in Second Temple Jewish literature meant "non-Jews," which in antiquity would have been roughly synonymous with "gentiles"; but with the advent of Christianity, gentiles came to be a term used to identify Christians in contrast with Jews. Thus, unlike the issues surrounding Ἰουδαῖος, my choice to use "non-Jews" is *not* primarily an issue of translation. A number of other factors influence my decision. First, the Greek word ἔθνη is usually translated as "gentiles."[58] Ἔθνη is the plural form of ἔθνος, which is usually translated as "nation" or "people." The singular form of ἔθνος is a general category used to identify various people groups, while the plural (in Jewish and Christian literature) is a contrasting term used to distinguish "everyone else" from one group, Jews.[59] When ancient Jewish and Christian texts use ἔθνη, the word (frequently) distinguishes between those who are Jews and those who are not, that is, non-Jews.[60] Luke regularly uses ἔθνη in this way in Acts.[61]

Second, in the study of ancient Christianity, "gentile" often carries supersessionist Christian meaning.[62] In the second century CE and beyond, ancient Christians began formalizing distinctions between Christians and Jews partly on the basis of the claim that Christianity made the salvation of the God of Israel available to "gentiles" (ἔθνη and *gens*).[63] Justin Martyr, for example, claims that the ἔθνη who have come to God through the crucified Christ are the *genos* ("lineage"; γένος) of Abraham (*Dial.* 11.5). Moreover, he argues, these Christians are the "true spiritual Israel" (Ἰσραηλιτικὸς ὁ ἀληθινός, πνευματικός).[64] Justin and others like him mined the depths of the Septuagint (LXX), especially the prophets, and routinely equated ἔθνη with Christians.[65]

Such claims are, of course, both rhetorical and part of a developing Christian anti-Judaism that took shape from the middle of the second century CE,[66] but they remain entrenched in some modern scholarship on this literature.[67] In the study of the New Testament, for example, scholars have often depicted Jesus and Paul as transcending the supposed ethnic particularity of Judaism in the way that they conceive of salvation for gentiles.[68] In studies of Acts, scholars have taken the "gentile mission" as a universalizing Christian mission that differed significantly from previous or contemporaneous Jewish interactions with gentiles.[69] Thus, "gentile," particularly in the context of the study of Christianity and of Acts, continues as a category of *religious* distinction, and implicit in this distinction is the contrast between gentiles who make up an ethnically "universal" Christianity and Jews who constitute an ethnically "particular" Judaism.[70] Such a contrast is precisely what I question in this book, and therefore the translation "gentile" undermines rather than serves the larger discussion of

Jewish identity and the formation of Christian identity in Acts.[71] I thus have chosen to use "non-Jews" as a translation of ἔθνη because I desire to highlight the fact that ἔθνη is an inherently ethnic (and religious and civic) classification that is only intelligible in its contrast with "Jews."

Chapter Overview

Each chapter of this book compares how Jewish identity was used in Acts to construct Christian identity as a subtype of Jewish identity. In the first chapter I discuss the uses of Ἰουδαῖος (Jew) in Acts and examine previous scholarship on the topic of Jewish identity. The remaining chapters "read" a selection from Acts alongside material remains, such as the Salutaris Foundation inscription and the sculptures of the Sebasteion in Aphrodisias, to compare the ways ethnic reasoning is used to negotiate identities in both contexts.

In chapter 1 I situate Acts historically and examine previous scholarship on Jewish identity and Acts. Much has been written on the author, date, and genre of Acts, but a consensus on these topics has yet to emerge. I argue that even given these ambiguities about authorship, date, and genre, it remains clear that someone living under Roman rule wrote Acts, an observation that is significant when examining the use of Jewish identity to construct a Christian identity in Acts. Because of this, Buell's concept of ethnic reasoning is helpful for understanding this writer's work. Scholars who discuss representations of Jewish identity in Acts often remain focused on determining the writer's stance toward Jews and Judaism. Such studies regularly defend one of two positions: Acts is pro-Jewish, or Acts is anti-Jewish. One common feature among scholars on both sides of this debate is the view that Acts presents Jews as an essential entity, "the Jews," developing a sharp contrast between "the Jews" and Christians. I depart from this approach, concluding that Acts uses Ἰουδαῖος as a hybrid ethnic designation that is simultaneously fluid and fixed in specific ways. Thus, the multiple meanings of Ἰουδαῖος do not contribute to the construction of an essential, oppositional category such as "the Jews." Rather, these meanings are strategically employed by the writer in order to create space to define Christian identity in Jewish terms and in a civic context.

In chapter 2 I test this conclusion in relation to a specific passage, Acts 2:5–13, and develop it in comparison with sculpted reliefs from the Sebasteion in Aphrodisias. Here I focus on religious activities and the construction of ethnic and civic identities more broadly, placing Acts within a wider material and cultural framework. Acts 2 lists Jews from various locations, ethnicities, and lineages. In this passage, the writer leverages the multiple meanings of Ἰουδαῖος in order to privilege the power of religious ideology—interpreted here as proper worship of the God of the Jews—as a mark of ethnic identity. In a similar way, reliefs from the Sebasteion in Aphrodisias created a visual list of *ethnē* that privileged religious imagery in the indexing of people groups. The reliefs use religious ideology—the veneration of Aphrodite and Roman emperors, for example—to indicate Aphrodisian identity and its relation to Roman identity to affirm some ethnic changes, while denigrating others, and to distinguish between ethnic groups. When "read" together, Acts 2 and the reliefs of the Sebasteion offer comparable ways of leveraging lists of ethnic groups in the negotiation of an identity for a specific rhetorical context. Acts 2 depicts Jews from various ethnicities in ways that highlight ethnic fluidity, while the Sebasteion represents various ethnicities as conquered in ways that emphasize that they are forever foreign and submitted to Rome, while Aphrodisians are imagined as allied with Rome and distinct from other conquered peoples.

I compare Acts with the Salutaris Foundation inscription from Ephesus in chapter 3, paying attention to how religious imagery provides a way to enact changes in ethnic and civic identities and examining the ethnic reasoning in Acts' narrative surrounding the so-called Jerusalem council (15:1–21) in relation to the depiction of Salutaris and the religious procession he sponsored. In both Acts and the inscription, the mythic past, ancestral customs, and gods are used to delimit ethnic identity, even while individuals and councils negotiate and manipulate those ethnic identities. By submitting the proper interpretation of the past, traditions, and the power of gods with the decisions of councils, both Acts and the Salutaris Foundation inscription authorize their respective councils to determine legitimate ethnic change through religious means. This happens even as they link these decisions to a distant, imagined past. More than this, they authorize individuals—namely, James and Salutaris—as agents fit to determine how and when ethnic change occurs.

In chapter 4 I build on the discussion of Acts and the Salutaris Foundation inscription and compare how each text uses ethnic reasoning together with civic and imperial space to produce unified identities. Focusing on Paul's visits to Jewish civic associations in Acts 15:30–18:23, I show how the repeated representation of civic space constructs a Jewish identity that includes proselyte non-Jews and at the same time makes an internal distinction between two Jewish identities: Christians and other Jews. Thus, the difference between Christians and non-Christians is one internal to Jewish identity. I then compare this to how the Salutaris Foundation regulates movement through the Ephesian cityscape in ways that both reimagine Ephesian identity and distinguish between "true" and other Ephesians. While Acts seeks to incorporate non-Jewish Christians into the Jewish community, the Salutaris Foundation seeks to marginalize those Ephesians who do not conform to the benefactor's desired construal of Ephesian identity. Finally, I examine how the literary representation in Acts of Paul's journeys throughout the Roman Empire also constructed a unified Christian identity that could be contrasted with the purported disunity of other Jewish civic associations.

I conclude with a summary of the findings followed by a brief reflection on the use of ethnic reasoning and the challenge of anti-Judaism in the interpretation of Acts today.

Recontextualizing Acts

Religious, Ethnic, and Civic Identity

Ὡς δὲ ἐπληροῦντο ἡμέραι ἱκαναί, συνεβουλεύσαντο
οἱ Ἰουδαῖοι ἀνελεῖν αὐτόν.

After some time had passed, the Jews plotted to kill him.

—Acts 9:31

Εἶπόν τε αὐτῷ· θεωρεῖς, ἀδελφέ, πόσαι μυριάδες εἰσὶν ἐν τοῖς Ἰουδαίοις
τῶν πεπιστευκότων καὶ πάντες ζηλωταὶ τοῦ νόμου ὑπάρχουσιν.

Then [the apostles in Jerusalem] said to [Paul],
"You see, brother, that there are many thousands of believers among the
Jews and they are all zealous for the law."

—Acts 21:20

Ἰουδαῖοι, JEWS, PLAY MULTIPLE ROLES in Acts. On one hand,
Luke's Christian heroes are law-observant Jews. On the other, the staunch
opponents of Christians and their message are also Jews. Some Jews re-
joice after hearing the Christians' preaching while others plot to kill them.
Between these two extremes, Jews interact with Christians and their message in various ways. It is no wonder that scholars have adopted divergent
opinions about Luke's portrayal of Ἰουδαῖοι, regularly interpreting
verses in opposing ways. Even so, their diverse interpretations often revolve around determining whether Luke was pro-Jewish or anti-Jewish.
Such an approach, however, is hampered by a static definition of "the Jews"

and ethnicity, categories that are hybrid and multiple rather than fixed states of being. Thus, the issue, I argue, is not Luke's pro- or anti-Jewish "attitude" toward "the Jews," as if Jewishness were (and is) a distinctive and separate bundle of characteristics and practices that can be identified and pinned down. Rather, the issue is Luke's constructions of Jews (both those with whom he agrees and those with whom he does not agree) and how such constructions fit into his narrative. By attending to the ethnic rhetoric present in the Lukan construction of Jewish identity in Acts, I demonstrate that Luke constructs "Jewishness" in ways that produce "Christian" as a distinctive kind of Jew in order to legitimate the place of Christians and their assemblies within the Roman *polis*.

In this chapter I situate my exploration within previous scholarship on Acts and argue that Lukan ethnic reasoning—as mediated by the cultural context of Greek cities under Roman rule—sought to create an alternate construal of Jewish and Christian identity. This alternate identity integrated Christian non-Jews into the civic hierarchy. I accomplish this task in three parts. First, I sketch the historical context of Acts and address the text's authorship, date, purpose, and context. Next, I provide a survey of scholarship on Jews and Judaism in Acts and attend to recent developments in interpretation that have emphasized the author's rhetoric rather than "attitude." Then I turn to the book itself and discuss four texts that highlight the value of ethnic reasoning and Buell's discussion of four uses of religious rhetoric in ethnic reasoning. I contend that Acts leverages the connection between gods, people, and places in its depiction of Jewish identity. Acts employs ethnic rhetoric in order to present all Christians as Jews and to privilege Christians as an ideal embodiment of Jewishness for the Roman-era *polis*.

Author, Date, Purpose, and Location

Since much of my argument depends on the similarity of rhetoric between Acts and contemporaneous material culture, it is helpful to establish a plausible historical and social context for the work. Acts is an anonymous text that was written near the beginning of the second century CE in order to legitimate Christians' place in the cities of the Roman Empire, and in those cities of the Greek East in particular.[1] I use "Luke" as a shorthand designation for the anonymous author of Acts, as scholars traditionally identify the author as the same person as the author of the Gospel of Luke, for a number of reasons.[2] The prefaces of both the Gospel of Luke and Acts are addressed to the same patron, a certain Theophilus, and the preface of Acts situates the narrative in relation to "the previous volume" (ὃ πρῶτος λόγος), presumably the Gospel of Luke (see Luke 1:1–4, Acts 1:1).[3] The connection between the two texts is therefore internally explicit.[4] In addition to the internal connection between the two works, there is also evidence that ancient authors associated Acts with the Gospel of Luke as early as the last third of the second century CE.[5] In recent years, however, a few scholars have questioned the value of the formal connections between the works for determining joint authorship, arguing instead that these are separate and distinctive works that were joined by a later editor for his or her own purposes.[6]

The particular focus of this book is Acts, so determining whether the same author wrote both the Gospel and Acts is not necessary. The Gospel simply does not address Jewish identity in the same way that Acts does.[7] For example, the Gospel uses Ἰουδαῖος five times (four of which occur during Jesus's trial and crucifixion), whereas Acts uses the term seventy-nine times.[8] The prominence of Jews and claims about Jews in Acts suggest that the writer was particularly concerned with describing the contours of this group when composing his second volume. This is likely the result of differences in narrative contexts: the Gospel's narrative centers on Judea and Galilee, the Jewish homeland, while Acts' narrative spans a broad section of the Roman world, the Jewish diaspora.[9] In this context "Jewishness" was by necessity more hotly contested.

Acts was written near the beginning of the second century CE but narrates events from the second third of the first century CE. Many scholars have sought support for an earlier date, ranging from 70 to 85 CE.[10] Still, an increasing number of scholars have persuasively argued for dates in the 90s and later.[11] Of scholars who support a date after 90 CE, Richard Pervo and Joseph Tyson are of particular interest. Pervo argues that Acts was written "in the suburb of the apologists," and he dates it to 115 CE,[12] while Tyson, echoing John Knox, contends that Acts offered a response to the ideas of Marcion, an early, second-century Christian who was condemned as a heretic by Irenaeus.[13] More will be said about the connection between Acts and Marcion later in this chapter, but now it is sufficient to say that in recent decades there has been a positive shift in support of a late-first-century/early-second-century date for Acts.

A central purpose of Acts is to offer a narrative legitimation of Christians' place in the city through a retelling of Christian origins and a positioning of Christians within the hierarchy of civic ethics. Though Acts does not have a single purpose—but rather a number of interconnected ones—scholars agree that a central goal of the writer was to defend Christian communities.[14] Opinions about the intended recipients of this defense vary widely: earlier historical critics argued that Acts sought to harmonize Jewish and gentile Christianities in order to create a single "Christianity"; others have contended that Acts was written to defend a particular (proto-orthodox) form of Christianity against the theological claims of other Christian groups or individuals; and still others assert that Acts was intended as a legal defense of a new religious movement before Rome.[15] The target audience for this defense is also a subject of debate. A number of scholars argue it was aimed at Christians rather than outsiders; from this point of view, Acts offered a legitimizing narrative of Christians rather than an apology designed to persuade outsiders. Philip Esler, for example, contends that early Christians desired assurance that their decision to "adopt a different life-style had been the correct one," and Luke sought to provide this reassurance.[16] Building on this perspective, I argue in subsequent chapters that Acts offers not only assurance to assuage Christian readers but also a way to identify Christians' place in the city based on the way that they honored the God of Israel and the prevalent relationships between gods and humans in antiquity. The writer of Acts does this, I argue, through the way that he represents Jewish identity.

We do not know where Acts was written, and scholars have not paid as much attention to its provenance as they have to its authorship and date.[17] Recently, however, Pervo has argued that Acts was written in Ephesus. As he points out, an important block of the narrative takes place in the famous Greek city, and the writer provides "local color," suggesting that he had some direct familiarity with it.[18] Pervo's proposal cannot fully settle the question of provenance, but even if Acts was not written in Ephesus, other evidence suggests that it was likely written from a Greek city under Roman rule. For example, the emphasis of the narrative is overwhelmingly urban and cosmopolitan, and the majority of its action focuses on Greek cities.[19] Also, Rome is both suspiciously present and curiously absent throughout the narrative, which fits a Greek urban setting. Greek writers regularly engaged Rome in this way, acknowledging its presence even as they defended Greek prestige over and against Roman hegemony.[20] Finally, the narrative revolves around interactions between central characters and civic associations within cities, specifically focusing on diaspora Jewish communities.[21] Christian communities, the writer presumes, are rooted in cities and develop within a context of Jewish civic associations.[22] As many have pointed out, Acts is urban.[23]

As a Greek literary text, as well as a document written by a Jesus follower (a "Christian"), Acts addresses a number of broader concerns facing elites who lived in Greek cities under Roman rule.[24] The arrival of Rome precipitated a significant change in the power structures of Greek cities, applying new pressures to old institutions, which could no longer function in quite the same way. As scholars of the "Second Sophistic" have shown, literary elites (like the author of Acts) responded to and aligned themselves with Roman authority by asserting a reimagined past and separate Greek identity while at the same time positioning themselves on a new imperial map.[25] Referencing the perceived value of "Greekness," elite writers and leading Greek citizens asserted ethnic connections between Greeks and Romans even as they defended the distinctive (and superior) qualities of "being Greek."[26]

The writer of Acts, like other Greek-speaking elites, also used practices and discourses associated with honoring gods to navigate a place in Roman society. In the ancient Mediterranean world, religious activity—the protocols and activities that regulated interaction with gods—was inherited. Populations had specific, ancestral gods and practices; they may (or may not) have considered these activities to be expressions of inward dispositions, but the emphasis in ancient literary and material evidence was on proper performance rather than on some sort of inner state.[27] People honored their gods according to specific ancestral customs/laws, and in return, gods protected and provided for their people.[28] Honoring the gods was therefore a matter of ethnicity as well as piety. During the Roman era, especially in Hellenized cities, interaction with gods was a constant part of life, and the veneration of the appropriate gods was a prerequisite for citizenship and membership on the city council (βουλή).[29] Honoring the gods was a way of establishing and enhancing piety in the *polis* and thereby a feature of "Greekness." Inhabitants worshipped gods throughout the city—at temples, altars, festivals, city council meetings, association gatherings, guild meetings, and domestic meals. Honoring gods through public and private sacrifices, processions, votive offerings, and benefaction was a regular *and* regulating part of life in the city.[30] Religious activity was, among other things, a civic designation, and the proper reverence toward civic gods was a central part of ensuring the prosperity of the city.

The writer of Acts was deeply informed by each of these features of urban life. Religious activity provided him (and other Greek writers at the time) with a way to enact changes in ethnic and civic identities. Moreover, it provided other writers and citizens with a way to connect with the mythic past, reaffirm and reformulate traditions, and legitimate authority.[31] These dynamics are present in other, nonliterary sources as well, such as epigraphy, architecture, and the honorific statuary that lined the processional ways in and out of the city center. As Laura Nasrallah has observed, both text and material served as a type of "memory theater" where the contemporary and the ancient were juxtaposed, thus "giving the appearance of mutually affirming religious values, ethnic identity, and certain ideas of aesthetics and *paideia*."[32] The implications of Acts' urban environment therefore should not be underestimated: not only is the narrative of Acts embedded in the Greek city, but the rhetoric of Acts is also firmly rooted in the rhetoric of the *polis*.

Interpreting Acts from within the discourses of the Greek *polis* is central to understanding the construction of Jewish and Christian identity in the text not only because the *polis* was a nexus of identity construction in the first and second centuries CE, as Simon Goldhill and others demonstrate, but also because Acts negotiates Jewish identity from within the *polis*.[33] The narrative of Acts develops around the Jewish associations that formed throughout the cities of the Mediterranean world. As the next section shows, many scholars have made important contributions to understanding Jewish identity in Acts, but room remains for further consideration of the ethnic rhetoric and the civic context of Jewish identity in the narrative.

"The Jews" and Judaism in Acts

Previous scholarship on Jews in Acts has often sought to locate "Luke's attitude" toward Jews and Judaism and has focused on whether Luke thought that "Christian" salvation remained available to Jews.[34] As previously mentioned, this scholarship falls into one of two broad camps: Acts is anti-Jewish, or it is pro-Jewish.[35] I argue that this dichotomy is problematic for understanding Acts because it masks the nuanced and complex way that Luke navigates Jewishness and relates Jewish and Christian identities. At the same time, it emphasizes a religious dichotomy between Jews and Christians while minimizing the civic, ethnic, political, and cultural aspects of ancient religious activities.[36] As just demonstrated, this dichotomous understanding of religion divorced from civic identity would have been at odds with an author immersed in the Greco-Roman *polis*.

When examining "Luke's attitude," many scholars have argued that Acts is essentially anti-Jewish.[37] Those who take this view acknowledge that the images of Jews in Acts are complex, but they consistently emphasize the writer's portrayal of Jewish opposition to the Christian gospel. They contend that in Acts the term οἱ Ἰουδαῖοι functions like a *terminus technicus* meaning "the Jews." "The Jews," on this reading, identify not only those Jews who oppose Christians, but also negatively signify all Jews who do not become Christians.

Scholars of this view have made a number of important observations about the representations of Jews in Acts. In his still-influential book *Theology of St. Luke,* for example, Hans Conzelmann saw a certain "hardening" of "the Jews" as the narratives of Luke and Acts unfold.[38] Luke, according to Conzelmann, divided the history of salvation into three phases: the period of Israel, the period of Jesus, and the period of "the Church."[39] With this division, Luke explained why it is "that Jews and Christians are in fact not distinguished" and at the same time "that they are sharply opposed to one another." As he then suggested, "Both statements are the outcome of the view that the Church represents the continuity of redemptive history, and to this degree is 'Israel.'"[40]

This construction of redemptive history in turn informed Conzelmann's understanding of Jews. Conzelmann claimed: "In the very usage of Ἰουδαῖος we can trace a certain hardening. . . . That the starting-point [of the gospel message] is in the synagogue is of course required by redemptive history. . . . [T]here is at the same time a reference to the cutting off of the Jews from redemptive history. We can say that the Jews are now called to make good on their claim to be 'Israel.' If they fail to do this, then they become 'the Jews.'"[41] For Conzelmann, Luke's Jews must legitimate their claim to "be Israel" by accepting the message of salvation from Paul and other disciples. In effect, Conzelmann understood Acts as identifying "the Church" as *verus* Israel and all non-Christian Jews as "the Jews."[42] In Conzelmann's reading of Luke-Acts, the writer viewed Christians as supplanting the Jews' place as the people of God.

Though a number of scholars have questioned Conzelmann's model of redemptive history for reading Luke and Acts, his observations about the increasing "hardening" against "the Jews" remain important in subsequent scholarship on the construction of Jewish identity in Acts.[43]

Ernst Haenchen developed Conzelmann's work and focuses his attention on how Jews fit into the purpose of Acts. Haenchen contends that Luke was "wrestling, from the first page [of Acts] to the last, with the problem of the *mission to the Gentiles without the law.*" According to Haenchen, this mission was both a theological and a political problem for Luke. Haenchen writes: "By forsaking the observance of the Jewish law Christianity parts company with Judaism; does this not break the continuity of the history of salvation? That is the theological aspect. But in cutting adrift from Judaism Christianity also loses the toleration which the Jewish religion enjoys. Denounced by the Jews as hostile to the state, it becomes the object of suspicion to Rome. That is the political aspect. Acts takes both constantly into account." For Haenchen, Luke's narrative attempts to create a theological and political bridge between Judaism and Christianity. Theologically, Luke needed this bridge because most Jews had rejected the claims of Christianity, calling into question Christian assertions of continuity with Judaism. Acts emphasized an initial Jewish acceptance of the Christian message in order to demonstrate a past connection between Judaism and Christianity.[44]

According to Haenchen's interpretation, Jewish rejection caused Christians to "turn" from Jews (see Acts 13:46, 18:6, 28:28).[45] Haenchen writes, "it was to the Jews that salvation was first offered, and offered again and again. It was not until they refused it by their vilification of Jesus that the emissaries of Christianity turned to the Gentiles."[46] Taken individually, these "turning" passages represent local situations, but taken together, Haenchen contends Luke had "written the Jews off."[47] By emphasizing the Jewish rejection of the Christian message, Acts justified the current (in Luke's day) separation between the two religions.

For Haenchen, Luke needed to connect Christianity with Judaism because of Roman views of religion. Romans tolerated Judaism because it was a "legal religion."[48] Judaism was a so-called *religio licita,* and Christians required a connection with Judaism in order to perpetuate a claim to be a legal religion in the Roman Empire.[49] With this connection established, Luke could claim that Christianity "had committed no πονηρά, nor crimes against Roman law."[50] Thus, Luke emphasized a theological connection between Judaism and Christianity for political and apologetic ends.[51]

Partly in response to Haenchen's thesis, Philip Esler conclusively demonstrated that Romans did not have a concept of *religio licita* during this period, a fact that seriously undermines Haenchen's interpretation.[52] No category of Roman law made religions legal or illegal; rather, the worship of gods was ancestral and traditional.[53] Since worship was ethnic, and proper worship placated ancestral gods, as Paula Fredriksen argues, Romans operated under a model of "pragmatic pluralism."[54] Variation in religious activities was permitted because "if *any* god is more powerful than *any* human, then such a posture simply made good sense."[55] Thus, Haenchen's claim that Acts emphasizes a connection between Jews and Christians, so that Christianity can be portrayed as a "legal religion," is no longer viable.

Moving beyond Conzelmann's and Haenchen's views that Acts depicts a hardening of "the Jews," Jack Sanders offered another forceful argument in defense of the view that the writer expresses an anti-Jewish attitude.[56] In multiple works, Sanders argues that Luke sees Jews, in their essence, as intransigent, opposed to God, hostile to the gospel, and murderers of Jesus.[57] Sanders understands the repeated use of the term οἱ Ἰουδαῖοι to be Luke's construction of an essentialist category, "*THE JEWS*," as he calls it. He argues that, though there are positive images of Jews throughout Acts, in the end Acts shows the author's true view. It "makes clear that Paul is done in, not by the religious authorities alone, not by Diaspora Jews alone, and not by Jerusalem [*sic*] alone, but by *THE JEWS*. Jewish opposition to Christianity is now universal and endemic."[58] This clear rejection of "*THE JEWS*" moves the narrative forward, Sanders claims, by means of a series of violent interactions between Paul and other Jews, each of which stems from Paul's gospel message.[59] Thus, Luke regularly uses the term οἱ Ἰουδαῖοι *in malam partem.*[60] Sanders writes: "At the end of the Acts the Jews have *become* what they from the first *were;* for what Jesus, Stephen, Peter, and Paul say about the Jews—about their intransigent opposition to the purposes of God, about their hostility toward Jesus and the gospel, about their murder of Jesus—is what Luke understands the Jewish people to be in their essence. The narrative shows how existence comes to conform to essence, the process by which the Jewish people become 'the Jews.'"[61] Jewish resistance toward the message of Paul represents the essence of all Jews everywhere for Sanders.

Sanders also contends that Acts has a consistently negative picture of Jews, despite an initially positive presentation in the opening chapters. Jews "*become* what they from the first *were,*" and Acts discloses this "truth" step by step in the narrative. Sanders, of course, does not personally support "Luke's attitude" (as he has described it); rather, he sees this presentation of "the Jews" as deeply problematic and therefore worthy of both detection and rejection by contemporary scholars.[62] In some instances Sanders overstates his case. For example, he claims that at the end of Acts Paul is "done in" by the Jews; however, the narrative of Acts is famously unclear about Paul's fate.[63] A number of other scholars have also observed that Sanders's negative view does not adequately take into account the positive images of Jews and Judaism present in the work.[64] In an attempt to expose and eliminate modern Christian anti-Judaism, Sanders appears to have exaggerated the scope of Lukan anti-Judaism.

Even so, Sanders's argument remains influential. Scholars have adjusted his claims, nuancing what Lukan anti-Judaism may mean, but the assumption of an overwhelmingly anti-Jewish movement of the narrative continues to guide discussions. In his essay titled "The Use and Meaning of (*Hoi*) *Ioudaioi* in Acts," for example, Augusto Barbi perceives "the Jews" as an essential category and sees no significant distinction between the uses of Ἰουδαῖος with or without the article.[65] He does, however, see a distinction between the way Ἰουδαῖος is used in passages that contain interactions with apostles and those that do not. Passages without such interaction are "neutral," and Ἰουδαῖος "clearly signifies that the persons belong to a race or to the religion of that race."[66] In passages containing interactions with the apostles, Barbi sees an "adversarial meaning" for the term. He writes: "If even when the author is aware that preaching addressed to the Jews is to some extent successful, he nonetheless uses (*hoi*) *Ioudaioi* without restriction, or other expressions even more indicative of a totality, to describe the opponents of the gospel and its preachers, then the term certainly does not have a neutral ethnico-religious meaning but refers to those members of Israel who have closed their minds to the preaching of the gospel."[67] On Barbi's reading, Ἰουδαῖοι does not mean the Jewish people per se but is a term denoting otherness. "This depiction of the *Ioudaioi* as enemies of the Christian community," he writes, is "a sign of a change in the mood of the Jewish people and of a growing rift between Christians and unbelieving Jews."[68] Barbi contends: "When Jews accept the gospel they become simply 'believers among the Jews' (21:20) and join the Christian community. When they reject the gospel, they become *Ioudaioi* in the adversarial sense.

The community of disciples is forced to distance itself from these Jews and their synagogues. It is from this group that a more continuous threat to the community and its missionary activity seems to come. Acts thus presents a 'very sad and tragic' picture of the 'Jews.'"[69]

Mitzi Smith has argued that Acts rhetorically constructs "the Jews" as Christians' "other," a fictive category produced by Luke for the purposes of rhetorical definition.[70] Smith first distinguishes between the Jewish people and "*the Jews*"—as she identifies them. She, like Sanders, contends that the articular plural uses of the Greek term Ἰουδαῖος (οἱ Ἰουδαῖοι) in the second half of Acts rhetorically construct an opponent of Christians, "*the Jews.*"[71] Luke does this by presenting *the Jews* as active participants in conflicts with Christians—*ekklēsia* in Smith's terms.[72] *The Jews* "are the ideal negatively romanticized opponents of the *ekklēsia* and its gospel message." Smith, like Sanders, does not see a "hardening" of *the Jews* as the narrative progresses. Rather, "*the Jews* consistently act the same way, and this consistency gives the impression that they are a predictable and unified group with respect to their response to the Gentile mission as Paul preached it." Thus, Luke "constructs *the Jews* so as to give the readers the impression that they are an authentically ubiquitous group that acts harmoniously, homogeneously, and violently to oppose the Gentile mission." *The Jews* in Acts are the consistent and uniform "other." Acts also connects *the Jews* with the Jewish people more generally. Smith writes: "Luke's narrative discursively creates the illusion that *the Jews* in Acts are Jewish people in general. The only power in Acts that is able to transcend the hostility of *the Jews* is the power of God, which, according to the narrative, is on the side of the *ekklēsia* and not on the side of *the Jews*." Though she initially distinguishes between *the Jews* and the Jewish people, Smith eventually blends them together into one homogenous category; all Jews become *the Jews*.[73]

In the end Smith, like Conzelmann, Haenchen, and Sanders, interprets the writer's portrayal of those Jews who oppose Acts' Christians as categorically identical to the Jewish people. Yet this interpretation remains problematic because it does not adequately account for the continuing Jewishness of most of the Christians in Acts' narrative. Jews who are also

Christians, like Peter, Stephen, and Paul, cannot remain Jewish if Luke discursively identifies *the Jews* with Jewish people more generally. From this perspective, when these Jews become Christians, their Jewishness is abandoned. As discussed below, Luke does not condemn or write off the Jewish people, but he does make a distinction between Christian Jews and non-Christian Jews.

Placing Acts in a different historical context allows a number of scholars to avoid this issue. With the exception of Smith, the scholars discussed above see Acts addressing a historical problem with the relationship between Jews and Christians.[74] Another group of scholars, however, argues that Acts addresses a problem of theological diversity in second-century Christianity. According to this view, Luke uses Jews to imagine Christian origins in a way that supports a vision of Christianity that is actually ambivalent toward Jews.

Joseph Tyson, for example, accentuates the "tension and ambivalence" of Luke's view of the Jewish people.[75] Building on the work of John Knox, Tyson reads Acts as participating in theological debates similar to those with the "arch-heretic" Marcion, the early-second-century Christian who was condemned as a heretic by Irenaeus, who claimed that the religion of Jesus and Paul differed completely from that of the Jewish scriptures. Luke counters Marcion's claims with positive images of Jews and of Jewish traditions in this story of the origins of non-Jewish Christianity. Yet, Tyson argues, in spite of these positive images, Acts remains anti-Jewish. The writer of Acts acknowledges that some Jews accept Paul's message but condemns the "Jews as a whole" for their rejection of the gospel. Tyson writes, "two facts seem clear: for Luke the mission to the Jewish people has failed, and it has been terminated."[76] Thus, Luke's battle against his (Christian) theological opponents results in the termination of the mission to the Jewish people.[77]

Shelly Matthews also argues that Acts responds to early-second-century debates within Christianity.[78] She writes: "Through the distinct coding of Jewish *symbols* as good and non-confessing Jewish *people* as bad, the rhetorical strategy of Acts aligns precisely with the *Adversus Judaeos* traditions of anti-marcionite Christians in the second century

and beyond."[79] Its positive valuation of Jewish customs and symbols notwithstanding, Acts remains anti-Jewish because it identifies Jews by their
hostility toward Christians. Matthews contends that "the proofs cited from
Jewish Scripture and other positive coding of Jewish symbols, along with
the highlighting of the Jewish credentials of its key protagonists, demonstrate that this community has the rightful claim on Israel's heritage."[80]
Placing Acts within the historical context of the *Adversus Judaeos* traditions
provides Matthews (and Tyson) space to explain the negative portrayal of
Jews while at the same time allowing the positive images to exist. The Christian Paul can both be "ethnically" Jewish and condemn the Jewish people.
Thus, on this view, Luke uses the concept of the Jews to make a theological claim against his opponents. He uses Jews to "think with."[81] Matthews's
proposal that Luke "thinks with" Jews provides space to consider the positive and negative ways that Acts represents Jews, without making a totalizing claim about "Luke's attitude" toward "the Jews" because Luke's
attitude is not clearly knowable and "the Jews" is not a fixed category.

Other scholars have seen in Acts a more positive view of Jews. They
set aside the conflicts between Christians and Jews that the writer portrays
and emphasize the fact that Jews accept the gospel before non-Jews do.
These scholars contextualize the representations of Jews historically as part
of an intra-Jewish debate and thus soften the distinction between Jews and
Christians (both Jewish and non-Jewish). As they argue, the Jewishness of
the apostles mediates the anti-Jewishness of other aspects of the narrative,
leaving the question of Luke's attitude toward Jews and Judaism unsettled.

In 1972, Jacob Jervell published a series of essays that challenged the
existing consensus that Acts is anti-Jewish and thus ignited an enduring
conversation about Jews in Acts.[82] Jervell contended that Luke goes to great
lengths to depict many Jews as accepting the gospel; he did not represent
the Jewish people rejecting the gospel but suggested that it is necessary for
Jews to accept the gospel before the message could go to non-Jews.[83] However, Jervell still viewed "the church" as supplanting Israel over the course
of Acts' narrative. Luke, according to Jervell, does not separate "the church"
from Israel or Judaism, but rather separates the unrepentant, that is, non-
Christian, portion of Israel from "true" Israel because it has "forfeited its

membership in the people of God" through its rejection of the gospel.[84] Jervell therefore calls into question the scholarly consensus of his time that understood "the Jews" in Luke-Acts as equal to all Jews. For Jervell, "the Jews" represent only those Jews who do not accept the gospel. Though this interpretation views Jewish identity in a slightly more positive light, the category remains largely religious in Jervell's reading of Acts, and the two religions—Judaism and Christianity—are distinguished from one another on the basis of their "beliefs." In Jervell's reading, only Jews who accept the gospel make up "true" Israel.

Robert Brawley has built on Jervell's work and also argues that Luke approaches Jews positively as a whole.[85] He contends, however, that Jervell overemphasized theological issues and failed to give adequate attention to the representation of social dynamics in Acts. For Brawley, Luke does not give up on Jews but responds to "Jewish propaganda and schismatic anti-Paulinism."[86] Luke, according to Brawley, defended and legitimated Paul and Christianity. In doing so, he left the door open for Jews to accept the Pauline gospel.[87]

Both Jervell and Brawley have emphasized the positive ways that Luke interacts with Jews, but their work still interprets Jews as a religious "other" in Acts. For Jervell, Luke showed the success of the message of Christian salvation among Jews, while for Brawley, Luke sought to legitimate Paul and his message and did so by contrasting Pauline Christians with "Jews." In the end, however, both Jervell and Brawley see Luke equating "the Jews" with a religion. For Jervell, "it is those Jews who are faithful to the law, *the real Jews*, the most Jewish Jews, who become believers," that is, trust in Jesus as God's Messiah.[88] For Brawley, Luke uses the traditions of the early church and "draws what he considers to be *authentic* Jews toward Christianity and *authentic* Christians toward Judaism."[89] Jews, on these readings, must become believing Christians in order to be "true Jews."

Both those who interpret Acts as anti-Jewish and those who interpret it as pro-Jewish often make similar assumptions about Acts, Jewish identity, and the formation of Christianity. First, they assume that Jewish identity in Acts is (or should be) primarily a religious identity. Discussions about Jewish identity revolve around the availability of Christian salvation for

Jews. Second, they argue that "the Jews" function as a clearly defined "other" throughout Acts. For Jervell, Brawley, and others who see Acts as pro-Jewish, Luke distinguished between *authentic* or *true* "Jews" and "the Jews." "The Jews" are an ethnically based religious group, and the distinction between "the Jews" and *authentic* Jews (i.e., Christians) lies in their "belief" or "nonbelief" in Christ. The distinctions are more clear-cut for those who see Acts as anti-Jewish or ambivalent toward Jews. Luke distinguished between "the Jews" and "Christians." Of course, some early Christians were Jews, but Acts constructs "the Jews" as an opposi-tional, ethnically based religious group, an opposition that transcends the individual ethnicity of a few Jewish Christians. Third, Acts depicts a re-ligion, Christianity, that opposed another religion, Judaism. "The Jews" serve as Christianity's "other," a distinction that delimits both groups in theological terms. The opposition that Christians face from "the Jews" allows the formation of distinct, unified groups. In each of these views, Acts identifies "the Jews" with a particular ethnic religion, Judaism, and identifies Christians, "true Israel," with a universal, belief-based religion, Christianity.

A few scholars offer a different approach to the topic of Jewish iden-tity in Acts. Marilyn Salmon, for example, asks whether Luke was an in-sider or an outsider in relation to Judaism.[90] If an outsider, then Acts is anti-Jewish and readings like that of Jack Sanders are correct. However, if Luke understood himself to be a Jewish insider, then Acts represents an intra-Jewish debate about how to best honor the God of Israel.[91] Salmon points to four aspects of Acts that indicate to her that Luke was an insider, in other words, that he perceived himself to be a Jew: he distinguishes be-tween sects of Judaism; he devotes significant space to questions of Torah observance; he focuses on the "gentile mission," which makes sense only as a Jewish concept; and he identifies Christians as members of a sect of Judaism.[92] Acts therefore represents Jews in ways that remain consistent with intra-Jewish discussions. Her focus on how Acts relates to Judaism moves the discussion of Jewish identity forward by shifting questions away from issues of salvation toward Luke's perceived social location and his own claimed identity in relation to Judaism.[93]

Philip Esler has also focused on the social location of Luke, showing how Luke used "legitimation techniques" throughout Luke and Acts.[94] Building on the influential work of sociologists Peter Berger and Thomas Luckmann, Esler defines legitimation as "the collection of ways in which an institution is explained and justified *to its members*," analyzing the relationship between theology and sociopolitical issues in Luke-Acts through the lens of social theory.[95] He contends that Luke "has shaped the gospel traditions at his disposal in response to social and political pressures experienced by his community."[96] This shift in focus also shifts the discussion of Luke's attitude toward "the Jews" to the way that Luke legitimated the separation between "Christian sectarians" and Jewish communities.[97] Esler argues that Luke wrote with a Christian community containing both Jews and non-Jews in mind and sought to show that "Christianity was a legitimate development of Judaism."[98] Esler's social legitimation model remains focused on two religions—Judaism and Christianity. However, by focusing on how Acts legitimated Christian communities rather than on Luke's attitude toward the salvation of "the Jews," he places Lukan rhetoric within a broader sociological framework. Jews are Luke's literary creation, Esler suggests, but they fulfill a social rather than a theological role.[99]

Attending to Acts' social setting in the Greek city, Lawrence Wills has also shifted the scholarly discussion about Jews in Acts.[100] Wills interprets Acts' Jews in light of the fear of urban uprisings in the Roman Empire, a fear the writer seems to share. Luke, according to Wills, "manipulates the stigma of *stasis* or *seditio* in a way that is profoundly Roman," repeating a broader Roman preference for "peace" in a way that renders "the Jews" as a social (rather than a theological) threat.[101] Wills writes: "The narrative method of Acts in regard to Jews is not to state the salvation-history dogma that their theology makes them wrong and lost—although the author probably believes this—but to *show* that Jews are every bit as disorderly and rebellious as one would expect from the fact that they were involved in three bloody rebellions in seventy years."[102] Luke juxtaposes "the Jews," who are portrayed as "scandalously bad citizens," with "the Christians," who are portrayed as model, orderly citizens. The emphasis

Wills places on Luke's use of Jewish identity as a means of navigating Christians' place in the Greek *polis* comes close to the approach I adopt in this book and supports Wills's reading that Luke is more concerned with the social status of Christians in relation to the Roman Empire than with the theological status of Jews.

Salmon's and Esler's emphasis on Luke's relationship to a Jewish community and Wills's emphasis on Luke's depiction of Jews in relationship to Roman fears of urban rebellion place Christians within their surrounding social context, shifting the discussion away from Luke's purported "attitude" toward Jews and toward Luke's use of ethnic-theological categories ("Jew" and "Christian") in his construction of Christian difference. Discussions of Luke's position in relation to Jews and Jewish identity have therefore become more complex. Still, the tendency to discuss Jewish identity in Acts as a matter of "the Jews" versus Christians continues to imagine clear boundaries between two social groups, Jews and Christians.[103] The religious aspects of Jewish and Christian identity are therefore considered separately from the social and theological categories of "Jewish" and "Christian" in Salmon's and Esler's treatments.

Eric Barreto also challenges the view that Luke held a totalizing, negative view of "the Jews" and argues that scholars have fundamentally misunderstood the function and use of ethnic discourse in analyses of Acts. Even "asking whether Luke's use of Ἰουδαῖος is positive or negative eliminates the possibility that the term is used descriptively, ambiguously, or ambivalently." Attention to ethnic discourse shows that "Luke constantly draws and redraws the referent of Ἰουδαῖος."[104]

Rather than emphasizing sites of opposition, as Barbi and many others have, Barreto catalogues the uses of Ἰουδαῖος under seven "heuristic headings" and highlights the variation and specificity of Ἰουδαῖος.[105] He argues that nearly all of the uses of Ἰουδαῖος in Acts identify a specific referent, an individual or group of people rather that an unbounded ethnic category.[106] He concludes, "For Luke, there is no essentialist meaning of Ἰουδαῖος, only a wide meaning potential befitting the ethno-cultural complexities of the ancient world."[107] According to Barreto, using "the Jews" to identify a single, fixed entity in Acts does not accurately reflect Luke's uses of the term Ἰουδαῖος or the ambiguity of ethnic discourse.

Barreto's conclusion that Ἰουδαῖος does not have an essentialist meaning in Acts provides a helpful entry into discussion of ethnic reasoning and the use of religious activities in the production of Jewish identity.[108] As discussed in the introduction, ancient Christians (and many other populations) produced ethnic and civic identities in part through honoring ancestral gods. According to Buell's analysis, ancient Christians used "religion" in four ways: to identify populations ethnically and distinguish between ethnic and civic groups, to establish guidelines for ethnic and civic change, to construe connections between previously distinct ethnic and civic populations, and to mark internal distinctions within a given ethnic or civic group. When applied to Jewish identity in Acts, the concept of ethnic rhetoric shifts the discussion of Jewish identity from Luke's attitude toward "the Jews" to how Luke uses religious activities to produce Jewish identity in Acts. What follows offers a few examples of how this approach enhances understanding of Jewish identity in the rhetoric of Acts.

Ethnic Reasoning and Jews in Acts

In the ancient world, religious activities were a means both of maintaining ethnic and civic identity and of creating ethnic and civic distinctions. Acts, of course, offers many examples of this dynamic. Throughout the work, Luke represents Jews constructing Jewish identity in ethnic and religious terms. Luke's Peter, for example, encourages a crowd of Jews to remember the oath that God made to "the ancestor David" (ὁ πατριάρχης Δαυὶδ), an oath that still applied to Peter's audience (2:29–30; cf. 3:13, 17). The promise of God is transmitted ethnically; that is, it works through lineage and maintains Jewish identity. Elsewhere, Stephen connects the appearance of "the God of glory" (ὁ θεὸς τῆς δόξης) to "our ancestor Abraham" (ὁ πατὴρ ἡμῶν Ἀβραὰμ) with the current situation of his Jewish audience (7:2). Thus Acts assumes an ethnic tie between the Jewish God and the Jewish people, past and present. More than a simple ethnic tie, God guides and rescues "his people" (7:33). Ethnicity determines how God interacts with humanity.

In a different way, Acts comingles religious and ethnic rhetoric in Paul's defense before Agrippa. Luke's Paul proclaims:

Τὴν μὲν οὖν βίωσίν μου [τὴν] ἐκ νεότητος τὴν ἀπ’ ἀρχῆς
γενομένην ἐν τῷ ἔθνει μου ἔν τε Ἱεροσολύμοις ἴσασι
πάντες [οἱ] Ἰουδαῖοι προγινώσκοντές με ἄνωθεν, ἐὰν
θέλωσι μαρτυρεῖν, ὅτι κατὰ τὴν ἀκριβεστάτην αἵρεσιν τῆς
ἡμετέρας θρησκείας ἔζησα Φαρισαῖος. καὶ νῦν ἐπ’ ἐλπίδι
τῆς εἰς τοὺς πατέρας ἡμῶν ἐπαγγελίας γενομένης ὑπὸ τοῦ
θεοῦ ἔστηκα κρινόμενος, εἰς ἣν τὸ δωδεκάφυλον ἡμῶν ἐν
ἐκτενείᾳ νύκτα καὶ ἡμέραν λατρεῦον ἐλπίζει καταντῆσαι.

All Jews know my way of life from my youth, a life spent from
the beginning in my *ethnos* and in Jerusalem. They have known
for a long time, if they are willing to testify, that, as a Pharisee,
I lived according to the strictest sect of our ancestral cult. And
now I stand on trial on account of the hope of the promise made
by God to our ancestors, a promise that our twelve tribes hope
to attain, as they earnestly worship day and night. (26:4–7)

Through Paul's claim, Acts ties Jewish identity to the continuing effect of
God's promise to ancestors. In the narrative of Acts, Jews use the connection between their God, his people, and ancestral customs to mark Jewish
identity.

Non-Jews also mark Jewish identity in ethnic and religious terms
throughout the narrative of Acts. While in Philippi, the owners of a slave
girl identify Paul and Silas as Jews. They then accuse them of stirring up
the city by announcing customs that Romans could not accept (16:20–21).
Jewish customs (including religious customs) were for Jews and were not
lawful for Romans.[109] In Corinth, Paul is again accused of transgressing
"the law."[110] However, this time leaders of the local Jewish community accuse him of acting contrary to Jewish laws and customs. The Roman proconsul Gallio, to whom these Jews appeal, would not judge such matters
and dismissed the case (18:12–17). In Ephesus, some silversmiths were concerned that Paul would persuade Ephesians to stop honoring Artemis
(19:23–31). Paul, a Jew, persuades non-Jews to worship in a Jewish way with
his claim that gods made with hands were not gods (19:26). The head sil-

versmith, Demetrius, argues that if Paul continues persuading people of this, the temple of Artemis would be scorned, and the goddess would be deprived of her majesty (19:27). Jews worshipping according to Jewish customs did not raise Ephesian ire, but when Jews encouraged non-Jews to do the same, these Ephesians responded with a near riot (19:38–41). In each of these three cases, Acts represents non-Jews connecting Jewish religious activity and ethnic identity.

Acts also uses religious practices to mark ethnic change in a way that was common among Jews in the Greek and Roman eras. As modern historians know well, Jews accepted non-Jews as full members of the Jewish community as proselytes.[111] Modern scholars continue to debate how ancient Jews understood the ethnic identity of these "converts." Were they now Jews?[112] Did they remain non-Jews who simply practiced Judaism?[113] Or were they somewhere in between?[114] It is probable that different communities accepted (or rejected) proselytes in different ways at different times. Because of this, it is important for the present argument to determine how Acts represents the ethnic identity of Jewish proselytes rather than to enter into the broader debate about the ethnic status of Jewish proselytes in the ancient world.

Acts identifies proselytes as Jews who simultaneously retain a distinction from those who are born Jews. In Acts 2:5–13 (a passage discussed in the next chapter) this complexity comes to the fore. Acts includes proselytes in a list of Jews from various ethnic groups (2:5, 10); therefore, proselytes are Jews. However, the same passage marks proselytes as distinct from born Jews (2:10), and later Acts distinguishes between born Jews and "pious proselytes" (σεβόμενοι προσήλυτοι; 13:43). In these cases, born Jews and proselytes make up two categories. As I argue in the next chapter, however, Luke presents both categories as Jewish. Ethnic reasoning provides a way of navigating the ambiguous representations of the ethnic identity of proselytes and their relation to Jewishness.

Acts uses religious activity to make ethnic connections between Jews and non-Jews of a different type as well. In the narrative depicting Paul in Athens, for example, Acts portrays some Athenian philosophers asking Paul about the "foreign deities" (ξένα δαιμονία) whom he proclaims because "all the Athenians and the resident foreigners would spend their time in nothing but telling or hearing something new" (Ἀθηναῖοι δὲ πάντες καὶ οἱ ἐπιδημοῦντες ξένοι εἰς οὐδὲν ἕτερον ηὐκαίρουν ἢ λέγειν τι ἢ ἀκούειν τι καινότερον) (17:21).[115] These Athenians identify Paul's deities as foreign and non-Greek. Acts, however, uses Paul's response to turn this claim around.

Luke's Paul contends that he revealed "the unknown god" (ὁ ἄγνωστος θεός), a deity who was already worshipped in Athens (17:23). Paul's god is not foreign, just unknown. Paul then claims that his god is "the God who created the world and everything in it" (ὁ θεὸς ὁ ποιήσας τὸν κόσμον καὶ πάντα τὰ ἐν αὐτῷ) and who "being master of heaven and earth does not live in handmade temples" (οὗτος οὐρανοῦ καὶ γῆς ὑπάρχων κύριος οὐκ ἐν χειροποιήτοις ναοῖς κατοικεῖ) (17:24).[116] Paul thus reveals the unknown god as the ancestral God of the Jews.

Paul then contends that the God of Israel made every *ethnos* of humans from one man and determined the geographic boundaries of each ethnic population (17:26). Moreover, humans live and move and exist (ἐν αὐτῷ γὰρ ζῶμεν καὶ κινούμεθα καὶ ἐσμέν) through God (17:28a). "Indeed," Paul proclaims, "we are even [this God's] offspring" (τοῦ γὰρ καὶ γένος ἐσμέν) (17:28b).[117] Each of these claims creates an *ethnic* link between the God of the Jews and *all* humans. The apparent ethnic distinctions between humans exist because God determined them. Thus, the God of the Jews is not a foreign deity; rather, he is the ultimate ancestor of all humanity according to Acts.[118]

Acts uses religious traditions to demarcate ethnic boundaries, navigate ethnic change, and make ethnic connections. But the book also uses religious ideology to assert and regulate differences among Jews. As discussed above, Acts distinguishes between Jews and proselytes. It also differentiates Jews by sect, lineage, and geographical origin. These distinctions are not neutral but are part of the broader ethnic reasoning of Acts. They offer a glimpse of how Luke privileges some ways of "being Jewish" over others.

For example, Acts often presents the Pharisees in a positive light and the Sadducees in a negative one.[119] The Sadducees become annoyed with the teaching of Peter and John (4:1), and jealousy fills them when they see the disciple's miraculous power (5:17). In contrast, the Pharisee Gamaliel does not hinder Peter and John's teaching and persuades others to do the same (5:34). Paul self-identifies as a Pharisee two times (23:6, 26:5; cf. 22:3). In the first instance, Acts leverages this identification to align Christians with the Pharisees and against the Sadducees (23:6–8). Paul claims that his trial stems from his Pharisaical view of resurrection. In the second instance, Paul makes the same claim (26:8); yet he does not connect his view of resurrection with a Jewish sect but with God's promise to "our ancestors" (26:7). Paul's trial stems from a connection between his God and his ethnic identity. Paul transmits God's promise ethnically. Such rhetoric does not create an ethnic distinction between those who share Paul's view and those who do not. That is, Paul is not saying that Sadducees are not Jews; rather, Paul's rhetoric regulates distinctions among Jews through ethnic reasoning. Acts thus legitimates Paul's view because it aligns with the ancestors and invalidates the view of those who oppose him. Acts asserts and regulates differences among Jews through their views of resurrection.

Conclusion

Acts was written within the context of a Greek *polis* sometime around the beginning of the second century CE. In his narrative of Christian origins, the author seeks to legitimate the identity of Christians, especially that of Christian non-Jews, by creating an alternate construal of Jewish and Christian identities. Many scholars have considered the depiction of Jews and Judaism in Acts and debated whether Acts is anti-Jewish or pro-Jewish. In this book, in agreement with Lawrence Wills, I emphasize the stylized ways that Acts represents Jews interacting in various civic contexts, especially in the narrative of Acts 15–18. With Barreto, I pay careful attention to the ethnic rhetoric the author of Acts uses and consider the ways that he constructs both Jewish and Christian identities. By placing both of these emphases together, I suggest that the writer of Acts uses the connection between gods, their people, and ancestral customs to produce a Jewish identity that is conducive to his depiction of Christian origins and identity.

Unlike later second-century writers such as Justin Martyr, he does not develop a theory of Christians as the embodiment of "true Israel." As I argue in the following chapters, Luke instead attempts to make room for Jesus followers within the category "Jew." Nevertheless, like these later writers, he attempts to suggest that Jesus followers are superior to others by characterizing some non-Jesus-following Jews as especially disruptive for the *polis*. Jesus followers remain "Jews" from the perspective of his ethnic reasoning, but he privileges them over other, non-Jesus-following Jews. Of course, Luke is not the only one at the beginning of the second century who makes such identity claims. In the subsequent chapters I consider Luke's ethnic rhetoric in relation to two examples of ethnic reasoning from Greek cities under Roman rule: the imperial temple complex in Aphrodisias and the Salutaris Foundation inscription from Ephesus.

TWO

Collecting Ethnē *in Aphrodisias and Acts 2:5–13*

TONGUES OF FIRE APPEAR. JESUS'S promise has arrived: a πνεῦμα ἅγιον ("Holy Spirit") fills the master's disciples, and they begin speaking in foreign languages (Acts 2:1–4). With the stage set for a momentous event, the author of Acts blithely informs his readers, ἦσαν δὲ εἰς Ἰερουσαλήμ κατοικοῦντες Ἰουδαῖοι . . . ἀπο ἔθνους ("there were living in Jerusalem Jews . . . from every *ethnos*") (2:5). He goes on to provide a list of these Jews' *ethnē*, a term usually used to denote the customs and homeland shared by ancestors.[1] These Jews are Parthians, Medes, Elamites, and residents of Mesopotamia, Judea, Cappadocia, Pontus, Asia, Phrygia, Pamphylia, Egypt, the parts of Libya belonging to Cyrene, visiting Romans, Cretans, and Arabs (2:9–11). In this first use of Ἰουδαῖος in Acts, Luke highlights the complexity of Jewish ethnicity in a way that evokes Roman-styled collections of *ethnē* and Rome's power to legitimate ethnic hierarchies and disguise ethnic change.

Acts 2:5–13 combines overlapping identifications of Jewishness in a single passage indicating that Acts takes Jewish identity to be multiple and hybrid. In this chapter I examine the ethnic rhetoric of Luke's list, focusing on the production of Jewish identity and difference in Acts 2:5–13. I argue that Acts 2:5–13 strategically combines multiple ways of being Jewish in a single passage, thereby emphasizing that Luke understood Jewish identity to be flexible. From Luke's perspective, Jewish identity could be inherited, or it could be achieved through proper ancestral customs as a *proselyte*.[2] Comparing this passage with civic identity produced by the sculptures of *ethnē* collected in the Sebasteion (imperial temple complex)

41

at Aphrodisias in Caria, I further suggest that Acts 2:5–13 and the Sebasteion both "collect" *ethnē* in ways that leveraged Roman imperial rhetoric, religious imagery, and ethnic lists to produce identity in ways that were rhetorically useful for their respective contexts. By juxtaposing Acts 2:5–13 and the Sebasteion, I highlight how Roman-styled population lists "fix" ethnic identities—producing identity and marking difference—in order to legitimate the identity of contested populations. I argue that the author of Acts lists Jews from various *ethnē* to highlight ethnic difference among Jews while simultaneously depicting a shared ethnic identification between Jews and proselytes. In a similar way, the benefactors for the Sebasteion leverage a collection of *ethnē* to highlight ethnic difference between conquered populations and Romans while also depicting an ethnic identification between Aphrodisians and Romans through their shared connection with Aphrodite. The Sebasteion produces both an intimacy between the Aphrodisians and the Romans and also a corresponding distance between the Aphrodisians and other *ethnē* by means of ethnic reasoning. Both Acts and the benefactors for the Sebasteion employ a Roman-styled collection of *ethnē* in ways that realign identities while at the same time characterizing their particular ethnic rhetoric as given or static.

Ethnic Rhetoric and Roman Imperial Propaganda

During the *saeculum augustum,* the use of art, architecture, and other forms of visual communication took a decisive turn toward standardization, with a focus on the emperor and Rome, as Paul Zanker observed decades ago. This gradual standardization of visual communication provided Romans with a means of projecting a patina of Roman imperial stability. Gathering together sculptures of the various populations that the Romans had "conquered" was one important way that the elite in Rome could use images to project imperial stability. By assembling images of conquered populations from diverse periods and locations into a single collection of *ethnē,* these Romans also projected an all-encompassing hegemony across time and space, displaying their power over the *oikoumenē,* the known world.[3]

In the city of Rome, the visual representation of ethnic groups often took the form of statues or images of conquered populations. For example, statues of fourteen *nationes* were stationed in Pompey's theater in the heart of Rome, and during the Augustan period, a *Porticus ad Nationes* was constructed. There, *simulacra omnium gentium* ("images of all the peoples") were erected, according to the fourth-century CE writer Servius. In the Forum of Augustus, a *tituli gentium* ("list of peoples") was crafted, according to Velleius Paterculus. Cassius Dio states that Augustus's funeral procession contained images of prominent Romans beginning with Romulus and his other (mythic) ancestors and incorporating into the procession bronze statues of τά τε ἔθνη πάνθ' ὅσα προσεκτήσατο ("all of the *ethnē* that were acquired by him").[4] As Nasrallah observes, "all the nations . . . followed the father of the empire."[5]

During the Roman era, the visual and rhetorical representation of ethnic populations became a powerful means of extolling Roman power over other ethnic populations. Geographical representation provided a visual language for Romans to project a political and cultural stability while at the same time naturalizing the very ethnic rhetoric that made such projections possible. This form of ethnic rhetoric marginalized and subjected those who were not Roman. Yet it could be used by non-Romans as well: in the provinces of Rome, others strategically manipulated and deployed such Roman imperial rhetoric for their own ends.[6]

In the context of this imperial propaganda, religious activities and protocols did not exist as a discourse distinct from ethnic rhetoric. Rather, these activities could operate as one more means of working within Roman claims to hegemony. Those in Rome used religious imagery and ethnic representations to authorize their power over subjected peoples visually and rhetorically because religion and ethnicity were not separate categories but were part of the larger discourse of peoplehood. This is evident in one of the most famous Roman-era population lists, which appears in Virgil's epic foundation myth of Rome, the *Aeneid*.[7]

Midway through the *Aeneid,* the goddess Venus/Aphrodite presents her son Aeneas, the legendary hero associated with the foundation of Rome and a progenitor of Augustus, with a shield crafted by Vulcan, the divine blacksmith. The shield contained images of "future" Roman triumphs (*Aen.* 8.626–728) in the form of Augustus accepting gifts from a long array of conquered *gentes* ("peoples") who spoke in different tongues and were adorned in diverse fashions and arms (8.720–23). The Nomad *gens,* the ungirt Africans, the Leleges, the Carians, the quivered Gelonians, the Morini, and the untamed Dahae all lined up to pay honor to Augustus (8.724–28).

Virgil's list can be viewed as legitimating the Augustan conquests of various *ethnē* religiously by linking Augustus to Aeneas and Aeneas to Aphrodite.[8] Augustus, the *Aeneid* points out, is the "son of a god" via Aeneas, the son of Aphrodite. Moreover, as the *Aeneid* repeatedly asserts, the founding of Rome and the rise of Augustus were mandated by fate and endorsed by Jupiter, who consistently intervened whenever this fate was threatened. The gods authorized Roman power and at the same time masked Virgil's rhetorical ideology as divinely sanctioned.

This style of population list proved useful outside of Rome as well, including among those from provincial and conquered *ethnē.* Both Philo, a Jew from Alexandria, and Josephus, a Judean Jew who composed his famous writings under imperial patronage in Rome, provide lists of *ethnē* similar to those found in Roman imperial rhetoric from the Augustan era. But they transform these lists to promote the view that Jews are both an independent *ethnē* and peaceful participants in Roman hegemony. Philo, writing from the middle of the first century CE, employs a Roman-styled population list to demonstrate the extent of Jewish influence in the Roman *oikoumenē.* In his *Embassy to Gaius,* he responds to emperor Gaius's attempt to desecrate the temple for the God of Israel in Jerusalem by erecting his own image in the temple precinct. Philo incorporates a speech of Marcus Julius Agrippa (10 BCE–44 CE)—grandson of Herod the Great, king of the tetrarchies of Philip and Herod Antipas, and friend of Gaius—in his own appeal.[9] Philo's Agrippa emphasizes the connection between Jerusalem and the Jews who lived around the world, exclaiming:

περὶ δὲ τῆς ἱεροπόλεως τὰ προσήκοντά μοι λεκτέον· αὕτη, καθάπερ ἔφην, ἐμὴ μέν ἐστι πατρίς, μητρόπολις δὲ οὐ μιᾶς

χώρας Ἰουδαίας ἀλλὰ καὶ τῶν πλείστων, διὰ τὰς ἀποικίας
ἃς ἐξέπεμψεν ἐπὶ καιρῶν εἰς μὲν τὰς ὁμόρους, Αἴγυπτον,
Φοινίκην, Συρίαν τήν τε ἄλλην καὶ τὴν Κοίλην
προσαγορευομένην, εἰς δὲ τὰς πόρρω διῳκισμένας,
Παμφυλίαν, Κιλικίαν, τὰ πολλὰ τῆς Ἀσίας ἄχρι Βιθυνίας
καὶ τῶν τοῦ Πόντου μυχῶν, τὸν αὐτὸν τρόπον καὶ εἰς
Εὐρώπην, Θετταλίαν, Βοιωτίαν, Μακεδονίαν, Αἰτωλίαν,
τὴν Ἀττικήν, Ἄργος, Κόρινθον, τὰ πλεῖστα καὶ ἄριστα
Πελοποννήσου, καὶ οὐ μόνον αἱ ἤπειροι μεσταὶ τῶν
Ἰουδαϊκῶν ἀποικιῶν εἰσιν, ἀλλὰ καὶ νήσων αἱ δοκιμώταται,
Εὔβοια, Κύπρος, Κρήτη.

As for the holy city, I must say what befits me to say. While she,
as I have said, is my fatherland, she is also the mother city not
of just one region, Judea, but of most of the others in virtue of
the colonies sent out at different times to the neighboring lands
Egypt, Phoenicia, the part of Syria called the Hallow and the
rest as well and the lands lying far apart, Pamphylia, Cilicia,
most of Asia up to Bithynia and the corners of Pontus, similarly
also into Europe, Thessaly, Boetia, Macedonia, Aetolia, Attica,
Argos, Corinth, and most of the best parts of Peloponnese. And
not only are the mainlands full of Jewish colonies but also the
most highly esteemed of the islands Euboea, Cyprus, and Crete.
(*Embassy*, 281–82)[10]

According to Philo's Agrippa, Jewish colonies, like their Roman counter-
parts, extended throughout the world. While Jews reside in diverse "fatherlands," they are united by Jerusalem, the Jewish "mother city."[11] Jews from
around the world pay tribute to their "mother city" while at the same time
retaining their connection to their various "fatherlands." As Cynthia Baker
writes, "this diverse array of Jews of diverse fatherlands nevertheless shares
with other Jews a sense of cultic piety toward the Holy City, broad patterns
of worship, and other ancient customs."[12] This dual, hybrid citizenship allows Philo's Agrippa to argue that a benefit to the temple in Jerusalem

would have positive repercussions throughout the Roman *oikoumenē*. Jews everywhere would honor the emperor that much more—just not as a deity.[13] Philo thus situates the Jewish refusal to honor Gaius as a deity at the temple in Jerusalem in relation to Jewish ancestral customs—the way that Jews revere the "mother city" no matter where they currently reside, the honor they impart to the temple in Jerusalem, and the prohibitions of images of the Jewish God. Through this Philo has shown that to honor Gaius as he desired would be an affront to Jews and, perhaps more important, to God. He uses a Roman-style ethnic rhetoric to accomplish this. While the rhetoric of the Augustan era used collections of *ethnē* to promote Roman dominance, Philo refracts imperial rhetoric away from Rome and toward Jerusalem in order to promote Jewish influence and Jewish piety toward their ancestral God.

Josephus also leverages the rhetoric available in a Roman model of listing *ethnē* in his *Judean War*. When Judea was on the edge of revolt in 66 CE, Josephus depicts Marcus Julius Agrippa II (ca. 27–93 CE), a Roman-supported client "king," trying to reason with a riotous crowd in Jerusalem. Agrippa, standing on the roof of his palace, extols the crowd not to take any action that the Romans could construe as revolt because Rome has destroyed all who opposed them. Agrippa then recounts the populations Romans had conquered, from the great Athenians and Spartans to the peoples of the Bosporus and the frontiers of Ister.[14] According to such reasoning, Rome's previous display of power over and domination of other peoples ought to dissuade a Jewish revolt because Romans always decimated whoever opposed them. More than this, Agrippa seeks to validate Roman power by reference to God's power. After recounting Roman conquests, Agrippa claims that the only recourse the Jews who desire to revolt have is to divine assistance. But even the Jewish God appears to be on the side of Rome, for a power like Rome could not arise apart from divine providence.[15] Agrippa uses a Roman style of collecting populations to display Roman power, in part by claiming that the Jewish God supported the rise of the Romans. As Josephus knew well when he wrote his *War*, Rome's previous displays of power and the claim of God's providence did not avert disaster for the Jews in Judea and in Jerusalem.

Using population lists to demonstrate influence across the known world, those in Rome—Pompey, Augustus, Virgil—displayed, organized, and paraded the populations of the *oikoumenē,* a rhetorical strategy that naturalized Roman hegemonic claims by repeated reference to and perpetual display of conquered *ethnē.* As the examples of Philo and Josephus show, however, "subject" peoples could adapt the habit of listing conquered peoples to their own ends, elevating their own *ethnos* even as they adopted an attitude of acceptance toward Roman dominance. In each case, the gods were said to be involved: Aeneas's shield underscored the importance of the divine origins of Rome through the visual representation of the peoples whom Rome would subjugate, above all by Octavian Augustus, the first Roman emperor. The spectacle of peoples subjected to Rome thus served to divinely sanction Roman dominance and to create an ethnic distinction between Romans and other populations.

The collections of statues of conquered *ethnē* in honor of Pompey and Augustus and the "collection" of *ethnē* in the *Aeneid* suggested that Romans rule and other peoples properly submit. This has the effect of stabilizing Roman dominance and marginalizing and subjugating outsiders along ethnic and religious lines. By naming Jerusalem as the "mother city" and celebrating the Jewish ancestral deity, Philo adjusts this claim and refracts it toward the influence of Jews in the *oikoumenē.* The Jews are also divinely appointed and protected, Philo argues, and they have spread their peaceable piety throughout the Roman world. For Josephus's Agrippa, Romans provide peace, and opposition to them will bring destruction. Moreover, if Jews rebel against the Romans, they are fighting against their ancestral God, since God must have authorized Roman dominance.

The examples of Philo and Josephus highlight the complexity of appropriating Roman ethnic discourse for other rhetorical ends. Philo reappropriated this rhetoric to emphasize God's power, Jerusalem, and the Jewish *ethnos,* but Josephus appeared to support Roman dominance and condemned those Jews who sought to resist it in relation to the power of God as well. These examples demonstrate that Roman-styled collections of *ethnē* provided a means for both those in Rome and those outside of Rome to navigate ethnic similarity and difference.

The collection of *ethnē* statues erected in the Sebasteion at Aphrodisias in Caria offers another example of the reappropriation and transformation of a Roman model by provincials.[16] Like Virgil, the elite Aphrodisians who commissioned the Sebasteion visually display the connection between Aphrodite and Aeneas, the forefather of Augustus. Like Josephus, they stabilize Roman hegemony by visually rehearsing Roman dominance over other *ethnē*. However, like Philo, they also use the rhetoric of an *ethnē* list to redeploy Roman hegemonic claims and to use them to bolster the importance of Aphrodite, the patron goddess of Aphrodisias.

Aphrodisian Identity, the Sebasteion, and Listing *Ethnē*

The so-called Sebasteion from the city of Aphrodisias exhibits how religious rhetoric could be embodied within the urban landscape and used to navigate ethnic difference.[17] The Romans exhibited their conquered peoples in Rome's theater and temple complexes, listing them in honorific inscriptions displayed in the Forum and elsewhere, and parading them through the city. The Aphrodisians also displayed the diverse *ethnē* under Rome's dominion, but differently. Aphrodisians celebrated their own status as a free city within the conquered *ethnē* that honor Roman hegemony. In this temple complex, Roman rule is valued positively as a divinely given inevitability, but so is Aphrodisian freedom, which, the reliefs in the Sebasteion imply, is rooted in the shared patronage of the goddess Aphrodite. Augustus, the *Aeneid* and other Augustan-era propaganda had argued, is the son of Aphrodite; Aphrodite is also the patron goddess of Aphrodisias.

In the first half of the first century CE, the city of Aphrodisias undertook the construction of an ornate temple complex composed of four structures and an elaborate collection of carved reliefs.[18] Situated along the road just to the east of the city's monumental temple of Aphrodite, the city's two agoras, and the theater, the temple complex occupied an important and central place in the city.[19] Two families dedicated the complex to Aphrodite, the Theoi Sebastoi (divine emperors), and the *dēmos*. The brothers Menander and Eusebes dedicated a monumental gate and a north portico, while Diogenes and Attalus, also brothers, dedicated a south portico and a temple of Aphrodite and the Theoi Sebastoi.[20] Construction of the Sebasteion likely began under Tiberius and was completed during the reign of Nero.[21] The four structures of the complex were an aediculated propylon (monumental gate) at the west end, a temple for Aphrodite and the imperial cult at the east, and two porticos separated by a paved walkway approximately fourteen meters wide.[22] The two-story propylon was joined with the north and south porticos in alignment with the existing road. At the other end of the complex, the imperial temple was situated on an axis with the porticos.[23] The material remains of the two-story propylon and temple are limited, but a significant portion of the porticos and the reliefs that lined them survive.[24]

Three colonnaded stories divide the twelve-meter-tall porticos horizontally. Doric capitals crown the columns of the first story; Ionic, the second; Corinthian, the third. Fifty rows of columns divide the façade of the north portico vertically. The slightly shorter south portico contains forty-five rows of columns. The space between the columns housed an estimated 180 sculptured relief panels of which archeologists have discovered the remains of more than sixty. The extant panels contain images based on three themes: the mythic past, Rome and the imperial family, and the allegorical representations of *ethnē* personified as captured females.[25]

Like the collections of images of *ethnē* stationed in Rome, the visual representations of ethnic groups in Aphrodisias made up an archive of Roman world dominance. Archeologists estimate the Sebasteion contained room for at least forty *ethnē* images; however, evidence remains for only sixteen people groups, one of which is the ἔθνους Ἰουδαίων ("*ethnos* of Jews"). This means that an image representing Jews as a conquered population likely stood in the Aphrodisian Sebasteion at the time when Philo was proclaiming Jews as colonizers in his letter to Gaius. Joining Jews were Arabians, Bessi, Bosporians, Callaeci, Cretens, Cypriots, Dacians, Dardani, Egyptians, Iapodes, Piroysti, Rhaeti, Sicilians, and Trumpilini.[26]

Joyce Reynolds has argued that the collection of images represents an Augustan expansion similar to the lists of Dio Cassius and others discussed above. However, R. R. R. Smith has observed that a number of the *ethnē* represented were not part of any Augustan expansion, and others

were not even part of the Roman empire when the Sebasteion was constructed.[27]

In spite of these facts, Smith convincingly connects the *ethnē* to Augustan imperial rhetoric. He writes, "The members so far could be understood as including a range of different parts of the Augustan empire, thus:
some from the civilized centre (the Greek islands, Egypt), some from beyond the frontier illustrating the effective reach of imperial power (Dacians,
Bosporans, Arabs), and many or most from the periphery, defining the Romanized side of the frontier (the northern and western *ethnē*)."[28] Even
though Augustus did not conquer a number of the peoples depicted, the
Sebasteion represents them as conquered ethnic groups. The silent women,
like the mute images paying homage to Augustus on Aeneas's shield, project a Roman imperial message: even unconquered *ethnē* submit to Roman
power and dominance.[29]

The *ethnē* reliefs of the Sebasteion depict Roman imperial dominance
over other populations, but they do so in Aphrodisian ways. Though not
impossible, it is not at all likely that the city's ancestral *ethnē,* the Carians,
were included among the conquered *ethnē* reliefs. Caria was not "conquered" by Rome, according to Aphrodisian rhetoric. The region probably remained a free ally of Rome until at least the first war with Mithridates
at the beginning of the first century BCE. During the war with the Pon-
tian king, Aphrodisias and a few surrounding cities fought on the side of
the Romans but eventually surrendered to Mithridates's forces. They were
later "recovered" by Sulla, who treated the entire region as Roman. Thus,
from a Carian perspective, the region was not conquered but annexed by
Rome.[30]

The image of Caria presented on Aeneas's shield, however, paints a
different picture of the region's status. There, Carians appear as a conquered population. Sitting among the conquered, the Carians pay homage
to Augustus as one among many other exemplars of Roman dominance and
provincial subjection. In spite of their differences, however, the models
of ethnic reasoning deployed by Virgil and in the Sebasteion remained
relatively consistent: both collect *ethnē* and arrange them in a religious
context—as divine gift described in a literary *ekphrasis* and a temple com-

plex, respectively—and both mark ethnic difference by referencing gods and their peoples. Virgil may have assumed that the Carians were just another conquered people, but the Sebasteion emphasized Aphrodisian ancestral ties with Rome instead, not Aphrodisian submission to Rome.

Even if the Carians were depicted among the personifications of the conquered peoples on the Sebasteion relief (which remains highly unlikely), the other reliefs strategically repositioned Aphrodisias as aligned with Rome. For example, a set of panels near the collection of *ethnē* depicted the life of Aeneas, the so-called founder of Rome, progenitor of Augustus, son of Aphrodite/Venus, and recipient of Vulcan's shield.[31] This collection of images reused a popular narrative of Rome's mythic origins, the same myth retold by Virgil. It also directly connected Aphrodisias and the city's patron goddess with Aeneas and the imperial center. The reliefs depicting the journey of Aeneas, coupled with the defeated *ethnē,* visually tied Aphrodisias to Rome while rhetorically undermining the ability of others, such as the conquered Jews, to claim such connections. Highlighting such "accidental" associations in a prominent place in the city and in stone perpetuated a close ethnic connection between Romans and the city of Aphrodisias.

The reliefs in the Sebasteion used religious images and activities both to identify Aphrodisians with Rome and to distinguish them ethnically from other conquered populations. By gathering conquered ethnic populations in a temple complex, the Aphrodisians literally carved their place into imperial and heavenly geography. This deployment of ethnic reasoning allowed them space to negotiate their place within the Roman world on their own terms, developing a specifically Aphrodisian idiom of a Roman model of ethnic rhetoric that connected Aphrodisias and the Sebastoi. This hybrid model of ethnic reasoning, which was at the same time pro-Roman and pro-Aphrodisian, combined conquered *ethnē,* the free city of Aphrodisias, and images of the shared patron goddess Aphrodite to place the city and its people on a Roman imperial map that favored their own *ethnē* over others.[32]

The list of *ethnē* in Acts 2:5–13 participates in a similar form of ethnic rhetoric but does so for a different rhetorical end, privileging Jews in the divine hierarchy rather than Carians. The Sebasteion used a collection of *ethnē* and the city's patron goddess to unite Aphrodisians with Rome and to privilege their place on an imperial map. In a similar way the list of *ethnē* in Acts unites Jews spread across the *oikoumenē*. Like Philo, the writer of Acts also portrays Jerusalem as the "mother city" of a peaceable and pious *ethnē* that has spread throughout Roman territory and beyond. Unlike the authors and Aphrodisian benefactors discussed thus far, however, Acts uses a collection of *ethnē* in ways that enable ethnic flexibility and legitimate ethnic change religiously.

Acts 2:5–13 and Jewish Identity in Acts

The narrative procession of Jews from every *ethnos* listed in Acts 2:5–13 provides an example of the author's technique for leveraging the hybrid and multiple character of ethnic identity, and Jewishness in particular, in his Christian origins construction project. Like the images of the Sebasteion, the passage presents a Roman-styled collection of *ethnē* to mark identity and difference. Also similar to the Sebasteion, the passage uses the latent ties between ethnic populations and their gods in ways that make it possible to realign ethnic identities.

The connection between Jewish identity and Christian identity is not apparent in the passage at first glance. After the outpouring of the Holy Spirit, the apostles begin speaking in various languages (2:4). This newfound linguistic gift allows them to speak to the Jews from around the world who live in Jerusalem. Luke writes:

(2:5) ῏Ησαν δὲ εἰς ᾽Ιερουσαλὴμ κατοικοῦντες ᾽Ιουδαῖοι, ἄνδρες εὐλαβεῖς ἀπὸ παντὸς ἔθνους τῶν ὑπὸ τὸν οὐρανόν. (6) γενομένης δὲ τῆς φωνῆς ταύτης συνῆλθεν τὸ πλῆθος καὶ συνεχύθη, ὅτι ἤκουον εἷς ἕκαστος τῇ ἰδίᾳ διαλέκτῳ λαλούντων αὐτῶν. (7) ἐξίσταντο δὲ καὶ ἐθαύμαζον λέγοντες· οὐχ ἰδοὺ ἅπαντες οὗτοί εἰσιν οἱ λαλοῦντες Γαλιλαῖοι; (8) καὶ πῶς ἡμεῖς ἀκούομεν ἕκαστος τῇ ἰδίᾳ διαλέκτῳ ἡμῶν ἐν ᾗ ἐγεννήθημεν; (9) Πάρθοι καὶ Μῆδοι

καὶ Ἐλαμῖται καὶ οἱ κατοικοῦντες τὴν Μεσοποταμίαν,
Ἰουδαίαν τε καὶ Καππαδοκίαν, Πόντον καὶ τὴν Ἀσίαν, (10)
Φρυγίαν τε καὶ Παμφυλίαν, Αἴγυπτον καὶ τὰ μέρη τῆς
Λιβύης τῆς κατὰ Κυρήνην, καὶ οἱ ἐπιδημοῦντες Ῥωμαῖοι,
(11) Ἰουδαῖοί τε καὶ προσήλυτοι, Κρῆτες καὶ Ἄραβες,
ἀκούομεν λαλούντων αὐτῶν ταῖς ἡμετέραις γλώσσαις τὰ
μεγαλεῖα τοῦ θεοῦ. (12) ἐξίσταντο δὲ πάντες καὶ διηπόρουν,
ἄλλος πρὸς ἄλλον λέγοντες· τί θέλει τοῦτο εἶναι;
(13) ἕτεροι δὲ διαχλευάζοντες ἔλεγον ὅτι γλεύκους
μεμεστωμένοι εἰσίν.

(2:5) Now there were Jews living in Jerusalem, devout men from
every *ethnos* under heaven. (6) And as a result of this sound a
crowd gathered and was confused, because each one heard [the
apostles] speaking in their own language. (7) Amazed and as-
tonished, they asked, "Are not all these who are speaking Galileans? (8) And how is it that we hear, each of us, in our own
language into which we were born? (9) Parthians, Medes,
Elamites, and residents of Mesopotamia, Judea and Cappadocia, Pontus and Asia, (10) Phrygia and Pamphylia, Egypt and
the parts of Libya belonging to Cyrene, and visiting Romans,
both Jews and proselytes, (11) Cretans and Arabs—in our own
languages we hear them speaking about God's mighty acts." (12)
All were amazed and perplexed, saying to one another, "What
does this mean?" (13) But others sneered and said, "They are
filled with new wine." (Acts 2:5-13)[33]

In the first verse (2:5), Luke identifies the gathered crowd as Jews, residents of Jerusalem, devout men, and men from every *ethnos*. Next,
through the mouth of the crowd, he identifies the disciples as Γαλιλαῖοι,
Galileans. Then, again through the singular voice of the crowd, he lists
ethnē in ways similar to the collections of conquered *ethnē* found in Roman
imperial *ethnē* lists and adapted by Philo and Josephus and in the images
of the Sebasteion. The way that Luke lists these Jews, describing them as

devout, living in Jerusalem, and from every *ethnos,* has two effects: it emphasizes the possibility of ethnic difference among Jews and simultaneously identifies proselytes as Jews. Both of these emphases will allow Luke to legitimate the Jewishness of Christian non-Jews later in Acts.

DEVOUT JEWS LIVING IN JERUSALEM

In Acts 2:5, Luke presents emigrant Jews who have made Jerusalem their home. A number of scholars have found this depiction to be jarring because they assert that it does not make sense for Luke to identify the men gathered in Jerusalem as Jews. These Jews are also from non-Jewish *ethnē,* these scholars point out, and therefore cannot be "Jews," properly speaking. Textual variants that do not include Ἰουδαῖοι in 2:5 have heightened speculation about this apparent contradiction. One important codex, Sinaiticus (א 01; fourth century), omits Ἰουδαῖος from the verse, removing the problem entirely, and the word order of a number of other manuscripts differs.[34] Perhaps the initial text of 2:5 did not contain Ἰουδαῖοι, and the gathered crowd was therefore not Jewish.

Prominent proponents of this point of view include Kirsopp Lake, who in 1933 proposed that Ἰουδαῖοι was a later addition.[35] More recent scholars such as Richard Pervo agree. He understands the presence of Ἰουδαῖοι in 2:5 as "a pedantic D-Text gloss that has entered the broader tradition."[36] Marianne Palmer Bonz questions the presence of Ἰουδαῖοι for another reason. She writes, "to speak of Jews dwelling in Jerusalem seems excessively clumsy for a writer of Luke's general skill."[37] Along similar lines, Bruce Metzger thinks that it is "remarkable" that Acts would state that Jews lived in Jerusalem, though he accepts that the word was likely included in the initial text. It is such a difficult reading, he suggests, that it must have been original.[38]

A number of factors beyond its status as a *lectio difficilior* support the presence of Ἰουδαῖοι in the earliest attainable text of 2:5, as other scholars have argued. First, important majuscules and manuscripts support the inclusion of Ἰουδαῖοι in this verse, and though a number do present a different word order, they include Ἰουδαῖοι nonetheless.[39] Second, as Jack

Sanders has pointed out, there is a reason to believe that Sinaiticus (ℵ 01) would omit Ἰουδαῖοι here, as it also omits Ἰουδαῖος in Acts 21:20, and it is the only major majuscule to do so.[40] These two verses (2:5 and 21:20) portray Jews in a positive light. In 2:5, Jews are "devout" (εὐλαβεῖς), and in 21:20, they are "ones who trust (in Christ)" (οἱ πιστεύοντες). Sanders contends that these two omissions indicate an anti-Jewish tendency in Sinaiticus.[41] Though Sanders's contention is by no means conclusive, it does provide one possible explanation for the omission of Ἰουδαῖοι in Sinaiticus. For the purposes of this study, it is assumed that the writer intended to include Ἰουδαῖοι here and that the textual variation can be attributed either to a later, theologically motivated editorial decision or to a scribal error. Though the text critical problems with this verse may never be fully solved, the inclusion of Ἰουδαῖοι within the text is further suggested by evidence internal to the narrative, especially the writer's ethnic reasoning. I argue that Ἰουδαῖοι fits the larger argument of the writer, enhancing his portrayal of Jewish identity.

Scholars who assume that Ἰουδαῖοι is in the text often interpret the writer's list as an enumeration of the diaspora Jews who had gathered in Jerusalem for Pentecost, along with other, resident Jews.[42] However, Luke's word choice makes it clear that the connection between these Jews and other Jews who dwell in Jerusalem was continual and not attributable to the swelled population of the city during the Pentecost festival.[43] These other Jews were κατοικοῦντες ("residing") in the holy city, and in Acts, κατοικέω always has the sense of "dwelling" or "residing" rather than "sojourning" or "visiting."[44] Thus, Luke presents emigrants from various homelands who have made Jerusalem, the ancestral home of the God of the Jews and mother city of the Jewish people, their permanent residence.

As noted above, Luke also identifies the Jews gathered as "devout men" (ἄνδρες εὐλαβεῖς). The term εὐλαβής occurs two other times in Acts, and both instances refer to a positive quality of Jews and suggest devotion with regard to Jewish ancestral customs.[45] The Jews who buried Stephen's stone-battered body and mourn his death are ἄνδρες εὐλαβεῖς (8:2), while a certain ἀνὴρ εὐλαβὴς κατὰ τὸν νόμον ("devout man according to the law"), Ananias, comes to the aid of Saul/Paul after God blinds him on the way to Damascus (22:12; cf. 9:10–19).[46] In all three cases, εὐλαβής identifies a positive quality that pious Jews possess.

Luke also states that these pious men are ἀπὸ παντὸς ἔθνους τῶν ὑπὸ τὸν οὐρανόν ("from every *ethnos* that is under the heaven") (2:5).[47] In Acts, the term ἔθνος in the singular refers to an ancestral people group, roughly equated with an "ethnic group," rather than a political territory, a nation. For example, the magical power of a certain Simon amazed τὸ ἔθνος τῆς Σαμαρείας ("the *ethnos* of Samaria") (8:9), and Cornelius was well spoken of by ὅλος τὸ ἔθνος τῶν Ἰουδαίων ("the whole *ethnos* of the Jews") (10:22). Luke's Paul claims that he spent his entire life among his own *ethnos* after stating that he was born in Tarsus (26:4). From this verse, it seems clear that Paul spent his life with Jews, his *ethnos*, while living outside of the "nation" of Judea. An ἔθνος in Acts is an ancestral or ethnic population (connected to an ancestral "homeland") rather than only a geographic or political boundary (a "nation"), and the ancestral people group that Luke refers to most often is, of course, the ἔθνος of Jews. In addition to the verses cited above, Luke's Paul refers to his *ethnos* two other times (24:17 and 28:19), and characters in Acts twice refer to the *ethnos* of the Jews as ἔθνος τοῦτο ("this *ethnos*") (24:2, 10).

Luke also uses ἔθνος in a generic way, referring three times to πᾶν ἔθνος ("every *ethnos*") (2:5, 10:35, 17:26). In Paul's famous Aeropagus speech in Athens, Luke also connects ἔθνος to ancestral populations rather than "nations."[48] Luke's Paul boldly proclaims, "ἐποίησέν τε ἐξ ἑνὸς πᾶν ἔθνος ἀνθρώπων κατοικεῖν ἐπὶ παντὸς προσώπου τῆς γῆς" ("[God] made from one [ancestor] every *ethnos* of humans that dwells upon the face of the earth") (17:26). A single ancestor unites every *ethnos*. In the story of Cornelius, Luke's Peter announces "ἐπ᾽ ἀληθείας καταλαμβάνομαι ὅτι οὐκ ἔστιν προσωπολήμπτης ὁ θεός, ἀλλ᾽ ἐν παντὶ ἔθνει ὁ φοβούμενος αὐτὸν καὶ ἐργαζόμενος δικαιοσύνην δεκτὸς αὐτῷ ἐστιν" ("I truly comprehend that God is not one who shows favoritism, but in every *ethnos* the one who fears him and does righteous acts is acceptable to him") (10:34–35). A single god, the God of the Jews, accepts people from every *ethnos*.[49]

These uses of ἔθνος in the singular raise questions about the use of the term in Acts 2:5. There, Jews are from every *ethnos,* while elsewhere in Acts, Jews are members of an *ethnos.* How can Jews both be an *ethnos* and be from other non-Jewish *ethnē?*[50] The common explanation, that Luke uses ἔθνος to mean "nation" or "country" rather than "ethnic group," does not hold. On this reading, these Jews left the realm of "every *ethnos*" and moved to Jerusalem. They came out from every "nation." Supporting such a view, Pervo writes, "'From every *country* under the sun' supplies the requisite intimation of that universality that will rise from firmly Jewish foundations."[51] Jews are from other "countries," and this marks the beginning of Luke's march toward a universal Christianity. In a similar way Bruce Malina and John Pilch write, "the passage then lists these Judeans according to where they lived among non-Israelites."[52] Again, Jews from other *ethnē* are simply Jews who come to Jerusalem from other locations.

The way that Luke uses the gathered Jews to list their *ethnē* in 2:9–11 pushes against this interpretation. Luke's crowd identifies the first three "countries" as their *ethnē,* not as "nations," but as ancestral populations who were connected to "homelands"—Parthians, Medes, and Elamites (2:9).[53] Jews are Parthians, not simply from Parthia. From these three *ethnē* Luke's crowd identifies themselves as (former) residents (οἱ κατοικοῦντες) of various regions—Mesopotamia, Judea, Cappadocia, Pontus, Asia, Phrygia, Pamphylia, Egypt, and the parts of Libya belonging to Cyrene (2:9–10). They then identify themselves as "visiting Romans" (οἱ ἐπιδημοῦντες Ῥωμαῖοι) (2:10), Jews, and proselytes. Finally, the crowd returns to listing their *ethnē.* They are also Cretans and Arabs (2:11). The list shifts from identifying *ethnē* to geographical locations and back to *ethnē.* This fluctuation creates a number of problems with claims that ἔθνος is a "country." Luke does not present Jews in a singular way; rather, he presents Jewishness as hybrid.

Scholars offer a number of interpretations for why Luke lists these Jews in this way. While their recommendations provide a number of important intertextual connections, I argue below that just as the Aphrodisians presented themselves in the Sebasteion as both Carian and Roman, Luke suggests that these Jews are both Jews and members of other *ethnē.* This is

not a Lukan innovation, but it does play a significant role in his later classification of Christians who are non-Jews. As the Aphrodisians are depicted
as a separate and free *ethnos* (Carians) with a mother city (Aphrodisias) who
are nonetheless ethnically united with Rome by their common ancestral
deity (Aphrodite) and their shared participation in Roman hegemony, so
Luke strategically represents these pious men as members of an *ethnos* (they
are Jews), who have a mother city (Jerusalem) and an ancestral deity (the
Jewish God), but they are also Cretan, Arab, Parthian, and Roman. Their
ethnic identity is not limited to their home *polis* and their shared ancestors
but can strategically incorporate others as well. As we will see, this imag-
ining of Jewishness has great payoff for Luke's construction of Christian
identity.

LISTING POPULATIONS, IDENTIFYING JEWS

Luke's list of Jews resembles Roman-styled collections of *ethnē*, but it also
resembles other ways of listing ancient *ethnē* and geographic locations.[54]
Previous scholarship on the passage has proposed a number of interesting
connections between the list in Acts 2:9–11 and other population lists. However, more can still be said about the ethnic rhetoric of Luke's list. In addition to Roman imperial propaganda, two other interpretations have
garnered the support of a number of scholars: the "list of nations" in Genesis 10 and the prophetic uniting of Israel during the end times.[55] These
three interpretations are not mutually exclusive; rather, they highlight the
range of possible intertextual contexts from which the author of Acts may
be working. The common thread that links this previous scholarship on
the inspiration or source of Luke's list in Acts 2:9–11 is the observation that
such population lists are used rhetorically to unite people.[56]

    In an extensive essay, James Scott suggests that Acts 2:9–11 should
be read in light of the so-called table of nations in Genesis 10 and the story
of the tower of Babel in Genesis 11.[57] Scott argues that "Genesis 10 provided
the fundamental point of orientation for describing Israel's place among the
nations of the world" in Jewish literature. He presents a convincing argument for some influence of Genesis 10 on later Jewish literature and pro-

vides some interesting connections between the table of nations and Acts 2:9–11, but his comparison does not explain all of the features of Luke's list, such as the inclusion of Jews and proselytes.[58]

Other scholars have contended that Acts serves as a reversal of Babel, the tale of language variation recorded in Genesis 11.[59] Scholars compare Genesis 10 and 11 with Acts 2:5–13 because both list ethnic groups and include discussion of diverse languages. They take interest in the linguistic dispersion in the story of the tower of Babel in Genesis 11 and apparent linguistic unification in Acts 2. The list of *ethnē* in Acts 2 resonates with some features of the table of nations and the tower of Babel, but these narratives do not exhaust the possible meanings of Luke's population list.[60]

Because of the apparent unification of Jews under the power of this spirit, many scholars have also argued that Acts 2:5–13 envisions the eschatological ingathering of Jews prophesied in the Jewish prophets, Second Temple literature, and rabbinic literature.[61] So, for example, the Septuagint version of Isaiah states:

> καὶ ἔσται τῇ ἡμέρᾳ ἐκείνῃ προσθήσει κύριος τοῦ δεῖξαι τὴν χεῖρα αὐτοῦ τοῦ ζηλῶσαι τὸ καταλειφθὲν ὑπόλοιπον τοῦ λαοῦ, ὃ ἂν καταλειφθῇ ἀπὸ τῶν Ἀσσυρίων καὶ ἀπὸ Αἰγύπτου καὶ Βαβυλωνίας καὶ Αἰθιοπίας καὶ ἀπὸ Αἰλαμιτῶν καὶ ἀπὸ ἡλίου ἀνατολῶν καὶ ἐξ Ἀραβίας. καὶ ἀρεῖ σημεῖον εἰς τὰ ἔθνη καὶ συνάξει τοὺς ἀπολομένους Ἰσραὴλ καὶ τοὺς διεσπαρμένους τοῦ Ἰούδα συνάξει ἐκ τῶν τεσσάρων πτερύγων τῆς γῆς.

> And it will be in that day, the Lord will continue to show his hand to be zealous for the remaining remnant of the people, who might be left from the Assyrians and from Egypt and from Babylon and Ethiopia and from Elamites, and from the rising of the sun until Arabia. And he will lift up a sign for the *ethnē*, and he will gather the lost ones of Israel and the dispersed of Judah, he will gather from the four corners of the earth. (11:11–12 LXX)[62]

The prophetic vision of an ingathering of Jews at the end of time may have informed Luke's list, but he appears to have interpreted the prophecy for his own purposes. The narrative setting of the list of *ethnē* and the larger context of Acts 2, again, point beyond this connection as well. In Acts 2:5 Luke writes that these Jews gathered in Jerusalem were already residents of the city *before* the outpouring of the spirit. They did not gather because of the spirit but were already κατοικοῦντες ("residing") in Jerusalem.

The speech of Peter that follows the list of ethnic groups also challenges the reading of Acts 2:5–13 as primarily referring to an eschatological ingathering of Jews. In his speech, Peter does not refer to the ingathering of Jews as described in texts like Isaiah 11 but points to a prophesy from Joel 3:1–5a LXX (2:28–32 NRSV) that indicates that the spirit is a symbol of the power of God and a precursor to the eschatological day of the Lord. Luke's Peter quotes Joel saying:

(2:17) καὶ ἔσται ἐν ταῖς ἐσχάταις ἡμέραις, λέγει ὁ θεός, ἐκχεῶ ἀπὸ τοῦ πνεύματός μου ἐπὶ πᾶσαν σάρκα, καὶ προφητεύσουσιν οἱ υἱοὶ ὑμῶν καὶ αἱ θυγατέρες ὑμῶν καὶ οἱ νεανίσκοι ὑμῶν ὁράσεις ὄψονται καὶ οἱ πρεσβύτεροι ὑμῶν ἐνυπνίοις ἐνυπνιασθήσονται· (18) καί γε ἐπὶ τοὺς δούλους μου καὶ ἐπὶ τὰς δούλας μου ἐν ταῖς ἡμέραις ἐκείναις ἐκχεῶ ἀπὸ τοῦ πνεύματός μου, καὶ προφητεύσουσιν. (19) καὶ δώσω τέρατα ἐν τῷ οὐρανῷ ἄνω καὶ σημεῖα ἐπὶ τῆς γῆς κάτω, αἷμα καὶ πῦρ καὶ ἀτμίδα καπνοῦ. (20) ὁ ἥλιος μεταστραφήσεται εἰς σκότος καὶ ἡ σελήνη εἰς αἷμα, πρὶν ἐλθεῖν ἡμέραν κυρίου τὴν μεγάλην καὶ ἐπιφανῆ. (21) καὶ ἔσται πᾶς ὃς ἂν ἐπικαλέσηται τὸ ὄνομα κυρίου σωθήσεται.

(2:17) In the last days it will be, God declares, that I will pour out my spirit upon all flesh, and your sons and your daughters shall prophesy, and your young men shall see visions, and your old men shall dream dreams. (18) Even upon my slaves, both men and women, in those days I will pour out my spirit; and they shall prophesy. (19) And I will show portents in the heaven above and signs on the earth below, blood, and fire, and smoky mist. (20) The sun shall be turned to darkness and the moon to blood, *before the coming* of the Lord's great and glorious day. (21) Then everyone who calls on the name of the Lord shall be saved. (Acts 2:17–21, quoting Joel 3:1–5a LXX)

Peter frames the list of *ethnē* around the outpouring of the spirit of God "on all flesh" (ἐπὶ πᾶσαν σάρκα) before the "Lord's great and glorious day." Acts 2:5–13 does not merely announce the eschatological gathering of Jews from the diaspora. The quotation of Joel 3:1–5a refracts the eschatological focus of Acts 2 away from the ingathering of Jews from the diaspora and onto the miraculous deeds of God that validate the centrality of the "Lord"—Jesus, in Luke's narrative world (2:22–35).

Though there are intertextual connections between Genesis 10–11, the eschatological ingathering of Jews, and Acts 2:5–13, these correspondences do not exhaust the possible meanings of Luke's list of *ethnē*. Roman-styled population lists like those depicted in the Sebasteion and in Virgil, Philo, and Josephus offer another lens through which to view this same material.

JEWISH IDENTITY AND ROMAN-ERA ETHNIC REASONING

Roman imperial propaganda regularly used ethnic rhetoric to legitimate Roman dominance over other populations. As Philo, Josephus, and the more extended discussion of the Sebasteion demonstrated, those outside of Rome employed Roman-styled *ethnē* collections for their own rhetorical ends. Gary Gilbert has also likened Luke's list of Jews from every "nation" to the Roman *ethnē* lists. He argues that Acts 2 "employs well-known political rhetoric to advance its theological convictions,"[63] writing: "The list of nations [in Acts 2] stands as one part of the larger narrative strategy that responds to Rome's claims of universal authority and declares that the true empire belongs not to Caesar but to Jesus, who as Lord and Savior

reigns over all people."[64] For Gilbert, "The list of nations provides one deployment of this literary strategy. The crowd gathered at Pentecost and
specified in the list of nations serves as an 'anticipatory element' that looks
forward to the time when all persons from throughout the inhabited world
will come under the authority of God, Jesus and the church."[65] The depiction of Jews from every ἔθνος thus anticipates the global mission of Acts
by presenting a universalized audience of Jews for the first public sermon
of one of Jesus's disciples. On this view, Acts 2 does not display complicity
in Roman dominance but resists that dominance in favor of a Jerusalem-
centered worldview. For Gilbert, "Luke-Acts dismisses the claim that Rome
was ruler of the world and speaks of the true *oikoumenē* created through
the Spirit, ruled over by Jesus, and mapped out by the list of nations in
Acts 2."[66]

Gilbert shifts attention from the context of Roman political rhetoric
to Christian theological argument in his interpretation of Acts 2. Romans
listed people groups to display their worldwide dominance; Luke, according to Gilbert, lists people groups to display the universal salvation
through Jesus.[67] Tertullian interpreted Acts 2 similarly, understanding the
list of people groups as "proof for the universal rule of Christ."[68] Indeed,
the list in Acts 2:9–11 includes *ethnē* that are outside of Rome's power, such
as the Parthians.[69] Gilbert concludes that Acts 2 presents a "geographic
catalogue" to "declare the inevitable expansion of Christianity and the universal power of God and Jesus throughout the world."[70]

Similarly, Marianne Palmer Bonz has compared the catalogue of conquered peoples on Aeneas's shield with the list of peoples in Acts 2.[71] She
argues that the catalogues are similar in length and structure and that Luke,
like Virgil, used a population list to represent "a collection of peoples from
the farthermost ends of the known world" in a way that symbolically testi-
fies to the "theological nature of the geographical conquests."[72] Bonz, like
Gilbert, provides an avenue for exploring the list of *ethnē* in Acts 2 that takes
the broader context of the Roman Empire into account and emphasizes the
universalizing aspects of both Rome's and Luke's message.

As Gilbert's and Bonz's comparisons demonstrate, Acts 2 fits into a
broader trend of ethnic discourse prominent in the Roman era. They both

argue that Roman-era ethnic rhetoric provided space for Roman writers and the author of Acts to make claims about ethnic identity and to bring diverse populations under the authority of a single ruler, whether that ruler is the emperor, God, or Jesus. Their interpretations do not, however, explain Luke's claim that it is Jews who make up his list of *ethnē*. One of the biggest payoffs of the Roman list of populations was the separation of Romans from the rest of the world. For this reason, these lists did not include the Romans themselves. Rather, they placed Romans at the top of an ethnic hierarchy and thus displayed the superiority of the Romans, who ruled over these other "inferior" populations.[73] One of the primary rhetorical benefits of such lists was therefore to articulate the superiority of the conquerors over the conquered, broadcasting Rome's sovereign power over a universalized "other" composed of various *ethnē* who were not classified as "Romans."[74] By listing *ethnē*, Roman writers and artists maintained and reified distinctions, identifying those who were "not Roman" as well as those who were. Even so, as demonstrated in the case of Aphrodisias, such lists could also allow local elites and writers both to align themselves with Rome and to distinguish themselves from other conquered peoples. As in Philo, Josephus, and the Sebasteion, local elites used lists of populations to show unity with Romans and distinctions from "other" conquered populations.[75]

Acts' list is best compared with this latter strategy: Luke integrates Jews into a collection of *ethnē* from all over the world, privileging Jews and presenting them as possessors of hybrid identities. A Roman model that universalizes populations under Roman control by listing ancestral populations provides a context for how Luke indexes populations with ancestral groups; however, it does not explain why Acts identifies all the *ethnē* first as Jews.

Cynthia Baker has offered a different comparison capable of addressing both Luke's interaction with Roman propaganda and his identification of all of the *ethnē* as Jews. She relates the ethnic rhetoric of Philo's *Embassy* with that of Acts 2 and argues that they are both examples of Jewish "multiethnicity"; both make universalizing claims but do so in such a way that the Jewish *ethnē* can identify with more than one ethnicity at the same time.[76] As she observes, Philo's list, discussed above, makes a universalizing claim about the dual nature of Jewish ethnicity while Acts' list points to "the universalizing mission that envisions every nation and every people united by the action of a single Holy Spirit."[77] Luke, according to Baker, thus reconceived the nature of ethnic unity around the Holy Spirit rather than dual ethnicity.

Gilbert, Bonz, and Baker helpfully emphasize the Roman propaganda evident in Acts 2:5–13 and highlight the universalizing effect of such ethnic rhetoric. They also interpret Luke's list as a means of refracting Roman universalizing propaganda away from the power of the Roman emperors and toward (the Jewish) God. However, focusing on the universalizing and unifying power of God can have the effect of masking the ethnic rhetoric of Acts. Acts 2 does use a known trope, Roman propaganda that listed conquered *ethnē*, but it does so in a way that also allows the author to claim Jewish identity of non-Jews through the concept of proselyte Jews.

JEWISHNESS AND LUKE'S ETHNIC REASONING

With the first occurrence of Ἰουδαῖος in Acts, Luke employs the word in a way that establishes the boundaries of the Jewish *ethnos* and reinterprets Roman imperial propaganda in ways that allow him to position Jewish identity as helpful to his construction of Christian identity. Though there were diverse iterations of Roman-styled collections of *ethnē*, the grouping of *ethnē* established identities and marked ethnic difference. Luke's list classifies Jews as members of various *ethnē* and thereby indicates Jewish sameness in the midst of ethnic difference. Jewish identity, like Aphrodisian identity, is hybrid. In this way, Luke's representation of Jewish identity compares well with Philo's depiction of Jews. Philo classified his Jews through genealogical language; they have a "fatherland" and "mother city." Luke classified Jews similarly; they are from other *ethnē* yet remain Jews.

Though conceptually similar, Luke's description of the hybrid ethnicities of Jews differs from Philo's in important ways. In the two places where Philo lists the various geographical locations where Jews lived, he carefully classifies these Ἰουδαῖοι as from other regions (χῶραι) rather than from other *ethnē*. They are Jews who identify themselves with their non-Judean "fatherlands." Philo, in *Embassy*, lists places where Jews have established "settlements" while Luke lists the *ethnē* from which Jews immigrated to Jerusalem. For Philo, Jews live in and establish settlements in various places; for Luke, Jews are Parthians, Medes, or Elamites. This ethnic hybridity provides space for Luke to represent Jews as becoming and being Parthians and other ethnic identifications by *ethnos*, while still remaining Jewish.

By highlighting Jewish ethnic hybridity and the flexibility of Jewishness at the first identification of Jews in Acts, Luke introduces the manner in which he will represent Jewishness throughout his narrative of Christian origins. After announcing that Jews from every *ethnos* have gathered in Jerusalem, Luke marks an ethnic distinction between the gathered crowd and the apostles. The crowd is shocked that the apostles, explicitly identified as Galileans, are speaking in the languages into which they, the gathered Jews, were born.[78] This is not to say that Luke seeks to avoid identifying the apostles as Jews. They are implicitly identified as such later in the narrative.[79] Rather, his labeling strategies highlight his emphasis on the hybridity and multiplicity of Jewishness. For Luke, some Jews can identify other Jews as Galileans without calling their Jewishness into question.

After making an internal distinction among Jews, Luke's univocal crowd then lists various *ethnē* and locations from where they came, in a way similar to the list provided by Philo's Agrippa. They are:

Πάρθοι καὶ Μῆδοι καὶ Ἐλαμῖται καὶ οἱ κατοικοῦντες τὴν Μεσοποταμίαν, Ἰουδαίαν τε καὶ Καππαδοκίαν, Πόντον καὶ τὴν Ἀσίαν, Φρυγίαν τε καὶ Παμφυλίαν, Αἴγυπτον καὶ τὰ μέρη τῆς Λιβύης τῆς κατὰ Κυρήνην, καὶ οἱ ἐπιδημοῦντες Ῥωμαῖοι, Ἰουδαῖοί τε καὶ προσήλυτοι, Κρῆτες καὶ Ἄραβες.

Parthians, Medes, Elamites, and residents of Mesopotamia, Judea and Cappadocia, Pontus and Asia, Phrygia and

Pamphylia, Egypt and the parts of Libya belonging to Cyrene, and visiting Romans, both Jews and proselytes, Cretans and Arabs. (Acts 2:9–11)

Unlike Philo's Agrippa, however, Luke includes Judea among the residences of these *ethnē*. Curiously, he also excludes many regions that show up with Jewish populations later in the narrative of Acts.[80]

As the discussion above indicated, many scholars have focused attention on determining a source for Luke's list. It is clear from these discussions that while he probably did intentionally invoke other lists, including those already found in Genesis and known across the Roman world, his list was adapted for his own purposes.[81] The odd appearance of Judea, like the inclusion of Ἰουδαῖοι in 2:5, has led many scholars to assume that the term, like Ἰουδαῖοι in 2:5, was either a later addition or a mistake.[82] Ancient authors had difficulty making sense of Ἰουδαία in 2:9 as well. Tertullian and Augustine, for example, thought the text should read *Armeniam*, and Eusebius in his commentary on Isaiah reads Συρίαν (Syria) when referring to Acts 2:9–11.[83] The reason for their confusion is clear: Why would residents of Judea be surprised that Galileans in Jerusalem spoke the native language of Judea?[84]

It is odd that Luke includes Judea in his list of places from which Jews emigrated. By syntactically connecting Judea with Cappadocia, Pontus, Asia, and other locations, Judea as the ancestral home of the ἔθνος Ἰουδαίων is deemphasized. Judea is just another location where Jews resided, not the privileged homeland of Jews and the temple for the God of Israel, according to this ethnic rhetoric. This stance has the corollary effect of decentralizing Judean identity for determining Jewishness. Luke highlights that these Jews are devout men and can be from Judea (and Cappadocia, Pontus, or Egypt); they are not merely "Judeans."[85]

Luke represents Jews as from other *ethnē* (2:5). He then includes, without qualification, the ancestral home of Jews, Judea, in his list of the residences of these *ethnē* (2:9). In Acts 2:11 a third variable, which will prove central to Luke's project, is introduced into the mix. Both Jews and proselytes made up the crowd of devout Jews (some of whom are from

Judea).[86] The presence of another overlapping variable in Jewishness adds a third level of complexity to Luke's already hybrid and multifaceted Jewish identity.

Luke rhetorically contrasts the Jews not with Christ followers but with proselytes, a term that usually marked a distinction between someone who is Jewish through lineage—a born Jew—and someone who becomes a Jew through a widely accepted means, namely, fidelity to Jewish ancestral customs, exclusive devotion to the God of Israel, and circumcision for males. Some Jews contested the meaning and value of the "conversion" of non-Jews, but for a significant number of born Jews, non-Jews could become Jewish as proselytes.[87] Luke shares this conviction.

For Luke proselytes are Jews, but he also retains an internal distinction between Jews and those who are Jews as proselytes. He has already categorized both those identified as Jews and those identified as proselytes in 2:11 as being Jews in 2:5.[88] On one hand, proselytes are Jews, but on the other, they remain distinct from born Jews. Luke's ethnic rhetoric resembles that of the Sebasteion in an important way. While the Sebasteion employed the mythical ancestral connection between Aphrodite, Aeneas, and Augustus to connect the Aphrodisians and the Romans, Luke uses the mythical ancestral connection established between Jews and proselyte non-Jews through observance of certain ancestral customs ordained by the Jewish God. Luke, like other Jewish authors, retains an internal distinction between those who are born Jews and those non-Jews who are integrated into the Jewish community,[89] yet he also clearly classifies them as Jews. By classifying these (former) non-Jews as Jews, Luke has created space that will allow him to identify Christian non-Jews as a type of proselyte Jew later on in the narrative.

The identification of proselytes as a type of Jew is, of course, not unique to Acts. Neither are the identifications of Jews from other *ethnē* (2:5) and Jews from Judea (2:9). They represent frequently attested examples of the multiple ways of "being Jewish" in antiquity.[90] However, the combination of these three identifications of Jewishness highlights the hybridity and flexibility of Jewishness at a critical moment in the beginning of Acts. Acts 2:5-13 strategically combines multiple ways of being Jewish in a single passage and articulates a fluid vision of Jewish identity. Jewish identity existed for Luke simultaneously dependent upon and independent of lineage. It could be inherited or achieved through proper ancestral customs. Like the Aphrodisians' use of the Aphrodite-Aeneas-Augustus connection to present Aphrodisian identity in terms of Rome, Luke uses the Jewishness of proselytes to present Jewish identity in terms that will be useful for his subsequent positioning of Christians in the civic hierarchy and his construction of Christian identity.

Conclusion

Reading Acts 2:5–13 in light of the types of ethnic reasoning presented both in the collections of *ethnē* found in Roman imperial propaganda and by other groups who reconfigured Roman-style lists for their own purposes suggests that Luke also redeployed a Roman-styled population list, but in this case to redefine Jewish identity. In a way similar to the presentation of *ethnē* in the Sebasteion, Luke depicted Jewish identity as multiple: Jews were Parthian and Jewish, Cappadocian and Jewish, Egyptian and Jewish, and so on. The distinction Luke draws is between Jewish proselytes and other Jews, not between Jews of Judea and "the nations."

The Sebasteion in Aphrodisias also used Roman-era propaganda depicting various *ethnē,* reimagining the city's place on the ethnic map by creating a representation of conquered *ethnē* that juxtaposed these conquered peoples to the Carians, who, the monument suggested, share a common ancestry with Augustus. The distinction there was between the unconquered Carians, who are Roman from the perspective of ancestors and gods, and the conquered, who remain non-Roman subjects of the superior Romans. The Aphrodisians ethnically identify themselves, through their connection to Aphrodite, with the conquering Romans rather than with the conquered *ethnē.* Aphrodisian identity is stable in the way it interacted with Aphrodite yet flexible in its interaction with Rome. Luke uses a similarly styled *ethnē* list to represent Jews from around the *oikoumenē.* He imagines Jewishness as stable in the sense that transcended ethnicity, yet flexible in its inclusion of non-Jews in the list of Jews as proselytes. In the next chapter I build on the claim that Luke identifies proselytes as Jews and continue to consider the ethnic reasoning in Acts by examining the so-called Jerusalem council of Acts 15 in light of the image of Jewishness privileged in Acts 2:5–13 and the material remains describing the Foundation of Salutaris from Ephesus.

THREE

The Jerusalem Council and the Foundation of Salutaris

IN THE ANCIENT MEDITERRANEAN WORLD, the protocols and activities that regulated interaction with the gods were generally inherited. Populations had specific, ancestral gods, and they kept their gods happy through proper veneration according to specific ancestral customs and laws. In return, gods protected and provided for their peoples. When traveling or living away from the ancestral home of their people and gods, immigrants regularly formed ethnic associations and continued to worship their ancestral gods while abroad. In 160 CE, for example, a certain Karpion dedicated an altar to Sarapis in the οἶκός ("house") of Alexandrians at Tomis, a city of Scythia Minor (west coast of the Black Sea).[1] In Puteoli (Campania, Italy), a Tyrian civic association sought financial support from the city council (βουλή) of Tyre to continue "sacrifices and services to the ancestral gods."[2] And there is, of course, extensive evidence of Jewish communities continuing their ancestral customs throughout the Greek and Roman eras.[3]

The veneration of a god or gods was not only a product of a given civic or ethnic identity, but also a means of indicating ethnic and civic identity. The activities and protocols that regulated interactions with gods could provide a means for maintaining and changing ethnic and civic identity, categories that faced constant slippage in antiquity.[4]

In the previous chapter I discussed the ways that the list of *ethnē* in Acts 2:5–13 and the Sebasteion presented religious imagery and employed ethnic reasoning to make identity claims and assert difference. I argued that Acts 2:5–13 depicted Jewish identity as fluid both by representing Jews as being from different *ethnē* and by including proselytes in the list of Jews. Proselytes are presented as simultaneously Jewish and something else. Jews from different *ethnē* are Jews as well as representatives of these other peoples. Jewishness, in this passage, transcends a single *ethnos* (2:5) and lineage (2:9) while also maintaining an internal distinction among Jews based on ancestry—both Jews and proselytes are identified in the same list as Jews.

In this chapter I continue the discussion of Jewish identity in Acts but shift focus from how the author represents Jewishness to how Acts uses the image of Jewishness constructed in Acts 2:5–13 to depict the Jewishness of Christian non-Jews in the Jerusalem council (15:1–21).[5] Comparing the ethnic rhetoric of Acts 15 with ethnic rhetoric of the Salutaris Foundation inscription (*IEph* 27), I call attention to wider negotiations of civic identity and within the context of formal public documents like this inscription. The Salutaris Foundation inscription, which contains the stipulations for a donation given by a wealthy citizen of Ephesus, provides a useful comparison with the Jerusalem council narrative in two primary ways. First, the inscription was composed within a decade or two of the likely publication of Acts and therefore offers a glimpse of a contemporaneous use of ethnic rhetoric. Second, a majority of the narrative of Acts takes place in an urban context, including in Ephesus. The Salutaris Foundation thus provides a securely dated and located example of the negotiation of identity within the city, demonstrating who had the power to influence identity claims and how such negotiations took place. Both Acts and the Salutaris Foundation leverage religious ideology in their respective forms of ethnic rhetoric in order to legitimate ethnic change, employing ancestral religious rhetoric, a shared sense of the flexibility of ethnic identity, and the authority of councils in ways that delimit the identity of contested populations and their religious activities. The depiction of an ancestral deity, the gestures toward the mythic past, and the centrality of ancestral traditions and customs are fundamental to both texts, as they leverage an ancestral god/goddess and protocols of veneration to justify their own ethnic claims.[6]

The Foundation of Salutaris

In 104 CE the Ephesian council (βουλή) ratified a civic foundation (διάταξις) proposed by Caius Vibius Salutaris, a wealthy Italian immigrant.[7] Salutaris dedicated twenty-nine statues for use by the *polis*, funded an annual lottery given out to at least 2,702 individuals on the eve of the goddess Artemis's birthday, and organized a regular procession of the statues that traveled from the Artemision—the world-famous temple of Artemis in Ephesus—to the city theater and back to the Artemision approximately every two weeks. The Salutaris Foundation inscription (*IEph* 27A–G) boasts an astounding 568 lines of text with letters ranging in size from one to four centimeters in height.[8]

The Foundation of Salutaris provides an example of Roman-era civic benefaction whereby civic elites could legitimate their status in a particular city. As Guy Rogers has argued, Salutaris's Foundation was more than a public proclamation of elite power; it also provided the Ephesians a means of dealing with an identity crisis caused by the increasing "Romanization" of this great Greek *polis* at the beginning of the second century.[9] The Foundation also serves as an example of how Salutaris and the Ephesian council imagined the connection between Artemis, the past, and the *polis*. For example, the distribution of "lotteries," a practice of handing out money to various Ephesians and Ephesian civic groups stipulated by Salutaris's Foundation, was largely symbolic and educational. The relatively small size of the distributions and the meager tasks required of the beneficiaries limited who could and could not enact Ephesian identity.[10] Taking care of statues or fulfilling ritual tasks, only a select group of citizens, city councilors, elders, and youths had access to these lotteries, which therefore maintained a very specific civic hierarchy. As Rogers explains, "The Ephesians themselves acted out the blueprint of Salutaris' contemporary civic hierarchy."[11] The Foundation thus provides an avenue to explore how civic elites utilized ethnic rhetoric to legitimate the identity of a contested population—elite Roman immigrants—while at the same time supporting the continuing dominion of Artemis over her *polis*.

The inscription also demonstrates how complex negotiations of identities took place through the display of writing. Statue bases, columns, walls, funerary monuments, and public buildings filled the urban space with visible reminders of the benefactions of leading citizens, and therefore also of their entitled belonging.[12] The Salutaris Foundation offers one important example of this form of belonging: the inscription re-creates an imagined past, validates this past through the repetition of a sacred procession enacted by present and future generations, and identifies what it meant to be Ephesian in a way that includes the Roman elite. The foundation actively participates in a widespread form of ethnic reasoning, but in a unique way and within the very specific context of early-second-century Ephesus. The strategies of inclusion and ethnic negotiation are particular to Salutaris and his Ephesian context, but the ideology of ethnic negotiation upon which he depends was shared, including by the author of Acts.

ROMAN-ERA EPHESUS

In the Roman era, Ephesus, like many Greek cities, expanded as an urban center. Shifts in architecture and demographics required corresponding adjustments to the understanding of the mythic past and the relationship between Ephesus and Artemis. In the midst of these civic changes, Artemis remained central to the identity of the city. The historian Strabo explains why this was the case in his *Geography*. He recounts an Ephesian foundation myth and the ancient history of the city and the monumental Artemision (14.1.20–24).[13] In the mythic past, the goddess Leto gave birth to Apollo and Artemis in the grove of Ortygia, which was located near Ephesus.[14] It was there that the Kouretes (Κουρῆται), a group of youths, banged their weapons and hid Leto from the jealous gaze of Hera.[15] The ancient inhabitants of the region subsequently built several temples nearby (*Geogr.* 14.1.20).

Later, according to Strabo, the Greek hero Androklos drove out the native Carian and Lelege inhabitants and established a Greek *polis* (*Geogr.* 14.1.21; cf. Pausanias, *Descr.* 7.2.8–9).[16] After the time of Androklos, epigraphic evidence shows that social groups in the city formed into five

different "tribes" (φυλαί) related to the early mythical founders of Ephesus.[17] As the Salutaris Foundation inscription shows, these tribes remained important into the Roman era.

Lysimachus, one of Alexander's generals, attempted to refound the
city in the early third century BCE under a new name, Arsinoeia, so that
he was not beholden to the authority of Artemis (and her priests).[18] His attempt to move the Ephesians to his new city initially failed. Not to be dis-
couraged, Lysimachus is said to have stopped up the sewers of the old
Ephesus after a heavy rainfall, forcing the Ephesians to move from the area
surrounding the Artemision to the newly walled area that was closer to the
harbor, the home of the city we call Ephesus from that point on.[19] Lysimachus's attempt to separate his city from Artemis did ultimately fail. The
name "Arsinoeia" disappeared after his death, and his *polis* was incorporated into the domain of Artemis and became known by the same name as
the city from which Lysimachus sought to separate himself, Ephesus.[20] As
Lysimachus's failed attempt to separate the city from Artemis demonstrates,
the connection between Artemis and Ephesus ran deep during the Hellenistic period. Strabo, writing in the first century BCE, participates in the
perpetuation of the connection between goddess and *polis,* Artemis and
Ephesus, by recounting the divine origins of the *polis* as the city was being
expanded in the Roman era.

In the early imperial period, a new civic center emerged southeast of
the harbor in a flurry of building projects.[21] The Ephesian cityscape was
redefined between the end of the first century BCE and the beginning of
the second century CE with the construction of a monumental Stoa Basilica, a "Roman" agora, a Prytaneion (the city's sacred hearth that became
home to the Kouretes), a significant renovation to the *bouleuterion* (the
meeting place of the city council), and the imposing temple dedicated to
the Flavian Sebastoi.[22]

By the beginning of the second century, the landscape of Ephesus was
in the midst of a significant shift, both because of these building projects
and also because of an influx of foreigners, like Salutaris, an Italian.[23] As
we will see, the Foundation of Salutaris participates in and legitimates these
changes through its depiction of Artemis, the sacred traditions and customs of the Ephesians, and the mythic past.

SALUTARIS AND HIS FOUNDATION

Salutaris is known only through the inscriptions and dedications from the first decade of the second century CE.[24] According to the Foundation inscription, he was of the equestrian order and "eminent in lineage and worth" (γένει καὶ ἀξίᾳ διάσημος) (*IEph* 27.14–16).[25] He was identified as part of the Italian tribe "Oufentina" (Οὐωφεντείνα), a Roman tribe that likely originated during the Republic (27.331).[26] Statue bases in Ephesus shed a little more light on his *cursus honorum*. He was stationed in Sicily as collector of port taxes (ἀρχώνης λιμένων ἐπαρχείας Σικελίας) and later as a grain authority for the *dēmos* of the Romans (καὶ ἀρχώνης σείτου δήμου Ῥωμαίων) (*IEph* 29).[27] He also spent some time in Africa (29.16–17). On the basis of the extant evidence it is likely that he held military posts during the reigns of Domitian and Trajan.[28] Salutaris's military career and service record, however, look "ordinary."[29]

Evidence suggesting when Salutaris moved to Ephesus does not exist, but it is clear from his *cursus honorum* that he was a relative newcomer when his Foundation was dedicated in 104 CE.[30] As a recent immigrant, Salutaris did not have a connection to the city's Hellenistic "tribes," which organized the city's citizens, or to its foundation by Greeks, which tied the city to its mythic past. He did, however, become an Ephesian citizen (πολείτης ἡμέτερος) and a member of the city council (βουλευτικόν συνεδρίον) (*IEph* 27.17).[31] As L. Michael White has argued, "Through civic benefaction [Salutaris] could move beyond the social status to which he might otherwise be limited in his own native context."[32]

The pinnacle of Salutaris's known benefactions was the Foundation he established in 104 CE. As mentioned above, it provided the money to commission and care for statues, an endowment from which various individuals and groups received distributions annually, and regular processions of the commissioned statues from the Artemision to the theater and back to the Artemision. The specific features of each aspect of the Foundation—statues, distributions, and processions—reimagine the bonds between Artemis, her people, and her *polis*.

ARTEMIS, HER PEOPLE, AND HER *POLIS*

The statues dedicated by the Salutaris Foundation assert Artemis's dominion over the *polis* while at the same time legitimating Roman authority in the city. Salutaris promised to dedicate twenty-nine statues to honor the city of Ephesus: nine type-statues (ἀπεικονίσματα) of Artemis, the city's founder (ἀρχηγέτης) and patron goddess, and twenty silver images (εἰκόνες)—five of which were related to the emperor Trajan (ὁ κύριος ἡμῶν αὐτοκράτωρ), his family, and Rome, while fifteen images represented (εἰκόνες προσωποποιούσα) various individuals and groups related to the Ephesian *polis*. Taken individually, the images honor Artemis, Rome, and Ephesus, but viewed as a collection, a carefully selected archive of what it meant to be Ephesian, the images represent how Salutaris and the Ephesian council negotiated Ephesian identity in relation to Artemis, Rome, and the city's mythic past.[33]

Salutaris first dedicated a golden image to Artemis and the Ephesian council (βουλή) and also statues to Artemis and the city elders (γερουσία), city youths (ἐφηβεία), and six "tribes" (φυλαί), respectively.[34] The combination of the images of Artemis with dedications to past, present, and future Ephesian elites depicts Ephesians as perpetually united under Artemis.

The statues of six Ephesian "tribes" are of particular interest for examining how Salutaris and the Ephesian council navigated the city's increasing "Romanization." As mentioned above, five Ephesian tribes traced their historical origins to the period shortly after Androklos established the Hellenistic city.[35] Independent inscriptional evidence exists for the five Hellenistic tribes—the Ephesians, the Karenaeans, the Teians, the Euonumoi, and the Bembinaeans—from the Hellenistic to the Roman periods indicating that the tribes had a continuing presence and influence in the *polis*.[36] For example, the extant portion of a list of temple officials (νεωποῖαι) from the imperial period includes members of four of the tribes (*IEph* 2948); and members of the tribe of the Teioi (φυλή Τηΐων) are associated with the dedication of the pavement of the Ephesian library (στρῶμα βυβλιοθήκης).[37] Tribes had reserved seating in the theater, and at least one individual is described as changing his tribal membership (*IEph* 956a).[38]

The tribal system indexed male citizens in Ephesus, as in other Greek cities; however, it is noteworthy that the number of tribes in Ephesus expanded with the arrival of the Romans.[39] The sixth tribe included among the images of the Hellenistic ones was of a more recent vintage: the tribe of the Sebaste, the tribe of the Roman emperors.[40] The tribal structure created an imagined Ephesian community that connected groups of citizens to the founding of the Greek city by Androklos and asserted a connection to the Hellenistic past through a shared tribe.[41] The incorporation of images of the tribes in Salutaris's Foundation builds on this existing social structure by honoring the tribal structure as a valid way to "be" Ephesian and by incorporating the tribal structure into the hierarchy of the *polis*. The processional images representing the tribes exist alongside the images of the Ephesian council, elders, and youths.

By incorporating the tribe of the Sebaste with the Hellenistic tribes, Salutaris's Foundation also integrates a version of the present that includes Rome in the recitation of the Ephesian past.[42] Salutaris's Foundation represents Greeks and now Romans as Ephesian tribes, thus reinscribing the established tribal structure to imagine a connection between the Hellenistic origins of the *polis* and Rome. The distribution of lotteries and the regular processions serve to legitimate the Ephesian identity projected by the statues that the Foundation commissioned.

SALUTARIS'S NEGOTIATION WITH THE EPHESIAN COUNCIL

As a public endowment, Salutaris's Foundation—along with its reinscription of the tribal structure—required the ratification of the Ephesian council, and by extension, the *dēmos*. The text of the inscription suggests that the council may have questioned Salutaris's legitimacy to serve as such a benefactor of Ephesus. In the opening lines of the inscription, the πρύτανις ("secretary/mayor") of the *polis*, Tib. Cl. Iulianus, who was an Ephesian and Italian like Salutaris, contends that Salutaris should be honored by allowing him to establish a foundation:[43]

ἐπειδὴ τοὺς] φιλοτείμους ἄνδρας περὶ τὴν [πόλ]ιν καὶ
κατὰ [πάντα ἀποδειξαμένοι]ζ στοργὴν γνησίων πολει[τῶν
ἀ]μοιβαί[ων χρὴ τυχεῖν τειμῶν πρὸς] τὸ ἀπολαύειν μὲν
τοὺς εὖ [ποι]ήσαν[τας ἤδη τὴν πόλιν, ἀποκεῖσθαι δὲ τοῖς
βο]υλομένοις περ[ὶ τὰ] ὅμοια ἁμι[λλᾶσθαι, ἅμα δὲ τοὺς]
ἐσπουδα[κ]ότας τὴν μεγίστην θεὸν Ἄρτεμιν [τειμᾶν, παρ'
ἧς γ]ε ίνεται πᾶσιν τ[ὰ] κάλλιστα, καθήκε[ι] παρὰ τῇ
πόλε[ι εὐδοκιμεῖν.

Since men who are munificent in the case of the city and on
every occasion show the affection of legitimate citizens should
have honors corresponding to the ones enjoyed by those who
have benefited the city in the past and laid up for those who are
desiring to compete in similar things, and at the same time [they
should have honors corresponding to the ones enjoyed by] those
who have been zealous to honor the greatest goddess Artemis,
from whom the most beautiful things come to all, it is fitting for
them to be esteemed by the city. (*IEph* 27.8–14)[44]

Iulianus asserts that the *polis* should honor present civic benefactors in the
same way that it honored past benefactors. He mentions three specific areas of benefaction: bringing honor to the *polis*, showing affection of genuine citizens, and being zealous for (Ephesian) Artemis. The lines that follow
present an image of Salutaris as just such a person (27.14–23).

By framing the Foundation in this way, the inscription symbolically legitimates Salutaris's Ephesian identity and situates him as one who
should be thrice honored by the city. First, he brings honor to the *polis;*
second, he is a genuine citizen; and third, he is an Artemis-lover.[45] Salutaris thus embodies the identity of a legitimate citizen (γνήσιος πολίτης)
of Ephesus.

The initial identification of Salutaris as a genuine citizen becomes poi-
gnant in light of two letters of recommendation from the two highest-
ranking Roman officials in Asia, the proconsul, Aquillius Proculus, and
the legate, Afranius Flavianus, which are included later in the inscription.[46]

Rogers suggests that the language of Flavianus's letter hints that the Ephesian council initially overlooked and possibly rejected Salutaris's Foundation proposal. If this was the case, then Salutaris sought recommendations from these regional Roman officials to garner the support needed for the Ephesian council to finally approve his endowment.[47] Afranius Flavianus, the *legatus pro praetor* of Asia, writes to the rulers and council of Ephesus in support of Salutaris.[48] He praises Salutaris's goodwill and affection toward the Ephesians, even if the majority did not notice (εἰ καὶ τοὺς πλείστους ἐλάνθανεν, ὡς ἔχει πρὸς ὑμᾶς εὐνοίας τε καὶ προαιρέσεος) (*IEph* 27.374–76).[49] By pointing out that Salutaris's goodwill went unnoticed previously, Flavianus's letter allows space for a new identification of Salutaris as Ephesian benefactor. Flavianus brings Salutaris's previously unknown generosity to the fore in order to validate Salutaris's inscription in two prominent places in the *polis* as a civic benefactor.[50] In this way, Salutaris also asserts his own Ephesian identity by establishing the Foundation, which would have also allowed those who shared Salutaris's foreign status, like Iulianus and even Flavianus, to represent themselves as ideal Ephesians in ways that supported a past structure of benefaction while at the same time allowing space to negotiate their own place as γνήσιοι πολῖται, legitimate citizens.[51]

Salutaris's Foundation uses images from the mythic Ephesian past to display a particular version of Ephesian history that is shaped by (and is amenable to) the realities of the Roman present. The images and their movement through the *polis* in regular processions combine the centrality of Artemis at the mythical origins of Ephesus with the more recent history of the Greek city and the Roman Empire in Salutaris's present. This version of the past supports the specific Ephesian identity proposed by Salutaris and approved by the leadership of the city.

Salutaris's Foundation therefore uses a backward gaze to legitimate the fluid present reality of Ephesus by creating an archive of (elite) Ephesian history and regularly parading it through the *polis*. Rather than just an example of embodied nostalgia, Salutaris's Foundation, in the words of Jaś Elsner, "vividly brings to life a culture of images" and uses them "symbolically to reenact the myths which linked Ephesian Artemis with her city and to perpetuate ritually the harmonious existence of the city within the empire."[52] Salutaris's Foundation uses Artemis, the tribal system, and the movement of images through the city as a form of ethnic reasoning to legitimate the place of Romans in the city of Artemis. It situates Artemis as the guiding image of his processions through the city, thus placing his own Foundation within the Ephesian mythic past. The addition of his "tribe," the Sebastoi, suggests that this innovation is traditional and connected to the Hellenistic city that Androklos founded. The movement of Romans and Ephesians through the city as a single entity—as a new Ephesian—reorients Ephesian identity around the city's Roman reality and excludes those who do not embrace such changes.

The Acts of the Apostles participates in a similar ethnic rhetoric with regard to Jewish identity and Christian identity. Salutaris expanded the Ephesian tribal system and capitalized on the city's custom of processing in honor of Artemis to situate himself as simultaneously Ephesian and Roman. The author of Acts uses God, the Jewish concept of the proselyte, and the movement of God's spirit across the known world as a form of ethnic reasoning that legitimated the place of Christian non-Jews in the Jewish community. Salutaris, his Foundation implies, can be both Roman and Ephesian. Christian non-Jews, Luke argues, can be both Jewish and whatever else they once were. Like the proselytes, their identity is hybrid, but Jewish nonetheless.

The Jerusalem Council and the Identity of Christian Non-Jews

Reading Acts 15 in comparison to the Salutaris Foundation inscription provides a new angle for assessing this complex, yet important chapter of Acts.[53] I argue that Acts 15 connects the identity of Christian non-Jews to the regulations for Jews and proselytes in Leviticus 17–18, suggesting that what is at stake in the debate about circumcision and the law of Moses is not whether or not Christian non-Jews should become Jews as proselytes, but rather who can claim the identity of a proselyte. The Salutaris Foundation provides an example of how an ancestral deity, an ancient system of organizing citizens within Ephesus, and the physical movement of images of the deity and her people could legitimate the Ephesian identity of Romans living in the city. The narrative of the Jerusalem council in Acts 15:1–21 also provides an example of how an ancestral deity, an ancient system of organizing populations, and the literary movement of God and his people could legitimate the Jewish identity of Christian non-Jews. Similar to the Salutaris Foundation, the Jerusalem council provides Luke's audience with a way of dealing with an identity crisis caused by the increasing presence of non-Jews among Christians. To deal with this crisis, Luke looks to the connection between the God of Israel, the mythic past, and the Jewish community to identify Christian non-Jews as proselyte Jews without circumcision.

The Jerusalem council (15:1–21) occupies a central place in the structure of Acts and ties together a number of themes present in the text's larger narrative arc.[54] The central issue at stake in Acts 15:1–21 is the identity of Christian non-Jews, an issue that was previously raised, but not explicitly resolved, in the narrative of Cornelius (10:1–11:18). Because the author of Acts has intentionally connected the Jerusalem council to Peter's interactions with Cornelius (15:7), it forms the basis for understanding the Jerusalem council in the narrative of Acts.[55]

THE CORNELIUS EPISODE (ACTS 10:1–11:18) AND GOD'S ACCEPTANCE OF NON-JEWS

The Cornelius episode narrates the first explicit entry of a non-Jew into "the Way" and marks the beginning of a wider acceptance of non-Jews among the Christians in Acts.[56] Like the Salutaris Foundation, Luke here participates in common ethnic discourses about identity, and the fluidity of Roman identity in particular. In Acts 10, Luke introduces Cornelius, a Roman centurion who was devout, gave alms, and prayed continuously to God (10:1–2). God commands Cornelius to send for Peter in Joppa (10:3–8). The next day, Peter receives a vision of clean and unclean animals descending from heaven. After the vision, a voice calls to Peter, "What God has made clean, you must not call profane" (10:9–16).[57] While Peter is still trying to figure out what the vision means, Cornelius's men arrive, and Peter travels to Caesarea with them (10:17–24). Upon his arrival, Cornelius conveys to Peter the story of the voice he heard (10:25–33), and Peter then proclaims, "I truly understand that God shows no partiality, but in every *ethnos* (ἐν παντὶ ἔθνει) anyone who fears him and does what is right is acceptable to him" (10:34–35).[58] Peter begins to preach the message God sent to the people of Israel, proclaiming "peace through Jesus Christ" (10:36–43). The Holy Spirit then comes upon Cornelius and his household while Peter is still speaking, and they are baptized (10:44–48).

Luke anticipates this monumental moment in the narrative expansion of the Christian message from the very beginning of Acts when Luke's Jesus says to his disciples, "You will receive power when the Holy Spirit has come upon you, and you will be my witnesses in Jerusalem, all Judea, Samaria, and to the ends of the earth" (1:8).[59] The introduction of Jews from every *ethnos* (ἀπὸ παντὸς ἔθνους) (2:5) at the initial outpouring of the Holy Spirit is reflected later in the narrative of Acts in God's acceptance of those in every *ethnos* (ἐν παντὶ ἔθνει) (10:35). The narrative that occurs between these two scenes describes the expansion of the message of Jesus from Jerusalem to Judea (8:1), to Samaria (8:4–25), and to the ends of the earth— represented, initially, by the Ethiopian eunuch (8:26–40).

Just as the Salutaris Foundation emphasizes the centrality of Artemis and Salutaris's identity as an Artemis-lover indicating and eliciting divine approval, Luke goes to great lengths to indicate that the acceptance of non-Jews was approved by God rather than by humans. In the Cornelius episode, Peter's visions (10:9–16), the prophetic message from the spirit (10:19), and an angel's appearance and message to Cornelius (10:30–32) all provide divine validation for the acceptance of non-Jews by the Christian Jews. Luke's Peter concludes by observing what Acts' narrative had already confirmed—"in every *ethnos* anyone who fears [God] and does what is right is acceptable to him" (10:35). In the narrative the acceptance of non-Jews among the Christians was initiated by God, confirmed by the Holy Spirit of that same God, and only then recognized by Peter and the other apostles.

After Cornelius and his household received the Holy Spirit, Peter returned to Jerusalem and some other Christian Jews "from the circumcision" criticized him for eating with uncircumcised men. Peter repeats the

narrative of the Cornelius episode along with the divine visions, the prophetic message from the spirit, and the angelic message to Cornelius, thus
highlighting the story's importance for the rest of Acts (11:1–17). The repetition of divine sanction by Luke mirrors the repeated appearances of
Artemis among the statues dedicated by the Salutaris Foundation. The
divine presence at every stage of the narrative legitimates the integration
of a Roman (Cornelius) into the community, just as ever-present Artemis
integrates Romans into the Ephesian community.

   After hearing Peter's retelling of the arrival of the Holy Spirit and Cornelius's baptism, the gathered Christian Jews, who previously opposed
Peter's action, proclaim in one voice, "God has given even to the *ethnē* the
repentance that leads to life" (11:17). The issue of the identity of non-Jews
appears settled: God had accepted pious non-Jews (ἔθνη) as they
were—without circumcision and without following the Jewish law. That is,
the God of Israel has accepted (some) non-Jews into the Jewish community
of Christians without requiring that they become proselyte Jews; God welcomes them as non-Jews. As the narrative of Acts unfolds, however, it becomes clear that the matter is not settled.

THE CHALLENGE TO THE ACCEPTANCE OF
NON-JEWS (15:1–5)

The relationship between the Jewish law, circumcision, and Christian non-
Jews was not settled in Acts with the Cornelius episode.[60] After Peter returns to Jerusalem, the message about Jesus spreads to Antioch, and
Barnabas and Saul/Paul gather money to support those who trust in Jesus
in Judea (11:19–30). After a brief interlude of events in Judea—Herod's mis-
treatment of James and Peter and ultimately Herod's death for not honoring God (12:1–25)—the narrative returns to Antioch, and the Christian
movement begins to expand.[61] The Holy Spirit speaks and sets Saul/Paul
and Barnabas apart for a special work (13:2). They set out and begin proclaiming the word of God in Cyprus (13:4–5), Pisidian Antioch (13:13–52),
Iconium (14:1–7), Lystra, and Derbe (14:8–20), and then they return to Antioch, where they stay for some time (14:26–28).

Certain Jews then come up from Judea to Antioch and begin teaching the Christian non-Jews that unless they are circumcised according to
the Mosaic customs, they cannot be saved (15:1).[62] Paul and Barnabas ve-
hemently disagree with these men from Judea, and the Christians in Antioch send Paul and Barnabas to Jerusalem to discuss the issue with the
apostles and elders there (15:2).[63] After arriving and being welcomed by the
Christian community, the Antioch delegation faces opposition from some
Christian Jews from the sect of the Pharisees who expand on the claim that
the Judeans made in Antioch.[64] They claim, "It is necessary for [the non-
Jews] to be circumcised and ordered to keep the law of Moses" (15:4–5).
Though a difference exists in the specific requirements of the Judeans who
traveled to Antioch and the Christian Pharisees in Jerusalem, they both de-
sire the Christian non-Jews to become proselytes through circumcision.[65]
That is, they desire that Christian non-Jews become Jews.[66]

In order to address this objection to the way that the Christians in
Antioch integrated non-Jews into their community, Luke, like Salutaris, depends upon the power of an ancestral deity and looks back toward the
mythic history of an ancestral population to legitimate his identity claims.
He situates God and the protocols for non-Jews from the past as the guiding factors of his description of the debate about the identity of Christian
non-Jews, thus identifying Christian non-Jews with the proselytes present
in the Jewish past.

PROSELYTE JEWS AND ETHNIC RHETORIC

As discussed in the previous chapter, Acts identifies proselytes as Jews
who nonetheless remain distinct from born Jews (2:9). According to
many ancient Jews, (male) non-Jews could become proselyte Jews through
circumcision. For example, the novella Judith indicates that a male and his
lineage can be added to the house of Israel through circumcision. An Ammonite, Achior, who initially despised the house of Israel, changed his
mind and "trusted firmly" (ἐπίστευσεν σφόδρα) in the God of Israel
after seeing the decapitated head of Holofernes (Jdt 14:5–10). He is circumcised (περιετέμετο τὴν σάρκα τῆς ἀκροβυστίας αὐτοῦ) and is

added to (προστίθημι) the house of Israel (14:10).[67] Circumcision, in this case, shifted Achior's identity from Ammonite to a member of the house of Israel.[68]

Josephus presents circumcision as a means for non-Jews to become Jews as well. He writes that Jewish identity is available not only to born Jews (τὸ γένος 'Ιουδαῖος) but also to non-Jews who follow certain Jewish customs (*Ag. Ap.* 2.210).[69] In his narrative, Josephus also indicates that circumcision changes the identity of non-Jews to that of Jews. His retelling of the conquest of the Idumeans by John Hyrcanus in the late second century BCE demonstrates how circumcision serves as a useful, though not uncomplicated, way to make non-Jews into Jews.[70] Josephus reports that John Hyrcanus gave the Idumeans an ultimatum: be circumcised and follow Jewish ancestral customs or leave their homeland (*Ant.* 13.257). The Idumeans chose circumcision, and according to Josephus, "from that time on they were Jews" (ὥστε εἶναι τὸ λοιπὸν 'Ιουδαίους) (*Ant.* 13.258). The ethnic rhetoric of Josephus notwithstanding, the Idumeans did not cease to exist as a distinct *ethnos*.[71] Josephus himself identifies prominent Idumeans, such as Herod, as both Idumeans and Jews.[72] In spite of this complexity, ancient authors represent circumcision as possessing the power to identify (male) non-Jews as Jews.

In the much-discussed story of the circumcision of Izates, the king of Adiabene, Josephus further illustrates that first-century Jews debated whether non-Jews should be circumcised or not in order to be genuinely Jewish (*Ant.* 20.38–48).[73] Izates follows a number of Jewish customs but desires to be circumcised because he believes that he will not genuinely be a Jew without it (μὴ ἂν εἶναι βεβαίως 'Ιουδαῖος εἰ μὴ περιτέμνοιτο) (20.38). His mother, Helena, persuades him that this would be political suicide. She pleads that he not go through with it because the inhabitants of Adiabene "would never bear to be ruled over by a Jew" (οὐκ ἀνέξεσθαί τε βασιλεύοντος αὐτῶν 'Ιουδαίου) (20.39). After questioning Helena's legitimacy as an interpreter of Jewish traditions, Helena's Jewish tutor, a former merchant named Ananias, persuades Izates not to be circumcised. Ananias argues that adherence to the other *patria,* ancestral customs, of the Jews is more important than circumcision, and Izates hesitantly decides against circumcision (20.40–42). Sometime later, however, Eleazar, a Jew from Galilee who was known for his strict interpretation of the Jewish *patria*, persuades Izates to "do the deed," and Izates is circumcised (20:43–46).

Josephus's description of Izates's struggle illustrates two points useful for discussion of the Christian Pharisees' claim and the debate surrounding the Jerusalem council in Acts. First, it shows that the issue of whether to circumcise non-Jews who wished to follow the Jewish *patria* was an intermural Jewish debate. One Jewish tutor thought it should be done; the other did not.[74] It was a matter of differing interpretations of Jewish *patria* for non-Jews based on the specific circumstances of Izates's situation. Second, it indicates that despite differing opinions about the circumcision of non-Jews, circumcision had the power to "shift ethnic identity." The Jewish tutors and Izates's mother, as Josephus describes them, think that circumcision will make Izates a Jew.[75] One Jewish tutor advocated it; the other did not. Neither disagree that through circumcision, Izates's perceived Jewishness would change definitively. It is clear that Izates became a Jew after his circumcision; however, it is unclear whether Ananias thought Izates was fully Jewish before his circumcision or whether he did not think that circumcision was necessary for non-Jews. As John Collins observes, "What is not clear is whether Izates was for a time, by way of exception, an uncircumcised proselyte."[76]

The story of Izates illustrates two sides of an internal Jewish debate about requirements for non-Jews who wished to follow the Jewish customs and join the Jewish people. The differences between the men from Judea who go to Antioch and Paul and Barnabas are thus analogous to the differences between Izates's two tutors, Ananias and Eleazar. The Judeans who travel to Antioch and the Christian Pharisees assume a position similar to that of Izates's tutor Eleazar, while Paul and Barnabas assume a position similar to that of Ananias that non-Jews do not need circumcision.[77] The Christian Pharisees think that Christian non-Jews should be circumcised and follow the Mosaic law to be saved. What remains unclear, to adapt Collins's observation, is whether Luke perceives Christian non-Jews as, by way of an innovation, uncircumcised proselytes.

THE RESPONSE OF PETER, PAUL,
AND JAMES (15:6–21)

In his description of the response to the dispute about whether Christian non-Jews should be circumcised or not, Luke, like the Salutaris Foundation, uses the decision-making power of councils to suggest that an innovative identification has divine sanction and is rooted in the ancient past. While the Salutaris Foundation utilized the Hellenistic tribal system to incorporate the tribe of the Sebaste into the ancient and mythic Ephesian past, Luke uses the Jewish acceptance of proselytes to incorporate in a novel way Christian non-Jews into the ancient Jewish past.

The apostles and elders in Jerusalem gather to consider the views of the Judeans and Christian Pharisees (15:6). Peter describes the divine authorization that he received during the Cornelius episode and points to God's acceptance of non-Jews "from long-ago" (ἀφ᾽ ἡμερῶν ἀρχαίων) (15:7). God did not distinguish between Jews and non-Jews then, so the apostles and elders should not do so now (15:8–9). Salvation comes through the grace of the Lord Jesus, a grace that has already been extended to non-Jews (15:10–11). Whereas the Judeans who went to Antioch and the Christian Pharisees claimed that the salvation of Christian non-Jews depended upon circumcision and adherence to the customs/law of Moses, Peter claims that salvation does not depend upon circumcision or the Mosaic laws, but upon the God of Israel. Paul and Barnabas then tell of the signs and wonders that God did in the *ethnē* (ἐν τοῖς ἔθνεσιν) in apparent support of Peter's assertions (15:12).

After hearing from Peter, Paul, and Barnabas, James provides an authoritative and resounding resolution to the conflict. James, like Tiberius Claudius Iulianus in the opening lines of the Salutaris Foundation inscription, proclaims the identity of Christian non-Jews as legitimate Jews like those proselytes inscribed in the Jewish past.[78] He remarks, "Simeon [Peter] has related how God first selected people in his name to take (them) out from the *ethnē* (ἐξ ἐθνῶν)" (15:14).[79] God's activity, James continues, agrees with the Jewish prophets, who wrote:

(15:16) μετὰ ταῦτα ἀναστρέφω καὶ ἀνοικοδομήσω τὴν σκηνὴν Δαυὶδ τὴν πεπτωκυῖαν... (17) ὅπως ἂν ἐκζητήσωσιν οἱ κατάλοιποι τῶν ἀνθρώπων τὸν κύριον καὶ πάντα τὰ ἔθνη ἐφ᾽ οὓς ἐπικέκληται τὸ ὄνομά μου ἐπ᾽ αὐτούς, λέγει κύριος ποιῶν ταῦτα (18) γνωστὰ ἀπ᾽ αἰῶνος.

(15:16) After these things, I will return and I will rebuild the dwelling of David which has fallen . . . (17) so that the rest of humanity and all *ethnē* upon whom my name is called might seek the Lord. Thus says the Lord who has been making these things (18) known from long ago. (Acts 15:16–18)

Luke's James uses a Greek translation of the prophet Amos to confirm that God has selected people to take out from the *ethnē* and that the Jewish scriptures predicted this beforehand.[80]

The two points of connection to Amos that appear most pertinent to Acts' context—πάντα τὰ ἔθνη, who seek the Lord, and the temporal marker ἀφ᾽ αἰῶνος—differ from known examples of LXX Amos. The text of the Göttingen Septuagint reads:

(11) ἐν τῇ ἡμέρα ἐκείνη ἀναστήσω τὴν σκηνὴν Δαυιδ τὴν πεπτωκυῖαν καὶ ἀνοικοδομήσω τὰ πεπτωκότα αὐτῆς καὶ τὰ κατεσκαμμένα αὐτῆς ἀναστήσω καὶ ἀνοικοδομήσω αὐτὴν καθὼς αἱ ἡμέρα τοῦ αἰῶνος. (12) ὅπως ἐκζητήσωσιν οἱ κατάλοιποι τῶν ἀνθρώπων καὶ πάντα τὰ ἔθνη, ἐφ᾽ οὓς ἐπικέκληται τὸ ὄνομά μου ἐπ᾽ αὐτούς, λέγει κύριος ὁ ποιῶν ταῦτα.[81]

(11) On that day I will raise up the tent of David that is fallen and rebuild its ruins and raise up its destruction, and rebuild it as in the days of old (12) in order that the rest of humanity and all *ethnē* upon whom my name has been called might visit it, says the Lord who does these things. (Amos 9:11–12)

LXX Amos does not include κύριος as the object of ἐκζητήσωσιν, thus shifting the meaning of the verb from "seek the Lord" in Acts 15:18 to "visit [David's reconstructed tent]" in LXX Amos 9:12.[82] LXX Amos either speaks of all humanity visiting the reconstituted house of David or the temple of the God of Israel, while Acts refracts the verb away from David's dwelling toward "the Lord"—Jesus in Luke's narrative.[83] The temporal marker also differs from LXX Amos. In Amos, ἀφ᾽ αἰῶνος does not appear at the end of 9:12 (Acts 15:18) but at the end of 9:11 and in a slightly different form: καθὼς αἱ ἡμέραι τοῦ αἰῶνος ("as in days of old"). Thus in LXX Amos the temporal marker is connected to David's dwelling—it will be rebuilt "as in the days of old"—rather than the connection with "the Lord who has been making things known from long ago" in Acts 15:17–18.

The use of ἀνθρώπος in 15:17 indicates that Acts' text depends upon the LXX, rather than a Hebrew *Vorlage*, even though it does not exactly correspond with a known LXX manuscript.[84] Regardless of whether the author had access to an edition of LXX Amos from which he drew his specific citation, the differences from the known texts of LXX Amos 9:11–12 and Acts 15:16–18 are significant for the religious ideology and ethnic rhetoric of James's statement. God had selected people and taken them out from the *ethnē* (15:14). The quotation that James attributes to the Jewish prophets supports this understanding by asserting that the Lord made known long ago that *ethnē* would seek him.

The quotation from Amos sets the stage for James's recommendation regarding the behavior of Christian non-Jews:

(15:19) διὸ ἐγὼ κρίνω μὴ παρενοχλεῖν τοῖς ἀπὸ τῶν ἐθνῶν ἐπιστρέφουσιν ἐπὶ τὸν θεόν, (20) ἀλλὰ ἐπιστεῖλαι αὐτοῖς τοῦ ἀπέχεσθαι τῶν ἀλισγημάτων τῶν εἰδώλων καὶ τῆς πορνείας καὶ τοῦ πνικτοῦ καὶ τοῦ αἵματος. (21) Μωϋσῆς γὰρ ἐκ γενεῶν ἀρχαίων κατὰ πόλιν τοὺς κηρύσσοντας αὐτὸν ἔχει ἐν ταῖς συναγωγαῖς κατὰ πᾶν σάββατον ἀναγινωσκόμενος.

(15:19) Therefore I judge that we should not trouble those turning from the *ethnē* to the God [of the Jews], (20) but we should

write to them to abstain from things polluted by idols, from fornication, from whatever has been strangled, and from blood.[85]
(21) For from ancient generations Moses has those who proclaim
him in every *polis* because he is read aloud in the Jewish assemblies every Sabbath.

James's advice that Christian Jews should not trouble Christian non-Jews
refers back to the claim of the Judeans who went to Antioch (15:1) and to
that of the Christian Pharisees in Jerusalem (15:5). Christian non-Jews who
turned from the *ethnē* to God (cf. 14:15, 15:3, 26:20) did not need to be
circumcised or follow the Mosaic law as some Christian Jews claimed;
rather, they were required to follow four general stipulations (15:20).[86]
The apostles and elders in Jerusalem accept James's four stipulations and
write a letter to the Christians in Antioch, Syria, and Cilicia (15:23). The
ruling from the Jerusalem council reverberates throughout the rest of Acts
(cf. 15:23–29, 21:25).

Just as Salutaris's turn to the tribal system places "Romans" into the
mythic past of the Greek *polis,* so also does the turn to LXX Amos and these
four stipulations situate Christian non-Jews in the Jewish sacred texts and
traditions. Though the precise meaning and origin of the four stipulations
remain unclear, and their connection to Moses proclaimed in every *polis*
(15:21) is puzzling, it is clear that Luke places Christian non-Jews into the
mythical Jewish past.[87]

Scholars generally regard the regulations Luke includes in Acts 15 as
ritual prohibitions that have the effect of allowing Christian non-Jews to
live among Jews.[88] Some emphasize that the prohibitions would allow table
fellowship between Jews and non-Jews, while others highlight that the prohibitions would limit the veneration of gods other than the God of the
Jews—that is, they are focused on idolatry.[89] Many scholars agree that the
specific regulations are based on the provisions of the so-called Holiness
Code for the non-Israelites living in the midst of Israel (Lev 17–18), and some
scholars emphasize the connection between Luke's prohibitions and what
would become the Noahide commandments present in an incipient form
in Jubilees and developed in rabbinic literature.[90] These four interpreta-

tions are not mutually exclusive, and challenges—in particular what to do with the prohibition of "a strangled thing" (τὸ πνικτόν)—remain unresolved in each interpretation.[91]

Those who understand Acts 15 as related to the Noahide commandments contend that the apostles sought to maintain an ethnic distinction between Christian Jews and Christian non-Jews. Non-Jews are to follow the seven stipulations in the Noahide commandments concerning "judgments, blasphemy, idolatry, uncovering nakedness, bloodshed, theft and living flesh" (t. 'Avod. Zar. 8.4).[92] Taylor sums up the implications of this view as follows: "James associates Gentile converts neither with Abraham nor with Moses, but with Noah. Gently but firmly, he keeps them at a distance from the Mosaic Covenant."[93] Yet this interpretation has to overlook another important aspect of this passage: Luke, for his part, explicitly ties Christian non-Jews and the prohibitions to Moses, not Noah (15:21). The four stipulations as Luke presents them therefore fit more easily with the stipulations of the Holiness Code for the proselytes living among Israelites—Jews in Luke's narrative world—than they do with the commandments in Jubilees and later rabbinic teachings regarding Noah's non-Jewish descendants.

Though the prohibitions in Acts 15:19–20 may have some relation to what would become the Noahide commandments, James explicitly ties them to the proclamation of Moses and by implication, his law. "Moses" is proclaimed in every *polis* every Sabbath from ancient generations (ἐκ γενεῶν ἀρχαίων) (15:21).[94] James connects prohibitions that are in general accord with Leviticus 17–18 and Moses's law read aloud in the Jewish assemblies. This supports granting Leviticus 17–18 priority over the Noahide commandments when seeking an appropriate intertextual context for Acts 15:19–21.[95] The inclusion of Moses, like Salutaris's inclusion of statues of Ephesian mythic heroes in his processions, solidifies a bond between the past and the present. Luke uses Moses like an image that symbolically reenacts the myths that linked Jews to their God through their lawgiver, Moses, just as Salutaris used Artemis to link the Ephesians with their goddess.[96]

Moving beyond a general accord between the four prohibitions in Acts and Leviticus 17–18, Isaac Oliver makes a strong case that the command to avoid the defilement of idols, *porneia*, strangled meat, and blood in Acts 15:20 is based on Leviticus 17–18.[97] He contends that "by the first century CE, many Jews probably read Lev 17:7–10 as a blanket prohibition against idolatry," thus lending support for such a connection.[98] Similarly the defilement of *porneia* generally corresponds with the sexual prohibitions in Lev 18:6–26, strangled meat with the prohibition of eating certain types of dead animals in Lev 17:15, and blood with Lev 17:10–16.[99]

Oliver deems the connection between Leviticus 17–18 and Acts 15 useful for Luke because Leviticus 17–18 contains regulations for Israelites and the *gēr* ("resident aliens") who live in their midst. The connection, according to Oliver, "helps illuminate the function of the decree for its targeted audience: to assist the governance of Jewish-Gentile relations within the Jesus movement."[100] He concludes, "Lev[iticus] 17–18 contain laws relevant for both Israelites and resident aliens, and readily presents itself as a model that could be appropriated and adapted for incorporating Gentile followers of Jesus into the early *ekklesia*."[101]

Stephen Wilson, however, earlier critiqued interpretations like Oliver's by pointing out that the translation of the Hebrew word *gēr* in the LXX of Leviticus 17–18 is προσήλυτος.[102] This translation "would suggest that first-century Judaism, and in all probability Luke himself, would not have seen these demands as relevant to Gentile Christians."[103] They were regulations for Jews and proselytes, a concept that had a different meaning in the LXX and in Luke's time, not for Jews and non-Jews and thus, according to Wilson, do not make sense in the context of Acts 15. From the traditional model of reading Acts 15 as a debate about whether Christian non-Jews should follow the laws of Moses or not, this critique is legitimate. From this perspective, the Christian Pharisees want the Christian non-Jews to become proselytes ("converts") (15:5) and Luke disagrees. According to Wilson, because the LXX uses προσήλυτος Luke "would not have seen these demands as relevant to Gentile Christians."[104] If the Jerusalem council is read from the perspective of ethnic reasoning in the *polis*, however, a different interpretation becomes possible.

As discussed above, the Salutaris Foundation inscription suggests that Salutaris negotiated (and perhaps renegotiated) the details of his Foundation with the Ephesian council and apparently needed the outside influence of two high-ranking Roman officials to finally gain the council's approval. It was the Ephesian council that possessed the power to rule on the way Salutaris sought to enact Ephesian identity. In a similar way, Luke presents his Jerusalem βουλή as possessing the power to regulate how to enact Jewish identity. In Acts 15, Luke equates the term προσήλυτος from the LXX of Leviticus with the concept of the proselyte from his own time. Luke's council thus incorporates an innovative way of identifying Christian non-Jews into the Jewish mythic past as embodied by Moses and regulated in Leviticus 17–18. The connection between Acts 15 and the regulations for Jews and proselytes in Leviticus 17–18 suggests that the issue at stake in the debate about circumcision and the law of Moses is not whether or not Christian non-Jews should become Jews as proselytes, but rather who can claim the identity of a proselyte.

A number of Jews in antiquity viewed male circumcision as a way that non-Jews could become Jews, as demonstrated previously.[105] Acts 15 questions the identification of circumcision with Jewish proselyte identity by pointing to the regulations for Jews and προσήλυτος (who were not circumcised) in Leviticus 17–18. Luke used the presence of the term προσήλυτος in LXX Leviticus 17–18, a term that meant "resident alien" at the time of the translation of the LXX, to identify Christian non-Jews as Jewish proselytes, a concept that indicated integration into the Jewish people, without circumcision. In Luke's view, the Levitical stipulations do not require Jewish proselytes to become circumcised. By basing their decision on laws promulgated by the "ancient generations," the Jerusalem council therefore reimagines proselyte identity and suggests that these stipulations were proclaimed "in every *polis*." Thus, James's ruling in Acts 15:14–21 reinterprets Jewish sacred texts in a way that places the Christian non-Jews, whom the Jewish God took out from the *ethnē* (15:14) and who have turned from the *ethnē* to God (15:19), into an ancient group, authorized by sacred narrative (15:17).[106]

James's ruling also challenges the contemporaneous identification of proselytes as equal with those who undergo circumcision by pointing to the presence of προσήλυτος without circumcision in Leviticus 17–18 (Acts

15:20–21). The Christian Pharisees propose Jewish proselytism for Christian non-Jews. James does the same, but the difference between them rests on interpretation rather than on identity. Acts 15:1–21 privileges his interpretation of the power of God and the authority of Jewish sacred texts over the well-known Jewish custom of proselyte circumcision. Based on the power of God and the Holiness Code in Leviticus 17–18, the Christian non-Jews in Acts are proselyte Jews, but without circumcision.

The Salutaris Foundation provides a comparative context for this interpretation of Acts 15. As this Foundation demonstrates, in antiquity, city councils possessed the authority to determine how to produce, enact, and enforce civic identity. At the beginning of the second century CE, these elite Ephesians used ancestral religious imagery, the flexibility of ethnic identity, and their authority to integrate Romans into the traditional Ephesian hierarchy. In a similar way, the Jerusalem council used Jewish religious imagery and traditions, the well-known concept of the proselyte, and the authority of these traditions to integrate Christian non-Jews into the Jewish community as a type of proselyte Jew.

Conclusion

Acts 15 positions the Jewish God, Jewish sacred texts, and the mythic past in ways that legitimate the Jewishness of Christian non-Jews by reasserting what is presented as the true meaning of προσήλυτος in the Septuagint translation of Leviticus 17–18. This rhetorical move minimized the need for the circumcision of non-Jews even as it preserved them as members of the Jewish *ethnē*. The Salutaris Foundation inscription from Ephesus deploys a comparable form of ethnic rhetoric—leveraging goddess, sacred traditions, and mythic past—to legitimate the identity of a contested urban population. Both pieces of evidence deploy ancestral gods for legitimating the ethnic identification of contested populations. Both decisions faced opposition but, Salutaris and Luke suggest, were ultimately accepted partly on the basis of the recommendation of individuals viewed as authoritative interpreters of sacred traditions. Salutaris leaned on the Roman proconsul of Asia, Aquillius Proculus, and the legate, Afranius Flavianus, while Luke turned to James, the brother of Jesus and leader of the Jerusalem Christians, for the legitimation of contested identities.

In the next chapter I consider the implications of reading the movements of Paul as depicted in Acts 16–20 in light of the ethnic reasoning in Acts 15:1–21. Building on the argument of this chapter, I examine the propagation of the ruling of the Jerusalem council by Paul throughout the Mediterranean world in comparison with the movement of statues through the city of Ephesus as regulated by the Salutaris Foundation.

FOUR

Moving Through the Polis, *Asserting Christian Jewishness*

ANCIENT CHRISTIANS, LIKE OTHER inhabitants of the *polis,* negotiated their various places in the city within and around material, civic topography. The gods, in ancient imagination, moved through cities in numerous ways as well—in processions, at sacrifices, during festivals and assemblies, and on coins. Their regular and regulating movements through space both perpetuated and altered civic identity, (re)asserting the centrality of the nexus of gods-people-place for civic identification. The movements of gods and their peoples can be understood as a form of ethnic reasoning.

In the previous chapter I argued that the Salutaris Foundation inscription (*IEph* 27), a civic benefaction approved by the Ephesian council in 104 CE, and the Jerusalem council (Acts 15:1–29) as described in Acts both offer examples of the negotiation of ethnic change. Furthermore, I contended that Salutaris and the writer of Acts set out to identify who can legitimately make these changes by reconfiguring the mythic past. This past, they argued, affirmed rather than undermined the adjustments in civic identity they recommended. The inscription honoring Salutaris and his Foundation suggested that the Ephesian council had the power to institute changes in ethnic identity and carefully positioned its founder, a Roman, as an Ephesian and within the Ephesian *polis.* Similarly, the writer of Acts suggested that the members of the Jerusalem council had the power to determine the boundaries of Jewish identity and then carefully portrayed the Jewishness of Christian non-Jews through an appeal to Jewish sacred texts. The Salutaris Foundation, employing its own form of ethnic reasoning, identified Roman immigrants to Ephesus as genuine Ephesians. In a comparable way, Acts 15:1–29 identified Christian non-Jews as proselyte Jews.

In this chapter I continue to explore how the Salutaris Foundation and Acts legitimated ethnic change, in this case by focusing on performance in geographical space. Both the Salutaris Foundation and Acts share a focus on geographical movement and deploy movement through space to represent and remap ethnic categories. Geography provides both those responsible for the inscription and the author of Acts with a way to enact and legitimate ethnic changes, which are made to appear "traditional" rather than innovative. As described in Acts, the Jewishness enacted in Paul's (and his God's) movements among the cities of the Mediterranean world unifies Christians while privileging them as an ideal type of Jewish community for the Roman-era *polis*.[1] This description of Paul's movements can be compared with the physical movement of Artemis and her entourage through Ephesus as mediated by the Salutaris Foundation. The movement of Artemis constructs a unified Ephesian identity while privileging the "Ephesianness" of certain Romans. A focus on the geographical reach of the God of Israel, in the case of the writer of Acts, or the Ephesian Artemis, in the case of Salutaris, mapped ethnicity onto space and time, naturalizing and reifying Jewish and Ephesian identities as if they were fixed, when in fact they were malleable and subject to constant reconfiguration.

I first discuss the processions sponsored by the Salutaris Foundation and then consider Acts' description of Paul's journey to propagate the Jerusalem council's decision (15:30–18:23). My treatment of the Salutaris Foundation processions focuses on the direction of the processions in relation to other processions held in honor of Artemis on her birthday and on the participants in the Salutaris Foundation's processions. My discussion of Acts concentrates on the three cities where Paul is depicted facing opposition from other Jews: Lystra (16:1–5), Thessalonica (17:1–10), and Corinth (18:1–17).[2] In these three *poleis*, Paul's engagement with local Jews demonstrates the Jewishness of "Christians" while also positioning Jesus followers as comprising a better Jewish community that contributes significantly to the stability of the *polis*, contrary to accusations from other Jews.

Moreover, the movements of Paul and his companions among and through
the various cities are represented as creating a unified Christian community that can then be contrasted with local Jewish associations, which are
depicted as disruptive and divisive.[3]

Artemis, Salutaris's Processions, and Claiming
Ephesian Identity

The images of Artemis dedicated by Salutaris and accepted by the Ephesian council provided space for a group of Ephesian elites to regulate the
movement of Artemis in the city. The Foundation reimagined the carefully
regulated official movements of Artemis through the streets of their *polis*
and performed Ephesian identity in a palpable, visible, and embodied way,
hierarchically arranging both the city and the city's population. As discussed in the previous chapter, the Salutaris Foundation commissioned
twenty-nine statues of Artemis and civic groups that enacted the Ephesian
identity of Roman immigrants to Ephesus and incorporated them into the
Hellenistic-based civic hierarchy. The regular movement of these images
bolstered the integration of Roman elites into the civic hierarchy; the particular way that Salutaris's Foundation regulated their movement also displayed the importance of the Roman presence in Ephesus.[4]

The movement of Artemis and her entourage through the streets of
the *polis* created a visual, dynamic link between the past and the present.
As Guy Rogers argues, the actions of all those involved—Salutaris, the
βουλή ("city council") the participants in the processions, and the
onlookers—"endowed the procession with whatever social significance it
held for Ephesians." Two characteristics of Salutaris's processions suggest
how they may have attempted to shape the social situation in Ephesus: the
route of the procession and the exclusion of the Kouretes, the mythical protectors of Artemis.[5]

According to Strabo, every year on the sixth of Thargelion (late April/
early May), the city of Ephesus celebrated the birth of Artemis with an
elaborate festival that included sacrifices along with the reading of entrails,
a cultic dance, music, and a procession from the Artemision to Ortygia,

the goddess's mythic birthplace located on the outskirts of the *polis*. According to legend, Ortygia was where Leto, the mistress of Zeus, gave birth to the divine twins Apollo and Artemis. Strabo wrote that when Leto rested after giving birth, Hera, Zeus's wife, began spying on her; the Kouretes, a group of young warriors, frightened the jilted goddess and concealed the birth of the divine twins from her (*Geogr.* 14.1.20). Each year, the Ephesian Kouretes reenacted this mythic scene at Ortygia, and after their performance, "it was time for the goddess Artemis to bestow her favor upon the Kouretes and the polis of Ephesos" once again. This yearly repetition reified the myth and reestablished Artemis as the great patroness of the city and honored her protectors.[6]

The annual celebrations of Artemis and her protection of Ephesus began in her temple, located to the northeast of the *polis* and outside of the city walls. To reach Ortygia, southwest of Ephesus, the procession moved from the Artemision along the Via Sacra, through the Koressian Gate into the city's Koressian district—the heart of the Greek *polis*—past the great theater and the Tetragonos Agora and continuing along to Ortygia. The festival according to Richard Oster "was one of the largest and most magnificent celebrations in Ephesus' liturgical calendar," stabilizing Ephesian identity around Artemis by annually circumnavigating the processional route between her temple and Ortygia, rehearsing the birth of the goddess and the role of the Kouretes.[7]

Unlike the annual festival in honor of Artemis's birth, the Salutaris Foundation processions occurred much more frequently. Nevertheless, Salutaris proposed, and the Ephesian council accepted, his Foundation's connection with the annual celebration by allowing him to distribute money to various groups on the eve of and the day of Artemis's birth. As a result the Salutaris Foundation, along with its processions, was directly linked with the annual procession from the Artemision to Ortygia in honor of Artemis. The Foundation's processions differed from the traditional celebrations of Artemis in other important ways: rather than traveling from the Artemision through the Koressian Gate to Ortygia, the Salutaris Foundation dictated that Artemis and her entourage move from the temple through the Magnesian Gate to the city theater, thus reversing the direction of the procession. The great goddess was also accompanied by a different set of practitioners. During the annual festival, Kouretes played a central role in the celebration; however, in the Salutaris Foundation processions, Kouretes did not participate. Instead, Salutaris and the Ephesian council overlooked this group that was central to the mythic foundation of Ephesus and included "Rome."[8]

THE PROCESSIONAL ROUTE

The processions described in Salutaris's inscription all began in the *pronaos* ("front hall") of the Artemision and continued to the Magnesian Gate rather than the Koressian Gate, where the procession surrounding Artemis's birthday entered the city.[9] At the gate, the temple wardens (φυλάκοι) handed the statues to the city's *ephebes*.[10] From there the processions could follow one of two paths around the city's upper agora.[11] One route would travel from the Magnesian Gate along the road south of the upper agora until it reached so-called Domitian Street and the base of the temple for the Flavian Sebastoi.[12] The more likely route, however, followed the walkway on the north side of the agora and passed through the magnificent Stoa Basilica that was donated by the famous Ephesian C. Sextilius Pollio at the beginning of the first century CE. The Stoa Basilica connected the north side of the agora with the *bouleuterion* (βουλευτήριον), a temple affiliated with Rome, and the Prytaneion—the official religious center of the *polis,* the home of Artemis in the *polis,* and the meeting place of the Kouretes. From the west end of the Stoa Basilica, the processions passed through the recently constructed chalcidicum and follow the street called the Embolos toward the traditional center of the city, the Tetragonos Agora.[13]

At the time of Salutaris's Foundation, the Embolos became a center for civic monuments, honorific tombs, and elite residences. A monument to Memmius, grandson of the famous Roman general Sulla, and a fountain stood on the north side of the street just beyond the chalcidicum. Farther down, on the south side of street, the tombs of the city founder, Androklos, and the sister of Cleopatra VII, Arisonë IV, stood near the elaborate, terraced *insulae* typically called the Slope or Terrace Houses. To the north of the colonnaded street, the Trajan fountain, Varius Bath, and the so-called temple of Hadrian also lined the street by the middle of the second century. By the second century, the Embolos was transformed from a largely uninhabited street for burials into a monument-lined tribute to Roman influence in Ephesus.[14]

Once at the bottom of the Embolos, Salutaris's processions would (eventually) move past the so-called Gate of Hadrian and the Celsus Library, past the traditional road to Ortygia onto Plateia, the street adjacent to the Tetragonos Agora, en route to the theater. The processions likely entered the theater through the south *parados* (entryway) since that was the location of the known copy of the Salutaris Foundation inscription. After each *ekklēsia* (assembly), the processions moved north toward the Koressian Gate, and the temple wardens would return the images to the Artemision.[15]

The images' progression through the *polis* enacted Ephesian identity in a way that used the past to stabilize a changing civic topography. The movement of the great Artemis of Ephesus in the form of the nine statues of her through the *polis,* dominated by the beginning of the second century CE with temples and monuments to the Roman emperors, reinforced and legitimated her rightful place in the *polis* even while the scope of her dominance was being renegotiated by elites like Salutaris and the members of the Ephesian council. The reversal of the processional route thus allowed Salutaris and the Ephesian βουλή space to reimagine Artemis's relationship with Ephesus. The parading of the city's patron goddess through the upper (Roman) agora first foregrounded the dynamic changes of the Ephesian cityscape in the first and second centuries CE. The statues of Artemis and the heroic Ephesians of the past thus created a visual link between Ephesus and its mythic history that emphasized the present power of Rome.[16]

THE PROCESSIONAL PARTICIPANTS

Artemis was not alone in Salutaris's processions. The great goddess was joined by images representing the ancient hierarchy of the *polis:* the tribes, city council, elders, and youths. She was also joined by statues representing

Rome: Trajan, Plotina, the Senate, *equites,* and the people of Rome. Together, the individual images formed a unified collection that processed
through the *polis* before "every assembly." During these processions, Ephesian Artemis was required to share a sacred retinue with the deified emperor and others. The movement of her images past the imperial monuments
that lined the processional route made this clear.[17]

The *ephebes,* a group of civic youths, carried the statues through the
polis. Rogers has persuasively argued that the processions and distributions
of the Salutaris Foundation provided a means of "educating" the city youths
into the institutional roles that they would fill as adult citizens of Ephesus.
By incorporating them into the processions, Salutaris's Foundation could
quickly become the way that the next generation of Ephesians viewed and
related to Artemis, Ephesus, and their own Ephesian identity.[18]

Perhaps more striking than the images and participants included in
the Salutaris Foundation is the conspicuous absence from the group of the
Kouretes, the mythical protectors of Artemis. No statue of the Kouretes was
included in the processions. The processions thus intertwined images from
the Ephesian past with the Roman present while their reversed direction
showed that the processions were distinct from typical processions that
honored Artemis and began at the Artemision. The fact that no evidence
exists in the Salutaris Foundation for either images or lotteries related to
the famous guardians of Artemis or the central location of Artemis in the
city, the Prytaneion, heightens the distinction between the civic hierarchy
that Salutaris's Foundation projected and that of the Hellenistic *polis.* Rogers states that "since there could be no Greek city at the site of Ephesos
without the prior condition of Artemis' birth in the grove of Ortygia, and
there could be no birth of Artemis without the K[o]uretes, the K[o]uretes
could reasonably claim that, without them, the Greek city of Ephesos would
not exist."[19] Salutaris's Foundation ignored this claim by excluding the
Kouretes from participation.

The exclusion is made all the more striking since the processions
likely traveled past the Prytaneion, with its inscribed list of Kouretes, on
the way to the theater. By conspicuously omitting this group of Ephesian
elites, Salutaris's Foundation significantly shaped how other (elite) Ephe-

sians could interact with the Artemision and allowed them to assert their
devotion to Artemis (and the Roman emperors) while at the same time marginalizing the status of the Kouretes and the centrality of the Prytaneion.
The participants in the processions thus displayed a particular version of
Ephesian history that excluded the Kouretes and was shaped by (and amenable to) the realities of the Roman present.[20]

Salutaris and the Ephesian council, which approved the Foundation,
deployed the Artemis-Ephesian-Ephesus bond in ways that legitimated the
changes that were taking place in the Greek *polis* under Roman rule. The
Salutaris Foundation regulated the movement of Artemis, joining her with
the Sebastoi and guiding her past the imperial temple and buildings dedicated by Roman Ephesians before moving to the Hellenistic-era portions
of the *polis*. At the same time, the Foundation avoided Artemis's historic
route toward Ortygia and marginalized the Kouretes.

The depiction of Paul's travels in Acts 15:30–18:23 also provides a
means of legitimating a changing identity—in this case, Jewish identity. In
ways similar to the Salutaris Foundation's use of Artemis, Ephesians, and
the urban landscape of Ephesus, Acts leverages the connection between the
God of Israel, Jews, and local Jewish communities in various cities to make
a claim about Jewish identity that privileges Christians as members of an
ideal Jewish community for the Roman-era *polis*. The Salutaris Foundation offers a record of a movement that (presumably) took place; by contrast, the writer of Acts tells a story about the movement of Paul and the
God he introduced to the Mediterranean cities he visited. Nevertheless,
both the literary movement of Paul in Acts and the actual movement of leading Ephesians through Ephesus seek to map civic topography according
to a particular set of images, defining landmarks, hierarchies, and points
of view. In the process, both works (one liturgical and the other literary)
work to manufacture and reify particular forms of ethnic identity.

The Jewish God, Paul's Travel, and Claiming Jewish Identity

In Acts, Luke carefully depicts the continuing presence of the Jewish God
corresponding with the movement of his emissaries throughout the cities

of the Mediterranean world. The avenues and sea routes that Luke's emissaries traveled, the places where they stopped and spoke, and the companions—both Jews and non-Jews—who joined them in "the Way" (ἡ ὁδός) indicate and demarcate Luke's Jewish and Christian identity. They create a visual, dynamic link between local Jewish associations and the communities that Acts represents Paul as founding. In the latter half of Acts, Jewish and Christian identity is produced and enacted largely in the cities of the Roman Empire. In the rest of this chapter I examine the ethnic reasoning implied in Luke's depiction of Paul's journey to proclaim the Jerusalem council's decree. Journeying to the *poleis* throughout the Mediterranean, Paul publicizes the council's understanding of Jewish identity, traveling through God's territories to announce the newly established policy, a policy that is represented as ancient and venerable (15:30–18:23). I compare the movements of the Salutaris Foundation processions with the travels of Paul in this passage, building on Nasrallah's contention that Paul's travels unify diverse groups of Jesus followers into a civic league. It also builds on Wills's assertion, discussed in chapter 1, that Luke presents local Jewish associations as disruptive for the city. I argue that the travels of Paul and his entourage fuse together the Christian communities in various cities as a cohesive and peaceful Jewish civic association under the authority of God and God's Messiah, Jesus, in contrast to other Jewish civic associations.[21]

Nasrallah situates Acts within the rhetorical context of the so-called Second Sophistic, the archaizing movement that revived and reinterpreted classical Greek culture for the Roman era.[22] She argues that "contemporaneous political and cultural discourses about Greek cities under Rome" best explain Paul's travels to cities in the latter half of Acts. "Moreover," she asserts, "through Paul's deeds and speeches in key sites . . . , Acts articulates a theological vision of how Christianity and its notion of one, true God can fit within a 'pluralistic' empire and its notions of ethnic difference." She compares the various sites that Paul visits—Lystra, Philippi, Thessalonica, and Athens—with Hadrian's creation of a Panhellenion, a civic league that bound Greek *poleis* with the Roman Empire in the middle of the second century CE. She observes four principal ways that the two intertwine: the creation of civic harmony or concord between cities; the centrality of discourses about identity; the juxtaposition of ancient and recent material in the production of "mutually affirming religious values, ethnic identity, and certain ideas about aesthetics and *paideia*"; and the creation of a "Christian parallel" to the Panhellenion through Paul's travels. She concludes that Acts "crafts a story of a city league formed by the ambassadorial presence of Paul," and "Christianity is constructed as the new Israel, as the rightful inheritor of these stories of salvation [of the people of Israel] and of God's activity in the world."[23]

Nasrallah's comparison of the geographical imagination of Luke with that of the Panhellenion demonstrates the importance of "mapping" for constructing identities. As the discussion of the Salutaris Foundation established, the specific mapping of the processional route through the Roman-centric portion of the *polis* before passing by monuments associated with the city's Greek past signified how Salutaris and the Ephesian council desired to represent Ephesian identity. Here I argue that Paul's movements both between various cities and within Jewish associations in those cities are examples of a similar form of "mapping" that creates a unified Christian identity. Yet, unlike Nasrallah, I argue that the writer seeks to map Christian identity as a type of Jewish identity. The writer crafts a unified, pan-Hellenic Jewish identity that includes Christ worship as a form of "being Jewish."

Wills, in an article written almost two decades before Nasrallah, considered the role of Jews in the latter half of Acts.[24] He examined the "stylized way in which Jews are often represented"[25] and found a pattern throughout the latter half of the book: missionary action, opposition from Jews and others, and Christian expansion.[26] In a revised and updated version of the article, Wills pays closer attention to how the mob scenes in Acts reflect "the common Roman assumptions about the nature of the masses and insurrection." The role of Jews in crowd scenes in Acts corresponds to the negative Roman assumptions about mobs and is contrasted with the newly "converted" Christians, whom Acts depicts as peaceful and respectable. "In Luke's hands," Wills contends, "the scriptures and traditions of Israel are transferred from Jews to this new *politeia,* Christians."[27]

Wills's interpretation provides a path for exploring the conflicts between Christians and other Jews in various cities in relation to their civic context. It situates Paul's interactions with Jews in the latter half of Acts in relation to Roman concerns about mob violence. His interpretation is fundamental to the reading of the conflicts the writer of Acts portrays, but with an important proviso based on the conclusion of the previous chapter: Acts (still) represents Christians as Jews, and the writer is working to reconfigure Jewishness to make this claim. Wills's helpful iteration of the so-called Jewish mob scenes therefore becomes a description of the writer's vision of appropriate ways of enacting Jewishness in the *polis* and not about the distance the writer seeks to create between Jews and Christians. The writer does not want to distance himself and his audience from Jewishness; rather, he suggests that Christians enact Jewishness appropriately, and non-Christian Jews do not. The discussion of the Salutaris Foundation demonstrated that the Ephesian council and Salutaris could appropriate Ephesian ancestral traditions and adapt them, all the while maintaining Ephesian identity. Artemis, the Ephesians, and Ephesus could be Romanized while remaining Ephesian, and Romans could become "Ephesianized" while remaining Roman. The Artemis-Ephesian-Ephesus nexus remains intact, but not without change. Similarly, the writer of Acts could maintain the Jewish God–Jews–Jewish association nexus even while claiming these identity markers for Christians who were non-Jews.

This observation provides grounds for fresh analysis of what Nasrallah describes as Acts' "Christian civic league" and Wills's conclusion regarding the transfer of the scriptures and traditions of Israel from Jews to Christians in the latter half of Acts. The Salutaris Foundation demonstrates that a wealthy Roman citizen of Ephesus could attempt to create a new Ephesus that forms around the Romanized urban center of the city and a transfer of ancestral customs from the priests of Artemis and the Kouretes by the Ephesian council. These Ephesians are still Ephesians, however. This malleability of Ephesian identity thus plays out along the gods-people-place nexus as the processions instituted by Salutaris move through the *polis*.

Luke's depiction of Paul's movements between and within cities of the Roman world provides an example of the malleability of identity but in this case of Jewish identity. But Paul does face opposition from other Jews: the circumcision of Timothy in Lystra (16:1–5), the jealousy of some Jews in Thessalonica (17:1–9), and the conflict with the leaders of the Jewish association in Corinth (18:1–17). These three scenes offer a sample of interactions between Paul and other Jews in civic spaces while at the same time typifying the gods-people-place nexus found throughout the ancient Mediterranean world and reflected in the Salutaris Foundation. Together these three episodes encapsulate the ethnic reasoning that occurs in the narrative as it describes the movement of the Jerusalem council's declaration identifying Christian non-Jews as proselyte Jews outward from the capital city. Like the Salutaris Foundation processions, these three episodes demonstrate that movement through civic space can provide a means of negotiating and unifying flexible identities in a changing present.

PAUL, TIMOTHY, AND HYBRID JEWISH IDENTITY

According to Acts, the Jerusalem council determined that Christian non-Jews did not need to be circumcised to turn to God (15:1–19). Rather, they were to follow four stipulations for the proselytes who lived among Jews (15:19–20, 15:29, 21:25), which were proclaimed in every *polis* for generations (15:20–21). Acts redeploys proselyte identity, thus identifying Christian non-Jews as Jewish. According to Luke's interpretation, circumcision was no longer the central symbol of Jewish proselytes, as it was for most historical Jews (and non-Jews) in the Roman era. Acts returns to the mythic past, to "Moses" and the Holiness Code of Leviticus 17–18 in Greek translation, to justify his identification of non-Jews as προσήλυτος without circumcision. His innovation was established long ago, the author claims. These four stipulations then become the means for Christian non-Jews to become Jewish. This identification becomes tremendously important for Acts' depiction of Jesus followers throughout the remainder of the narrative, particularly those Christian non-Jews dwelling in the *poleis* of Asia.

Luke's Paul does not move through the cities of the Roman world alone. The inclusion of the emperors and the tribe of the Sebaste and the exclusion of the Kouretes in the Salutaris Foundation processions demonstrated that the identity of traveling companions matters. The individuals and groups either selected for participation or ignored provided a physical means of unifying Ephesian identity according to the Ephesian council's proclamation. In a similar way, the travelers who deliver the Jerusalem council's decree in Acts provide a literary means of unifying Christian identity in relation to Jewish identity in the *polis*. Luke takes great care to narrate the selection of Timothy as Paul's traveling companion, but before Timothy can join Paul, he must be circumcised. When read through the lens of ethnic reasoning, the circumcision of Timothy provides a symbol of the malleability of Jewishness that Luke's Paul carries with him from *polis* to *polis*. Thus, I argue, Luke's Timothy, like Salutaris's tribe of the Sebaste, legitimates the ethnic identity of a contested population: Christian non-Jews in Acts.

After receiving the Jerusalem council's decree, the Christians in Antioch send Paul and his new companion Silas, a leader of the brothers in Jerusalem and prophet (15:22, 32), to visit the *poleis* Paul and Barnabas had visited (15:36) and to proclaim this "good news" for non-Jews throughout the Mediterranean (16:4). At Paul's first stop, Acts narrates a puzzling episode.[28] The first event that Luke depicts after the Jerusalem council's decision that Christian non-Jews do not need to be circumcised is the circumcision of a Christian non-Jew, Timothy, by Paul:

(16:1) Κατήντησεν δὲ [καὶ] εἰς Δέρβην καὶ εἰς Λύστραν. καὶ ἰδοὺ μαθητής τις ἦν ἐκεῖ ὀνόματι Τιμόθεος, υἱὸς γυναικὸς Ἰουδαίας πιστῆς, πατρὸς δὲ Ἕλληνος, (2) ὃς ἐμαρτυρεῖτο ὑπὸ τῶν ἐν Λύστροις καὶ Ἰκονίῳ ἀδελφῶν. (3) τοῦτον ἠθέλησεν ὁ Παῦλος σὺν αὐτῷ ἐξελθεῖν, καὶ λαβὼν περιέτεμεν αὐτὸν διὰ τοὺς Ἰουδαίους τοὺς ὄντας ἐν τοῖς τόποις ἐκείνοις· ᾔδεισαν γὰρ ἅπαντες ὅτι Ἕλλην ὁ πατὴρ αὐτοῦ ὑπῆρχεν. (4) Ὡς δὲ διεπορεύοντο τὰς πόλεις, παρεδίδοσαν αὐτοῖς φυλάσσειν τὰ δόγματα τὰ κεκριμένα

ὑπὸ τῶν ἀποστόλων καὶ πρεσβυτέρων τῶν ἐν Ἱεροσολύμοις.
(5) Αἱ μὲν οὖν ἐκκλησίαι ἐστερεοῦντο τῇ πίστει καὶ
ἐπερίσσευον τῷ ἀριθμῷ καθ' ἡμέραν.

(16:1) Paul went on also to Derbe and to Lystra. There was a disciple there named Timothy, the son of a Christian (πιστῆς) Jewish woman, and his father was a Greek. (2) He was well spoken of by the brothers in Lystra and Iconium. (3) Paul wanted Timothy to accompany him; and taking him he circumcised him because of the Jews who were in those places, for they all knew that his father was a Greek. (4) As they passed through the *poleis,* they delivered to them for observance the decrees that had been reached by the apostles and elders in Jerusalem. (5) So the assemblies were strengthened in faith and increased in numbers daily.

With Timothy's circumcision, Luke has surrounded the Jerusalem council's decree with two examples of two different groups of Jews—Christian Pharisees in Jerusalem and Jews in the region of Lystra—affirming the malleability of Jewishness through male circumcision. Thus other Jews view Jewishness as malleable but in terms different from the apostles and elders. This juxtaposition provides space for Luke to forcefully assert the Jewishness of those who move through the Mediterranean with Paul to proclaim the deeds of God. I argue that Luke uses Timothy's Jewish identity to show that Jewishness is malleable in the hands of Jews, just as the Ephesian identity of Romans is malleable in the hands of Salutaris and the Ephesian council.

Timothy's identity, in particular his ethnicity, plays a central role in interpreting his circumcision.[29] Previous scholars have seen the story of Timothy's circumcision as Luke's attempt to insert a connection between Jewish Christianity and gentile Christianity in the earliest days.[30] Many more recent scholars, however, now view Timothy's circumcision as necessary because he is a Jew; the Jerusalem council's decision did not alleviate Jews's obligation for circumcision, and so he was circumcised to meet this criterion.[31] Shaye Cohen, however, persuasively argues that a straight-forward reading of Acts 16:1–5 indicates that Timothy is not a Jew by lin-eage. As Cohen points out, the limited evidence that does survive suggests that the Jewish matrilineal principle of lineage had not yet developed by the first century. Thus, that principle cannot have applied in Timothy's case, and therefore Timothy would not be Jewish on the basis of the iden-tity of his mother.[32] Furthermore, Cohen concludes, Jews from the sur-rounding regions would more likely view Timothy as a non-Jew because his father was Greek (16:3). On this reading, Luke depicts the circumcision of a non-Jew.[33] Though Timothy's circumcision was no longer necessary, in Luke's eyes, for Timothy to be Jewish (on the basis of the Jerusalem coun-cil's ruling), Paul's circumcision of Timothy affirms that circumcision re-mains a legitimate way to become Jewish, even though it is no longer required of Christian non-Jews.

Acts depicts Paul, who staunchly opposed the teaching that Chris-tian non-Jews needed circumcision (15:1–2), as actively circumcising Tim-othy (16:3), even though the narrative has just confirmed Paul's view that Christian non-Jews do not need to be circumcised (15:10–21, 23–29). The narrative suggests that by means of circumcision Timothy becomes Jew-ish in this way so that he can accompany Paul as he moves throughout the Mediterranean. Cohen's interpretation demonstrates that it is not likely that Luke followed the matrilineal principle for Jewish identity.

In contrast to Cohen, Eric Barreto interprets Timothy's circumcision as an example of the complexity of ancient identity categories. He argues that Luke purposefully leaves Timothy's ethnic identity hybrid, and that identity remains multiple even after his circumcision.[34] A single ethnicity for Timothy is never defined in Acts, and thus his circumcision serves as an "open ethnic symbol," sufficient for Jews in the region but in no way con-clusive for determining his ethnicity.[35] Barreto contends that Timothy is "an emblem of this theologically rich negotiation of ethnic difference" that Luke uses throughout the rest of Acts.[36] Timothy's circumcision indicates that "ethnic diversity and hybrid identities are not an obstacle for this move-ment of Christ followers but an opportunity to reach all peoples not by erasing their differences but by participating in the complexities of ethnic discourse."[37] To Barreto, Timothy can remain both Jewishly circumcised and not-Jewish at the same time.

Barreto highlights the possible hybridity of Timothy's identity and allows ambiguity in that identity before and after his circumcision. This is a helpful reminder of the complex and fluid way that ancient identity was constituted. However, Cohen's observation that Luke suggests that Jews from the regions around Lystra would have known that Timothy's father was a Greek (16:3) and therefore perceived him to be a non-Jew before his circumcision remains persuasive.[38] As I argued previously, circumcision was a way for non-Jews to become Jews, even if Luke supported another way for that to occur.[39] For most ancient writers, both Jews and non-Jews, circumcision was a tangible way for a male to mark his Jewish identity, regardless of his lineage or previous connection with a Jewish community.[40] Timothy's circumcision confirms this point of view. However, the suggestion that Timothy was a non-Jew by lineage does not address why Acts depicts the event at all, let alone after the Jerusalem council's decree.

The ruling of the Jerusalem council indicates that even if other Jews (like the Christian Pharisees of Acts 15:4) deemed Timothy's identity to be initially hybrid, Luke and his Jesus followers could view him as a Jewish proselyte before his circumcision. As the discussion of proselytes in the previous chapter showed, Luke does acknowledge that circumcision is a way for non-Jews to become Jews; however, Luke offers another way for non-Jews to become proselyte Jews, namely, by being accepted by the God of Israel and by receiving the Holy Spirit (15:8–9). Therefore, Timothy was, in a sense, already Jewish before his circumcision. He was a non-Jew who became a twice-proselyte Jew—first through the power of God, and then by the hand of Paul.

As an example of ethnic rhetoric, Timothy's identity serves as a symbol of the ethnic complexity of Christian communities, as Barreto has observed.[41] However, because Timothy became a proselyte Jew (first through the power of God, and then through circumcision), he is not only a symbol of Christian ethnic diversity; rather, he embodies the Jewishness of Christians, even those who may be considered non-Jews by some. As Paul's traveling companion, Timothy narratively proclaims the multiple ways of becoming Jewish, including the Jerusalem council's redefinition in terms based on Moses and the Jewish ancestral traditions for ancient προσήλυτος. By depicting Paul's desire to "take" (ἐξελθεῖν) Timothy with him on his journey, Luke incorporates Timothy, as a symbol of the Jewishness of Christians, into Paul's moves from *polis* to *polis*.

Timothy's embodiment of the Jewishness of Christians as regulated by Jews is similar to the "Ephesianness" of Romans as regulated by Salutaris and the Ephesian council. The Ephesian council approved incorporating into the Salutaris Foundation processions images of the emperors and the tribe of Sebaste, thereby incorporating "Rome" into the existing Ephesian hierarchy and tribal system. This had the effect of calling that same structure into question. Similarly, Timothy perpetually proclaims his Jewish identity through his joint movements with Paul.[42] Timothy, like Salutaris's tribe of the Sebaste, legitimates the ethnic identity of contested populations: Christian non-Jews in Acts.

THE ONES WHO TURN THE *OIKOUMENĒ* UPSIDE DOWN

The Salutaris Foundation carefully regulated the physical movement of Artemis and her entourage through Ephesus. Similarly, Luke regulates Paul's literary movements in Acts. While the Salutaris Foundation created a pattern of processions that physically transferred images of Artemis and others from the Artemision through the *polis* and back to the goddess's temple, Luke creates two overlapping literary patterns with regard to Paul's movements. Throughout Acts, Paul's movements revolve around his departure from and return to Jerusalem.[43] This pattern is perhaps most strikingly illustrated in the fact that Luke does not complete it at the ending of Acts.[44] Acts ends with Paul in Rome.

A second pattern emerges while Paul is away from Jerusalem, as Wills has observed:[45] Paul enters a city, finds the Jewish community there, and after facing opposition departs from the Jewish association to form a new community. Just as each of the movements of Artemis through Ephesus unified Ephesian identity in a particular way, I argue that each of Paul's movements in individual cities unifies Christian identity in a particular way. Moreover, just as the exclusion of the Kouretes from Salutaris's processions privileged one way of being Ephesian over others, Luke's depiction of opposition to Paul by some Jews privileges one way of being Jewish in the *polis* over others.

According to the writer of Acts, as Paul, Silas, and Timothy are strengthening the Christian assemblies in the *poleis* around Lystra, the Holy Spirit guides them on their way (16:6). They depart for the regions of Phrygia and Galatia, having been forbidden by the spirit of Jesus from entering Asia (16:6). From there they travel to Mysia (16:8–11) and on to Macedonia. While in Philippi, a leading city of Macedonia, the owners of a slave girl with a Pythian spirit accuse Paul and Silas of disturbing the *polis* because they are Jews and advocating customs that are not permitted for Romans "to adopt or to do" (παραδέχεσθαι οὐδὲ ποιεῖν) (16:20b–21). After the two men are beaten and thrown into prison, Luke turns the slave masters' accusation on its head by revealing that these Jews are also Romans (16:37–38).[46] The Roman magistrates (στρατηγοί) who threw them in prison are forced to apologize to Paul and Silas and then ask them to leave the *polis* (16:39).

From Philippi, Paul and Silas continue their divinely inspired travel to Thessalonica, where Paul locates the Jewish association and, "as was his custom" (κατὰ τὸ εἰωθὸς), joins their weekly meetings to discuss the Jewish sacred texts (17:1–2). There he argues that Jesus is the Christ (17:3). Paul persuades some Jews along with some God-fearing Greeks and leading women to join him and Silas (17:4). This causes jealousy in some Jews, and so they gather a group of ruffians from the agora and stir the *polis* into an uproar (17:5). Since they cannot find Paul and Silas, they drag a previously unmentioned Jason and some other Christians before the city rulers. The mob proclaims, "These ones who turn the *oikoumenē* upside down have also come here, and Jason welcomed them. All these people act contrary to the decrees of Caesar, saying that there is another king, Jesus" (οἱ τὴν οἰκουμένην ἀναστατώσαντες οὗτοι καὶ ἐνθάδε πάρεισιν, οὓς ὑποδέδεκται Ἰάσων· καὶ οὗτοι πάντες ἀπέναντι τῶν δογμάτων Καίσαρος πράσσουσιν βασιλέα ἕτερον λέγοντες εἶναι Ἰησοῦν) (17:6–7). After hearing this accusation, the city leaders and the crowd are disturbed and take a security from Jason and the other Christians (17:8–9).[47]

Paul and Silas sneak to the nearby town of Berea and find the Jewish association there (17:10). That community welcomes their message and searches the Jewish scriptures to check its accuracy (17:11). Again, Paul and Silas persuade Greek women and men of high standing (17:12; cf. 17:4). Some Jews from Thessalonica hear of Paul's work in Berea and attempt to stir up the crowds there as well (17:13), but the Christians send Paul off to Athens, while Timothy and Silas stay behind (17:14–15).

As ethnic rhetoric, the way Luke describes events in Thessalonica emphasizes the Jewishness of Christians and marginalizes other Jews in the *polis* in three ways: (1) the Christian community forms within an existing Jewish community on the basis of debate about the interpretation of Jewish ancestral texts; (2) benefactors of the Jewish association join Paul and Silas, privileging their group's place within the *polis;* and (3) the Jews who do not join Paul marginalize their place in the *polis* by forming a mob and accusing Christians. Each of these three points asserts the Jewishness of Christians while also using movement through the city to marginalize other local Jewish associations. Acts, like the Salutaris Foundation, uses Paul and other Jews' movements through a *polis* to emphasize certain ways of enacting ethnic identity while marginalizing others.

Luke grounds Paul's reenactment of Jewishness in Thessalonica in a Jewish association and through interpretation of Jewish scriptures, specifically the interpretation and meaning of messianic prophecies (17:2–3).[48] The interpretation of the messiah in the Jewish scriptures inspires Paul's following, and a subgroup forms within the Jewish association in Thessalonica. Among them "some" (τινες) Jews, a "great many" (πλῆθος πολύ) God-fearing Greeks, and "not a few" (οὐκ ὀλίγαι) leading women are persuaded and join with Paul and Silas (17:4). Until this point in the narrative scene, the two travelers have taught only at the Jewish association, so the "pious" or "God-fearing" (σεβόμενοι) Greeks must be understood as somehow affiliated with the Jewish community in Thessalonica before Paul and Silas's arrival.

Historically, "Godfearers" appear to have been non-Jews who honored the God of Israel.[49] Such Godfearers are present throughout Acts (φοβούμενοι [10:2, 22, 35; 13:16, 26]; σεβόμενοι [13:43 (combined with προσήλυτος and likely meaning "pious"), 50; 16:14; 17:4, 17; 18:7]) and play an important literary role.[50] In Acts Godfearers also often serve as benefactors for Jewish communities.[51]

In Thessalonica, the literary shift of allegiance from the leaders of the Jewish association to Paul and Silas by many Godfearers and the leading women suggests a shift of support from the former Jewish association by a group of benefactors, benefactors who could contribute to the financial and social stability of the Jewish association in Thessalonica. As Pervo comments, "by siphoning off a number—which could not in any circumstances have been very large—of the God-Fearers, Paul had deprived their community of important financial and political support."[52]

For Luke, the support of the Godfearers and the leading women is also symbolic. They serve as representatives of the broader *polis*, with its own civic structures, patterns of benefaction, and place on the gods-peoples-place nexus. Some of the non-Jewish inhabitants of the city who could serve to socially legitimate the Jewish association in the *polis* now legitimate Christians as an embodiment of Jewishness in Thessalonica. As discussed in the previous chapter, the Salutaris Foundation inscription depicted a similar form of symbolic support in the form of letters from the proconsul of Asia, Aquillius Proculus, and legate, Afranius Flavianus. Just as these high-ranking Roman officials legitimated Salutaris's "Ephesian-ness," so the Godfearers and leading women symbolically legitimate the Jewishness of the Christian gathering. This inspires jealousy in other Jews.

Luke's depiction of these Jews forming a mob as a result of jealousy undermines their accusation that Paul and Silas are the ones who are turning the *oikoumenē* upside down. These Jews "stirred up the *polis*" (ἐθορύβουν τὴν πόλιν) (17:5). Grabbing ruffians from the market, storming the house of Jason, dragging him and some others before the city officials—they are the ones doing the act of which they accuse those joining Paul of doing.[53] These Jews expand their disruptive ways to the *oikoumenē* when they travel to Berea, stirring up and inciting the crowds (σαλεύοντες καὶ ταράσσοντες) there even though the Jewish association from that city welcomes Paul and Silas and their message (17:13). The movement of these Thessalonian Jews from *polis* to *polis* both unifies and marginalizes their identity.

As if the actions of these Jews does not undermine their accusation enough, Luke also depicts the city officials hesitating when they offer their response (17:8–9). These officials, along with a gathered crowd, were "disturbed" (ἐτάραξαν), Luke reports, leaving out exactly what may have disturbed them. Perhaps the reader is to infer that the accusation that Christians are turning the world upside down was disturbing, or that the officials were disturbed that the Christians came to Thessalonica at all, or they were disturbed that the Christians would dare to claim a king other than Caesar. Luke's depiction of the city officials' response, however, suggests that they were worried about the events taking place in their *polis* rather than the rest of the *oikoumenē;* they took money as a security from Jason and the others; they did not look for Paul or Silas; and they did not report the matter to the nearest Roman officials. The Christians put up the required security, and order was restored to the *polis*. Paul continues his journey, creating, sustaining, and uniting Christian assemblies throughout the *oikoumenē*. Luke leaves the rabble-rousers from the Jewish association in Thessalonica looking divided, disruptive, and defeated.

The scene in Thessalonica serves as an example of the way that Jewishness in the latter half of Acts becomes reified, in part, through performances in civic space, similar to the way the Salutaris Foundation procession enacted "Ephesianness." The specific regulations for the movement of Salutaris's processions, beginning at the Magnesian Gate in the Roman-centric portion of the city and then moving through the streets of Ephesus, could legitimate the Ephesianness of certain Romans in the city. In Thessalonica, Paul first enters the city through the metaphorical "gate" of a Jewish association. By placing Paul in a Jewish association first, Luke thus privileges Jewishness as the first entry point of the *polis* in a way similar to how the Salutaris Foundation processions privileged the "Romanness" of Ephesians by first passing through the Roman-centered upper agora. Moreover, this situates the Jewishness of Paul and those who follow him in stark contrast to those who oppose him. The civic movement of those Jews who oppose Paul—from their association (17:1) to the agora (17:5) to the home of Jason (17:6) to the civic authorities (17:6–7) and to a neighboring *polis* (17:13)—reifies this negative portrait. Jews who oppose Paul are represented as perpetually troublesome. In both cases, the movement through civic space delimits identities in ways that are rhetorically useful for their respective authors. Luke repeats this negative image of Jews who oppose Paul and develops a positive image of the Jewishness of Christians in the depiction of Paul in Corinth.

THE FORMATION AND LEGITIMATION OF A JEWISH ASSOCIATION IN CORINTH

Acts' narrative of Paul in Corinth (18:1–17) uses ethnic reasoning to legitimate the Jewishness of Christians in the *polis* while marginalizing Jews who oppose Paul as a divisive influence on the city. Before arriving in Corinth, Paul travels from Berea to Athens, the symbolic center of the Greek cultural world, without Timothy or Silas (17:15).[54] While waiting for them to arrive, he becomes upset (παρωξύνετο) when he sees that the *polis* is full of idols.[55] He begins debating in the Jewish association and in the agora (17:17). When given the opportunity to explain his teachings to some Athenians in the Areopagus, he proclaims the power of God (17:22–31).[56] In his stylized declaration, Paul "tries to establish proper human relations with the divine, and ... proper human relations with each other" in large part through ethnic rhetoric.[57] After hearing Paul's claims, some mocked the "babbler," and others invited him back, but others still trusted in God and joined with Paul (κολληθέντες αὐτῷ ἐπίστευσαν) (17:34; cf. 2:12–13).

After leaving Athens, Paul arrives in another prominent Greek city, Corinth.[58] There, he meets two Jews who were recently forced out of Italy because of Claudius's decree expelling πάντας τοὺς Ἰουδαίους ἀπὸ τῆς Ῥώμης ("all Jews from Rome") (18:1–2). Paul joins Aquila, Ποντικὸν τῷ γένει ("a Pontean by *genos*"), and his wife, Priscilla.[59] He stays with them, helping them in their work as tentmakers until Silas and Timothy arrive in the *polis* (18:5). Here again, Acts indicates the hybridity of Jewish and other ethnic identities in the narrative.

While waiting for his companions to arrive from Macedonia, Paul also debates with those who gather every week in the Jewish association (συναγωγή).[60] After Silas and Timothy arrive in Corinth, Paul "was wholly absorbed with the message, testifying to Jews that the messiah is Jesus" (συνείχετο τῷ λόγῳ διαμαρτυρόμενος τοῖς Ἰουδαίοις εἶναι τὸν χριστὸν Ἰησοῦν) (18:5).[61] When Silas and Timothy arrive, Luke's Paul thus shifts his focus from Jews and Greeks in the Jewish association to speaking with Jews. This shift results in a change in response to Paul's message by (some) Jews in Corinth. These Jews begin resisting Paul and defaming him, so he departs from their association and enters the home of a Godfearer who lives next to the Jewish association hall (18:6–7). After Paul begins work from this new location, a Jewish association leader, Crispus, and his household join Paul's community (18:8). Following Crispus's actions, many Corinthians "trusted" and were initiated into community meeting at Titius Justus's home through baptism (18:8).[62]

One night Paul has a dream and hears the voice of the Lord (ὁ κύριος) (18:9), who tells him, "Do not be afraid, but speak and do not be silent because I am with you and no one will do you harm for I have many people in this city" (μὴ φοβοῦ, ἀλλὰ λάλει καὶ μὴ σιωπήσῃς, διότι ἐγώ εἰμι μετὰ σοῦ καὶ οὐδεὶς ἐπιθήσεταί σοι τοῦ κακῶσαί σε, διότι λαός ἐστίν μοι πολὺς ἐν τῇ πόλει ταύτῃ) (18:9–10).[63] With this vision from the Lord, Luke's Paul remains in the city for a year and a half before a group of Jews in Corinth confront him (18:11). They take him before the tribunal, Gallio, and accuse him of persuading people to worship God contrary to the law (18:12–13). Gallio dismisses their complaint (18:14–16), and all those around begin beating a Jewish association leader, Sosthenes, in front of an indifferent Gallio (18:17). After the beating of Sosthenes, Paul remains in Corinth for a "considerable number of days" (ἡμέρας ἱκανάς) (18:18) and then departs for Syria, making stops in Ephesus, Caesarea, and Jerusalem before spending some time in Antioch (18:19–22) and heading back to the regions of Galatia and Phrygia (18:23).

As in Thessalonica, Luke's depiction of Paul in Corinth uses ethnic rhetoric both to marginalize the local Jewish association in the *polis* and to reinforce the Jewishness of Christians in the city. The scene in Corinth also develops these two themes from Thessalonica in three important ways for discussing Jewish identity and the ethnic rhetoric of Acts. First, it narrates a response by Paul to opposition from Jews (18:6). Second, it depicts Christians separating from a Jewish association in Corinth (18:7–8). And third, it portrays Christians and Jews disputing in the civic sphere (18:12–17). In each of these cases, Luke demonstrates the Jewishness of Christians and privileges their place in the *polis*.

PAUL RESPONDS TO HIS OPPOSITION

As in Thessalonica, when Paul begins testifying in earnest in the Jewish association, he faces opposition (cf. 19:8). This time, however, he shakes out his garments and says to them, "Your blood is on your head. Clean [of your blood], I will now go to the *ethnē*" (ἀντιτασσομένων δὲ αὐτῶν καὶ βλασφημούντων ἐκτιναξάμενος τὰ ἱμάτια εἶπεν πρὸς αὐτούς· τὸ αἷμα ὑμῶν ἐπὶ τὴν κεφαλὴν ὑμῶν· καθαρὸς ἐγὼ ἀπὸ τοῦ νῦν εἰς τὰ ἔθνη πορεύσομαι) (18:6).[64] Paul's actions and words represent a symbolic discharge of responsibility, as Joseph Fitzmyer and others have claimed, though many scholars have attempted to narrow the meaning of Paul's actions and words further.[65] Interpretations of Paul's saying range from a simple removal of responsibility to "a reference to the death of the Jews, presumably by violence (bloodshed)."[66] Pervo moderates this view, but he also claims that Paul's actions suggest that "those who reject his [Paul's] message will bear the consequences."[67] On this view, Paul condemns those Jews who oppose him and leaves them to their own destruction.

The relationship, however, between Paul's claim to be "clean" (καθαρός) and the connection with blood (αἷμα) indicates that his statement is not necessarily a condemnation of those Jews who opposed him, but could merely represent a removal of Paul's responsibility for and to them.[68] Paul makes a similar statement to the elders of the Christians from Ephesus, also connecting αἷμα and καθαρός. He exclaims, καθαρός εἰμι ἀπὸ τοῦ αἵματος πάντων ("I am clean of the blood of all [of you]") (20:26).[69] Paul follows this proclamation with an exhortation to the leaders of the Christians in Ephesus saying, "I commend you to God and to the message

of his grace" (20:32). After telling those gathered that they would never see
him again, Paul prays with the Ephesians, and "there was much weeping
among them all" because they would not meet again (20:37–38). Paul's declaration to these Ephesians that he is "clean of the blood of all" need not
imply condemnation, indicate negative consequences, or suggest bloodguilt
for "the Jews"; rather, it suggests a general release of responsibility. Paul
has commended the Ephesians to God and encouraged them "to shepherd
the assembly of God" (20:28). His statement in Corinth, when read in light
of 20:26, serves as a release of responsibility that does not necessarily entail a verdict of destruction or a condemnation of Jews more generally.[70]

After Paul's proclamation in Corinth, he turns to non-Jews (ἔθνη)
(18:6).[71] This turn does not imply a corresponding condemnation of "the
Jews" either;[72] rather, as Brawley also argues, Luke more likely employs
Paul's turn to non-Jews as a means of further legitimating Paul's mission in
Acts.[73] Moreover, the context of Acts 18:1–17 suggests that Paul's turn is primarily locative and not "religious" or "ethnic." When read in relation to
the Salutaris Foundation processions that began at the Roman-centric upper agora and then moved to the Hellenistic portion of the city, Paul's turn
from Jews to non-Jews establishes a connection between the Jewish association and those Jews and non-Jews to whom Luke's Paul turns. Both
groups are represented as Jewish, just as both the Roman and non-Roman
citizens of Ephesus were Ephesians, or at least they were from the perspective of the Salutaris Foundation. As in Thessalonica, Paul enters the *polis*
through the metaphorical "gate" of a Jewish association. In Corinth, however, Luke's Paul forms a new Jewish community.

THE ASSOCIATION IN TITIUS JUSTUS'S HOME

After facing conflict, Paul leaves the Jewish association hall, heads next
door, and forms his own Jewish association in Corinth:

(18:7) καὶ μεταβὰς ἐκεῖθεν εἰσῆλθεν εἰς οἰκίαν τινὸς
ὀνόματι Τιτίου Ἰούστου σεβομένου τὸν θεόν, οὗ ἡ οἰκία
ἦν συνομοροῦσα τῇ συναγωγῇ. (8) Κρίσπος δὲ ὁ

ἀρχισυνάγωγος ἐπίστευσεν τῷ κυρίῳ σὺν ὅλῳ τῷ οἴκῳ
αὐτοῦ, καὶ πολλοὶ τῶν Κορινθίων ἀκούοντες ἐπίστευον
καὶ ἐβαπτίζοντο.

(18:7) And after departing from there, he entered into the house
of a certain venerator of the [Jewish] God named Titius Justus,
whose house was next door to the [Jewish] association hall. (8)
And Crispus, a leader of the Jewish association, with his whole
household trusted in the Lord, and hearing, many of the Corinthians were trusting and being baptized.[74]

Like Jason from Thessalonica, Luke makes no mention of Titius Justus in
Acts beyond his brief statements here. Luke identifies him as a Godfearer
(σεβόμενος τὸν θεόν) without a qualification like "proselyte" (cf. 13:43).
If Luke is consistent in his designations, this suggests that Titius Justus is
a non-Jew.[75]

Paul's turning to non-Jews indicates a locative change that leads to
the formation of a new Jewish association in Corinth. Nevertheless, the
move from the Jewish association hall to the home of a Godfearer whose
residence bordered upon (συνομορέω) the meeting place of the previous
Jewish association reveals, at the very least, that Luke imagines a continued social proximity of the two groups. Now two Jewish associations exist
next door to each other in Corinth.[76]

Paul's move from the Jewish association to a neighboring house indicates that Paul is no longer responsible to the leaders of the Jewish association who opposed him. He founds a new Jewish association with its
own location in the civic hierarchy. Titius Justus serves as one of its benefactors by hosting the community in his home, and Crispus, a leader of the
Jewish association (ἀρχισυνάγωγος; *archisynagōgos*), legitimates the new
Jewish community both for Jews and for Corinthians by joining Paul.

As discussed in relation to the Salutaris Foundation, the specific
people included and excluded from the processions served to both legitimate the Ephesian identity of the participants and marginalize those who
were excluded. The explicit inclusion of an *archisynagōgos* in Paul's new

community in Corinth serves a similar function. Because of ambiguity in the identification of *archisynagōgoi*, Crispus can serve to legitimate both the Jewish identity of Paul's community and its place in the hierarchy of Corinth.

Archisynagōgos, a term that appears twice in Acts 18, occurs frequently in inscriptions from the Greco-Roman period.[77] Evidence from the inscriptions indicates that *archisynagōgoi* is a term denoting both a functionary in a Jewish community (cf. Acts 13:15) and a benefactor of the community. Tessa Rajak and David Noy have catalogued the relevant evidence and contend that *archisynagōgos* became associated specifically with Jewish communities in the Greco-Roman world and that the term describes a range of ways that Jews and (possibly) non-Jews could connect with Jewish associations in civic contexts.[78] Rajak and Noy observe that often *archisynagōgoi* "operate essentially like Greco-Roman benefactors within a 'euergetistic' framework."[79] *Archisynagōgoi* could serve liturgical roles and as benefactors of a Jewish association.

Interpreting *archisynagōgos* as both a functionary and honorific title helps explain Luke's connection between Crispus "trusting in the Lord" (ἐπίστευσεν τῷ κυρίῳ) and the subsequent "trusting" and baptism of many Corinthians.[80] On one hand, Crispus's initiation marks an ethnic association leader's shift from one Jewish association to another. On the other, it indicates the connections between a patron of a Jewish association and a broader civic context.

After Luke's Crispus affiliates with Paul, many "Corinthians" join Paul's group as well. Luke depicts a titled donor/benefactor of the Jewish association in Corinth moving to support Paul. This triggers a flow of Corinthians from one Jewish association to another.[81] Luke presents these Corinthians following a recognized civic benefactor in the formation of a new Jewish civic association.

The claim that "Corinthians" join Paul is also significant for the civic identity of Paul's association. Corinthian identity, Ephesian identity, and Jewish identity were malleable and contested, negotiated, disputed, and leveraged by elites and citizens, patrons and clients.[82] The claim of Corinthian identity therefore conveyed a connection to the Greek past with its associated civic status and honor embodied in this Greek *polis*. By affiliating Corinthians with Paul's group, Luke makes a claim for the place of Paul's group on the Corinthian civic hierarchy. Thus, Crispus, as a civic benefactor, serves as the bond connecting Corinthians with Paul's Jewish association. Many Corinthians join Paul's new Jewish association after hearing that a recognized civic patron and leader of another Jewish association, Crispus, joins Paul.

This sequence again situates Jewish identity as hybrid. As a leader of the Jewish community, Crispus is affirmed in his Jewishness, yet he demonstrates his role as a Corinthian by influencing other Corinthians to join Paul's Jewish association. Like Luke's Paul, the Jew who is also Roman, and Salutaris, the Roman who is also Ephesian, Crispus is Jewish while also Corinthian.[83]

Luke's inclusion of Crispus creates space to legitimate Paul's understanding of Jewish sacred traditions (e.g., the Messiah is Jesus, Christian non-Jews do not need circumcision according to Moses) while at the same time maintaining the Jewishness of Paul's gathering in Corinth. This dual negotiation highlights the way Acts leverages the gods-people-place connection in civic and ethnic space to situate Jesus followers as Jews. As the scene in Corinth unfolds, Luke presents Christians as a better Jewish association for the *polis*.

THE JEWS BEFORE GALLIO

Acts again highlights the Jewishness of Christians' civic and ethnic space in the affair with Gallio:

(18:12) Γαλλίωνος δὲ ἀνθυπάτου ὄντος τῆς Ἀχαΐας κατεπέστησαν ὁμοθυμαδὸν οἱ Ἰουδαῖοι τῷ Παύλῳ καὶ ἤγαγον αὐτὸν ἐπὶ τὸ βῆμα (13) λέγοντες ὅτι παρὰ τὸν νόμον ἀναπείθει οὗτος τοὺς ἀνθρώπους σέβεσθαι τὸν θεόν. (14) μέλλοντος δὲ τοῦ Παύλου ἀνοίγειν τὸ στόμα εἶπεν ὁ Γαλλίων πρὸς τοὺς Ἰουδαίους· εἰ μὲν ἦν ἀδίκημά τι ἢ ῥᾳδιούργημα πονηρόν, ὦ Ἰουδαῖοι, κατὰ λόγον ἂν

ἀνεσχόμην ὑμῶν, (15) εἰ δὲ ζητήματά ἐστιν περὶ λόγου καὶ
ὀνομάτων καὶ νόμου τοῦ καθ᾽ ὑμᾶς, ὄψεσθε αὐτοί· κριτὴς
ἐγὼ τούτων οὐ βούλομαι εἶναι. (16) καὶ ἀπήλασεν αὐτοὺς
ἀπὸ τοῦ βήματος. (17) ἐπιλαβόμενοι δὲ πάντες Σωσθένην
τὸν ἀρχισυνάγωγον ἔτυπτον ἔμπροσθεν τοῦ βήματος· καὶ
οὐδὲν τούτων τῷ Γαλλίωνι ἔμελεν.

(18:12) But when Gallio was proconsul of Achaia, the Jews rose
up against Paul in one accord and led him to the tribunal (13)
saying, "This guy is misleading people to venerate the [Jewish]
God contrary to law." (14) When Paul was about to open his
mouth, Gallio said to the Jews, "If there were some crime or se-
rious wrongdoing, Jews, I would be justified in accepting your
complaint; (15) but if you have questions about words and names
and your own law, see to it yourselves; I do not desire to be a
judge of these things." (16) And he dismissed them from the tribunal. (17) Then seizing Sosthenes, the *archisynagogos,* they
all beat him before the tribunal. And none of these things was
a concern for Gallio.

Luke here provides another insight into how Paul's community relates to
other Jewish associations.[84] In this narrative climax of Paul's time in
Corinth, Luke uses the highest-ranking Roman official depicted in Acts,
the proconsul Gallio, to silence Paul—which goes against the Lord's command to Paul (18:9)—and to proclaim that the problems some Jews had with
Paul were indeed a matter of intra-Jewish debate rather than of civic or public importance.[85] The Jewish community in Corinth, Paul and the association that met at Titius Justus's home included, needed to deal with these
issues themselves according to this Roman regional official.[86]

In his discussion of Gallio's ruling, Steve Walton points out that by
granting legal immunity to Paul, Gallio "*de facto* treats the group meeting
in Titius Justus' house as a subspecies of Judaism."[87] In the terms of ethnic rhetoric, Luke's Gallio identifies both the previously existing Jewish association and those now gathered in Titius Justus's home as part of the

Jewish community in Corinth.[88] C. Kavin Rowe also contends that Gallio's response marks the disagreement between Paul and the Jews who accuse him as an "intra-Jewish theological debate."[89] Since this was an intra-Jewish debate, Gallio did not need to rule on the matter. The charge against Paul is not that he introduced foreign customs (cf. 16:21) but that he persuaded people to venerate the God of Israel contrary to law. Luke thus uses Gallio to legitimate the Jewishness of Paul's community.

Luke's representation of the conflict in Corinth does not stop with Gallio's ruling, however. After Gallio drives Paul and his accusers from the tribunal, πάντες ("bystanders") grab Sosthenes, an until-now-unmentioned *archisynagōgos* in Corinth, and beat him before he can get away from the tribunal. Gallio is indifferent to these events (18:16–17).

The narrative referent of πάντες is ambiguous.[90] No matter who are included in the "all," Luke depicts the beating of a benefactor in the center of the city. This has the narrative effect of shaming Sosthenes and his Jewish association.[91] Some scholars understand πάντες as referring to only the Jews who have accused Paul and take the mobbing as frustration at the dismissal of the legal case.[92] Malina and Pilch, for example, see Sosthenes's beating as a public shaming by other Jews for his failure to obtain a favorable verdict.[93] Moyer Hubbard contends that πάντες makes the most narrative sense as referring to Paul's Jewish accusers *and* the Greeks who gathered in the Corinthian agora. He points to the fact that Luke has identified no group other than Jews in the scene. But, he contends that the verses depict a common Roman fear—the uprising of the urban masses. He concludes that it is a mistake "to reduce this incident to simply or even primarily racial enmity and ignore the wider socio-economic issues fueling such disturbances throughout the Greco-Roman world." The fear of urban unrest adequately explains how Luke depicts Sosthenes's beating.[94]

Given the nature of the accusations and Gallio's response, it is likely that Luke's πάντες included both Greeks and Jews, some of whom were also Christians.[95] Those individuals whose identity could be questioned, like Titius Justus, had the most to lose if Paul was found guilty of persuading people to venerate the God of Israel contrary to Jewish ancestral customs. Paul's neck is on the line, but the legitimacy of his community, especially Christian non-Jews, is also at stake.

Luke therefore uses the beating of an *archisynagōgos* to situate the Jewish associations in a civic context. The public beating of Sosthenes is significant for the status of his Jewish association. The beating of a bene-factor in the heart of the *polis* shames the entire association. Sosthenes's shame is heightened when contrasted with Crispus. Jews and Greeks alike publicly shame a benefactor of one Jewish association while the benefactor of Paul's Jewish association inspires "many Corinthians" to honor God. Through the mob violence of the indiscriminate πάντες, Luke establishes Paul's Jewish association both as a legitimate Jewish association and as at-tractive to the citizens of Corinth.

After Sosthenes is beaten, Paul remains, undisturbed, in Corinth (18:18). He eventually leaves for Syria, taking Priscilla and Aquila with him. He stops in Ephesus, Caesarea, and Jerusalem, spends time in An-tioch (18:19–22), and heads back to Galatia and Phrygia (18:23). Luke brings this journey of Paul, which began when Paul left Jerusalem (15:35), to a close. Paul and his companions have traveled the Mediterranean and expanded their reach from Antioch to Macedonia, Greece, and Asia while delivering the decision reached by the apostles and elders. They en-couraged the assemblies in the *poleis* (16:4–5), thus creating a unified, em-pirewide community of Christians populated by Jews—born Jews, like Paul, and proselytes, like the Christian non-Jews.

Conclusion: Gods-People-Places and Ethnic Rhetoric

In 104 CE, Salutaris proposed, and the Ephesian council approved, a foun-dation that enacted a change in the way that Ephesians interacted with Artemis and their *polis*. The great goddess could now travel with the em-perors as her companions, and she processed through their space and under the shadow of their temples, avoiding the route to the place of her mythic birth. Salutaris and the Ephesian council negotiated Ephesian identity for the Roman-era *polis* through their ancestral goddess, her people, and the urban landscape of her *polis* in ways that unified Ephesian identity in a changing present. Salutaris's Foundation legitimated this ethnic change by deploying the ancestral connections linking gods, their people, and their geographical place. Thus, ethnic reasoning provided a means of identifying wealthy Romans as Ephesians in relation to Artemis, Ephesians, and Ephesus.

At the outset of his journey depicted in Acts 15:30–18:23, Paul desires to see how the communities he had previously formed are doing (15:36). Throughout the rest of the journey, he repeatedly creates, strengthens, and encourages Christian associations in the *polis*. When taken together, Paul's movements through narrative space—Lystra, Philippi, Thessalonica, Athens, Corinth, and beyond—calls into existence a unified identity for his association within the Roman-era *polis*. Paul journeys with God, guided by the Holy Spirit and the spirit of Jesus. He travels with Timothy, the symbolic representation of the Jewishness of Christians, whom he leaves behind, thus extending his own unifying presence once he departs a given location. Paul and his entourage fuse the Christian community, not as a civic league, but as a cohesive Jewish association under the authority of God and God's Messiah. They do this in stark contrast to the local Jewish associations they encounter along the way. Reading Paul's movement from Jerusalem through the Roman world and back to Jerusalem in relation to the movement of the Salutaris Foundation processions provides a path for comparison of the ethnic rhetoric of Acts' depictions of Jews within the context of the Roman-era *polis*. Ethnic reasoning provides a means of identifying Christian non-Jews as the ideal Jews for the *polis* in relation to God, Jews, and their local associations.[96]

Christian Non-Jews and the Polis

AS WE HAVE SEEN, THE IMAGES OF Jewish and Christian identity in Acts of the Apostles exist within a much wider context of ethnic claims in the Roman-era *polis*. These claims, and the ethnic, civic, and religious identities they describe, did not specify or identify static or fixed categories but were enacted in specific rhetorical situations. Identity labels were negotiable and remarkably flexible, intersecting with one another in complex and meaningful ways. Within this meaningful intersection, ancient authors, civic benefactors, and other "cultural producers" found the space to inscribe social, cultural, religious, and political change. The writer of Acts, for his part, capitalized on this fluidity by depicting Jewish identity in such a way that the category included Christian non-Jews without circumcision. In his account, "the Jews" were not simply a theological foil for Christians; rather, Jewishness was an ethnic identity, but simultaneously and inseparably a religious and civic identity as well. From this point of view, "being Jewish" was an inherited characteristic that regulated one's place within a *polis* but also was an achievable identity that could be attained through proper worship and other mechanisms. Among first- and second-century Jews, the claim that honoring the God of the Jews in specific ways could make one "Jewish" was not innovative; rather, adherence to this God was an accepted way of assimilating non-Jews into a Jewish community from at least the Second Temple period on. Many Jews would have agreed with Luke that such non-Jewish adherents to the God of Israel could become Jewish proselytes. Not every Jew would have accepted the Jewishness of proselytes, but as Acts 2:5–13 suggests, the author of Acts agreed with those who did. From this perspective, proselytes are Jewish even as they remain distinct from those who are Jewish by lineage. One can be both Jewish and Carian, both Jewish and Cretan, both Jewish and Roman, or a non-Jewish *Jewish* proselyte, for example, and still qualify for the label "Jew" in ancient civic space.

Similar forms of multiple, hybrid, and fluid ethnic reasoning are found throughout Roman-era cities, and not only among Jews. Carved into walls, fashioned into images of the divine and the mundane, and enacted through civic processions, the hybrid character of ethnic categorization was both referenced and performed in a variety of media. Thus, the benefactors who commissioned the Sebasteion in Aphrodisias of Caria linked the mythical ethnic tie between Aphrodite, the city's patron goddess, and Aeneas, the legendary founder of Rome, legitimating Aphrodisian Romanness even as they preserved Carian difference. At the same time, they deployed a Roman model of ethnic rhetoric that depicted subjected populations as a collection of conquered *ethnē*, promoting a distinction between their own city and those other conquered populations. Aphrodisians portrayed themselves as "Roman," and others as less so.

In a similar way, Salutaris and his Foundation from Ephesus represented wealthy Roman immigrants as "true" Ephesians who honor both Artemis Ephesia and the Roman imperial family. Though they remained Roman, they were also integrated into the mythical, religious hierarchy of the city, incorporated into the tribe of the Sebaste, and therefore placed within the ancient civic tribal structure. Salutaris, native of the area surrounding Rome, appears to have viewed himself as being every bit as Ephesian as any other resident of the city. The involvement of Salutaris and those like him in the ancient hierarchies of Ephesus was thereby normalized, legitimating the changes occurring in the city at the beginning of the second century CE.

Acts also utilized religious, ethnic, and civic identity markers to navigate social change. In Acts 15, the narrative of the Jerusalem council emphasized the power of God to determine how non-Jews could be welcomed into Jewish communities that venerated Jesus as Messiah. God, Acts claimed, accepts non-Jews without circumcision, a symbol that, by the Roman period, had come to indicate how a non-Jew joined the Jewish people and became Jewish. To justify this acceptance of non-Jews without circumcision, Luke's James pointed to instructions regarding the προσήλυτοι drawn from Leviticus (LXX). By connecting the portion of the Jewish scriptures that used the term προσήλυτος to the debate surrounding the circumcision of Christian non-Jews, Luke used the archaic meaning of the term προσήλυτος, meaning "resident alien" in the LXX, to affect the concept of the Jewish proselyte. These ancient proselytes, Luke argued, did not need circumcision, but they had to follow a set of standard, "well-known" regulations. So too, his Christian non-Jews did not need circumcision but only a set of regulations to be identified as proselytes. Acts thus played on the flexible meaning of proselyte in ways that both undermined contemporaneous claims that equated proselyte identity with circumcision and bolstered James's own assertion that his regulations, which did not require circumcision of Christian non-Jews, were both ancient and ancestral. With this innovative move, Luke identified Christians, both born Jews and proselytes, as Jews, independent of circumcision. This move provided space for Luke to situate Christian communities as another Jewish community within the city.

As Paul moved throughout the Mediterranean world in Acts 15–18, he proclaimed the Jerusalem council's message about the acceptance of non-Jews. In a few places, Paul and his traveling companions faced opposition from the leaders of local Jewish communities, an opposition that Luke situated within both Jewish and civic discourses. By combining Paul's movements with his interactions with Jewish communities in various cities, Luke depicted Christian communities as a unified Jewish association that stretched beyond civic boundaries and across the Mediterranean. Moreover, by juxtaposing Christian leaders like Paul with the leaders of other local Jewish associations, he represented Christian communities as a better, more peaceful type of Jewish community for the *polis*, utilizing geography to naturalize a specific, Christianized form of Jewish identity. Luke thus positioned Christian communities in relation to Jewish associations and within broader civic structures in ways that legitimated the place of Christians within the Roman-era cities of the Mediterranean world.

Throughout this book I have pushed against the view that Christian identity is un-ethnic and, in turn, a dichotomized view of Jews and Christians in Acts, particularly one that views "Jew" as an ethnic category and "Christian" as its universalizing, nonethnic opposite. I argued instead that Acts' rhetoric of Jewish and Christian identity should be situated within the context of Roman-era cities, in which ethnic, civic, and religious identities were inseparable. Placing Acts within this broader ethnic discourse emphasizes the Jewishness of Christians, even in Acts. When one reads Acts with an eye to the writer's ethnic reasoning, it becomes clear that Luke did not represent Jews as a static group but instead presented Jewish identity in multiple, hybrid, and complex ways that allowed for the identification of Christian non-Jews as Jews. Debates and conflicts between Christians and other Jews in places like Jerusalem (5:17–42, 7:1–8:3, 22:1–21), Antioch (13:13–52), and Rome (28:17–31) are therefore presented as intra-Jewish debates about the implications of following the God of Israel. Luke also employs the ethnic, religious, and civic aspects of Jewish identity to privilege those Jews (and non-Jewish Jews) who follow Jesus. For example, near the end of Acts, Paul speaks to a Roman tribunal in Greek, identifying himself as a Jew and a Tarsian of Cilicia (21:39–40). Then when Paul addresses the crowd gathered in Jerusalem in the "Hebrew dialect" a few verses later, he identifies himself as a Jew who was born in Tarsus but educated in Jerusalem according to the ancestral laws (22:2–3). In a world of competitive identity claims, Paul's dual self-identifications—first as a Tarsian and second as someone who had been born in Tarsus—are not insignificant. They are a form of ethnic reasoning that enables Paul to embody multiple ethnic categories simultaneously. Luke is highly attuned to the importance of such ethnic claims.

Luke also situates Christians ethnically within the civic hierarchies of every city where they show up. For example, Paul claims to know the identity of the unknown god that the Athenians honor (Acts 17:23). This god, according to Paul, is the God who made all *ethnē* from a single ancestor (17:26). Moreover, Paul here argues that humans are the γένος of this God (17:28, 29), a rhetorical claim that is reminiscent of the Aphrodisian-Carian claim to be "Roman" by means of a shared divine ancestry. Luke situates the God of the Jews within the pantheon of Athenian deities as the Highest God while at the same time claiming that all humanity is linked ethnically both to one another and to this God. Luke thus uses ethnic and religious rhetoric to inform and guide Paul's speech in Athens and to establish a relation between Athenians and the God of Israel.

As attention to ethnic reasoning has further demonstrated, Acts' so-called Christian universalism—that is, salvation is now available to all through Christ, not just to Jews—should be abandoned in its current form. If Acts marks all Christians as Jews and Christian communities as Jewish communities, as I have argued, then the concept of "Christian universalism" should be understood as a particular form of "Jewish universalism." Non-Jews can join Jews if they become Jewish through Christ. On one hand, this interpretation shifts the discussion away from whether Acts is anti-Jewish or not toward how Luke imagines an intra-Jewish debate about the Jewishness of non-Jews who venerate Jesus. On the other hand, it does not alleviate an incipient supersessionist impulse of Acts—Christians have still used Luke's narrative to appropriate the God of Israel and Jewish scriptures as their own. It is within this double deployment of Jewishness that Luke is able to situate Christians as both Jewish and distinct from other Jews. It is also how later Christian interpreters are able to quickly reposition Christians as the "true Israel," even as they are becoming more and more distinct from their Jewish origins, and it is how early Christians quickly move from identifying as a Jewish sect to positing anti-Jewish interpretations of Acts and Christianity. These features of Acts' interpretive history haunt Luke's images of Jews and Jewishness in Acts and cannot and should not be separated from interpretations of the historical document.[1]

This reconsideration of the intersection between ethnic, religious, and civic identity in early Christian rhetoric reconnects life in the *polis,* ethnic identity, and religious practices, demonstrating that these connections were both inextricably bound up, one to another, and fundamental to the development of Christian identity in Acts and beyond. As we have seen, the civic, the ethnic, and the religious were intertwined throughout the *polis,* and Luke both understood and made the most of this phenomenon. Reading Acts in an urban context shows that Luke was engaged in close conversation with the visible, material, and practical signs of civic life. His decision to represent Christian communities as unified, peaceful Jewish civic associations, partly by identifying Christian non-Jews as Jewish proselytes, shows that his polemic was directed at particular Jews, not at Jewishness in general, which he sought to claim for his version of Christian ethnic identity. Through this form of ethnic reasoning, Acts situated Christians in the city's bustling topography as Jews.

Notes

1. I use the term "Christian" to identify those who honored the God of the Jews and Jesus as his messiah. The author of Acts did not use the term "Christian" in this way, but it remains heuristically useful for this book.

2. The terms "Christian," "Jew," and "pagan" are, of course, problematic. See discussion of "Christian" and "Jew" below and discussion of "pagan" and "paganism" in O'Donnell, "Demise of Paganism." See also Fredriksen, *Paul*, 34–35.

3. I use the terms "hybrid" and "hybridity," rather uncritically, according to their dictionary definitions meaning mixed or composed of two or more parts rather than according to the critical examinations of these terms in postcolonial studies. A full analysis of the rich and important lineage of these terms is beyond the scope of this book. In brief, see Homi Bhabha ("Signs Taken as Wonders"), who writes: "Hybridity is the revaluation of the assumption of colonial identity through the repetition of discriminatory identity effects. It displays the necessary deformation and displacement of all sites of discrimination and domination" (164).

4. The modern term "synagogue," which is a transliteration of the Greek term συναγωγή, can mean both the building where a Jewish community gathers and the Jewish community itself. I use "association," in part to distinguish Jewish communities from their places of meeting and in part to highlight the similarities between Jewish communities and other associations that gathered in the ancient *polis*. In antiquity other associations also used the Greek term συναγωγή. See discussion in Harland, *Dynamics of Identity*, 25–26, 40. However, on the use of συναγωγή in Acts and its distinction from ἐκκλησία, see Trebilco, "Why Did the Early Christians Call Themselves ἡ ἐκκλησία?," 440–60.

5. See discussion in Buell, "Challenges and Strategies," 39–44; Buell, "Early Christian Universalism"; and Buell, *Why This New Race?*, esp. 138–65.

6. In these ways, Luke's use of Jewishness pushes against conservative and liberal interpretations of Jews in Acts. Shelly Matthews has observed that by embracing Jewish scriptures, Acts also appropriates them, thus allowing Christians to supersede Jews as the "true" Israel (*Perfect Martyr*, 34–36).

7. Cadbury, *Making of Luke-Acts,* 245. See also Nasrallah, "Acts of the Apostles"; and more recently Billings, *Acts of the Apostles and the Rhetoric of Roman Imperialism.*

8. Throughout this book, I use the transliterated terms *polis/poleis* and English words "city"/"cities" interchangeably.

9. See Concannon, *When You Were Gentiles,* xi–xii.

10. For ancient Christian literature see, for example, Buell, "Producing Descent/ Dissent"; Buell, "Rethinking the Relevance of Race"; Buell, *Why This New Race?;* Buell, "Early Christian Universalism"; Buell and Johnson Hodge, "Politics"; Knust, *Abandoned to Lust;* Johnson Hodge, *If Sons, Then Heirs;* Johnson, *Ethnicity and Argument;* Nasrallah and Schüssler Fiorenza, eds., *Prejudice and Christian Beginnings;* Barreto, *Ethnic Negotiations;* Kuecker, *Spirit and the "Other";* Baker, "Early Christian Identity Formation"; Kok, "True Covenant People"; Concannon, *When You Were Gentiles.*

11. See discussion of the term "proselyte" in chapter 2.

12. See, for example, Knust, *Abandoned to Lust,* esp. 143–63.

13. Brubaker, *Ethnicity Without Groups,* 11. The so-called instrumentalist view was advocated by Fredrik Barth (*Ethnic Groups and Boundaries*). This differs from the "primordial" view of ethnicity commonly associated with Clifford Geertz (*Interpretation of Cultures*). However, see Richard Jenkins (*Rethinking Ethnicity,* 44–45), who notes the problems with associating these views with Barth and Geertz.

14. Jenkins, *Rethinking Ethnicity,* 9–15, 41–51, quotation from 50.

15. Hall, *Ethnic Identity,* 182.

16. Cohen, *Beginnings,* 5. Cohen uses the language of "imagined communities" developed in Anderson, *Imagined Communities.*

17. Buell, *Why This New Race?,* 6.

18. Of Smith's numerous publications on nationalism, see Smith, *Ethnic Origins of Nations;* Smith, *National Identity;* and Hutchinson and Smith, "Introduction," esp. 6–7. See also the discussion of Christians, Jews, and the problems of nationalism in Acts in Jennings, *Acts,* 20–24.

19. Barth, *Ethnic Groups and Boundaries.*

20. Buell, *Why This New Race?,* 7. See also Stoler, "Racial Histories"; and Malkin, "Introduction."

21. See discussion in Jenkins, *Rethinking Ethnicity,* 40–51.

22. On the ways that the core and boundaries of ethnic identifications can change, see Ann Laura Stoler's work on Dutch identity in colonial Indonesia (*Carnal Knowledge and Imperial Power*).

23. Stanley Stowers has critiqued Buell's constructivist view of ethnic identity and argued that ancient Christians' "claim that [their] recently formed group is

an ancient ethnicity is not the same as a population that has lived for hundreds of years on land passed down with practices that form the belief that these people inherently belong to this land" ("Review of Why This New Race?, 730). However, generations of work on ethnicity and national identity demonstrate that the claim to be "a population that has lived for hundreds of years" is rhetorical and "imagined" in ways similar to the claims of a more recent group. On "imagined" ethnicities, see Anderson, *Imagined Communities*.

24. Craig Keener, for example, writes about the "Gentile mission" in Acts: "While maintaining Judaism's theological exclusivism, the Christians rejected ethnic exclusivism and hence could combat negative perceptions attached to many other Jews" (*Acts*, 1:509). See also Ernst Haenchen, who, commenting on Acts 15:35 ("Whoever fears God and does what is right is acceptable to him") writes "there is no racial barrier to Christian salvation" (*Acts of the Apostles*, 351).

25. Buell, *Why This New Race?*, 1–5. On my reading, "rhetorical situation" not only includes the rhetorical or literary context of a specific use of language of peoplehood but the larger discourses from which such uses arise. That is to say, the rhetorical situations extend beyond texts and into larger cultural and material contexts.

26. On ethnicity and Roman identity, see Woolf, *Becoming Roman;* and Wallace-Hadrill, *Rome's Cultural Revolution*, 3–37; on Corinthian identity, see Concannon, *When You Were Gentiles*.

27. See the important works of Hall, *Inventing the Barbarian,* and Woolf, *Becoming Roman*.

28. See, for example, Whitmarsh, "Reading Power in Roman Greece"; Preston, "Roman Questions"; and Peirano, "Hellenized Romans."

29. Throughout this book, I use "Jewish God," "God of Israel," "God of the Jews," and "God" interchangeably to identify the deity that the author of Acts calls θεός in order to highlight the ethnic connection between gods and their peoples in antiquity. When the author of Acts speaks of θεός, he refers to the deity of the Jewish scriptures and venerated by Jews (and those others who wished to worship the God of Israel).

30. On the issues surrounding claims about the identity of Jews in Alexandria, see Barclay, *Jews*, 48–81, esp. 60–71.

31. Quotations from Nock, *Conversion*, 19, 17, respectively. Nock refers to religions in the fifth and fourth centuries BCE. However, the same can be said of the connection between religion, ethnicity, and civic identity in the Roman era. See also the discussion of the importance of civic religion in Sourvinou-Inwood, "What Is Polis Religion?"; Paula Fredriksen has pointed out on numerous occasions that in the ancient world, "gods run in the blood" ("'Mandatory Retirement,'" 232). Cf. Fredriksen, "Judaizing the Nations,"

235. See also Steve Mason ("Jews"), who writes, "An ancient *ethnos* normally had a national cult . . . , involving priests, temples, and animal sacrifice. This cannot be isolated from the *ethnos* itself, since temples, priesthood, and cultic practices were part and parcel of a people's founding stories, traditions, and civic structures" (484). Buell writes, "the boundaries between religion, ethnicity, civic identity and philosophy were often blurred in antiquity" (*Why This New Race?*, 37).

32. Buell, *Why This New Race?*, 2, 41–49. By fluidity, Buell and other ethnic theorists do not suggest that ethnic and racial identities are all fluid in the same way or to the same extent. For example, an identity may be deployed in fluid ways (emphasizing one of multiple ethnic identities in a given situation), or it may be changed through adaption and appropriation of ethnic identifiers. The "fluidity" in each case is determined in negotiation with the "borders" of the ethnic identity and the "core" identifiers of a relevant ethnic classification.

33. On the implications of this move, see Matthews, *Perfect Martyr*. Matthews argues that the narrative of Stephen's stoning (Acts 7:1–8:3) is important for Acts' construction of early Christians as legitimate and distinct from Jews.

34. Jacob Jervell famously argued that the varying responses to the (Christian) gospel divided people of the God of Israel (*Luke and the People of God,* 41–74). See also Matthews, *Perfect Martyr,* 71–72. Matthews argues that Stephen's speech and subsequent stoning mark a significant shift in the separation of Christianity from Judaism. "The Jews" are guilty for Jesus's and Stephen's deaths and are no longer the people of God. See my discussion of Matthews in chapter 1.

35. Chapters 2 and 3 provide several examples of this phenomenon.

36. As Buell notes, scholars also must acknowledge how racist readings of these texts "haunt" their interpretation in ways that do not allow for their separation. See Buell, "Challenges and Strategies"; and Buell, "Christian Universalism."

37. On the date, audience, and location of composition of Acts, see chapter 1.

38. Scholars have long noted the importance of cities and civic life for the narrative of Acts. See Nasrallah, "Acts."

39. "Religious worlds" is a concept developed by scholar of religion William Paden, who contends that religions create worlds and that the concept of religious worlds facilitates comparison of religious beliefs and practices (*Religious Worlds,* esp., 51–65).

40. For a similar "reading" of ancient Christian literature and material remains, see Nasrallah, *Christian Responses;* and Concannon, *When You Were Gentiles.*

41. Mattill and Mattill's 1966 bibliography of Acts lists 210 entries stretching fifteen pages on "Archeology and Geography" (*Classified Bibliography,* 193–208).
42. C. Kavin Rowe understands this claim to be ironic: the author of Acts knew that the glory of Artemis was surpassed by Christ (*World Upside Down,* 41–49).
43. See, for example, Bruce, *Book of the Acts,* 399.
44. Trebilco, "Province of Asia," 348–49.
45. Wood, *Discoveries at Ephesus,* 68–96; Heberdey, Wilberg, and Niemann, *Das Theater in Ephesos.*
46. Pervo, *Acts,* 5–6.
47. Some scholars use the existence of archeological remains described in Acts as a means of proving the historical accuracy of a given scene. A paradigmatic example of the use of archeology as a "proof text" of Acts is found in McRay, "Archaeology."
48. Nasrallah, *Christian Responses,* 12.
49. See discussion above and Buell, *Why This New Race?,* 41.
50. The original construction of the Sebasteion in Aphrodisias is dated to the reign of Tiberius (14–37 CE); however, there was a significant renovation under Claudius (41–54 CE). The Salutaris Foundation inscription is dated to 104 CE. On the dating of Acts, see chapter 1.
51. See Pervo, *Acts,* 5–6; however, see the caution in Fitzmyer, *Acts of the Apostles,* 54–55.
52. See, for example, Malina and Pilch, *Social-Science Commentary;* and Baker, *Identity, Memory, and Narrative.*
53. For a thorough discussion of the translation of Ἰουδαῖος in scholarship, see David Miller's three essays "Meaning of Ioudaios," "Ethnicity Comes of Age," and "Ethnicity, Religion and the Meaning of Ioudaios." Early discussions surrounding the translation of Ἰουδαῖος developed in the study of the fourth Gospel. See, for example, Schram, "Use of ΙΟΥΔΑΙΟΣ," 101–30; and Ashton, "Identity and Function." More recent discussion has surrounded the translation of Ἰουδαῖος in Josephus. On one hand, Steve Mason ("Series Preface" and "Jews") argues that "Judaean" is a better translation; on the other, Daniel Schwartz ("'Judaean' or 'Jew'?") contends that "Jew" is a better translation (see also S. Schwartz, "How Many?").
54. So Mason, "Jews."
55. Levine, *Misunderstood Jew;* Schwartz, "'Judaean' or 'Jew'?"; Runesson, "Inventing Christian Identity"; Schwartz, "How Many?"
56. Johnson Hodge, *If Sons, Then Heirs,* 12. Johnson Hodge opts to transliterate rather than to translate Ἰουδαῖος. She explains that she revised her previous

translation of Ἰουδαῖος with "Judean" and used the transliterated term *Ioudaios* because of the modern implications of removing "Jews" from ancient texts (*If Sons, Then Heirs,* 11–15). For Johnson Hodge's previous position, see Buell and Johnson Hodge, "Politics"; and Johnson Hodge, "Apostle to the Gentiles."

57. See Schwartz, "How Many?," esp. 221–30.

58. "Gentile" is from the Latin *gentilis,* a term used in the Latin Vulgate to translate ἔθνη. See "Gentile, Adj. and N.," OED Online (Oxford: Oxford University Press, 2015), http://www.oed.com/view/Entry/77647.

59. The distinction between Jews and gentiles is comparable to the distinction between ancient Greeks and barbarians. However, the Greek word βάρβαρος is transliterated as barbarian in both the singular and plural forms while ἔθνος is not. On the creation of barbarians in Greek tragedy, see Hall, *Inventing the Barbarian;* in Jewish literature, see Rajak, "Greeks and Barbarians in Josephus."

60. Paul is ambiguous in his use of ἔθνη to identify non-Jews who are "in Christ." In some cases he identifies them as ἔθνη, and in others he distinguishes them from ἔθνη. See, for example, Gal 2:14–15; 1 Thess 4:3–5; 1 Cor 5:1, 12:3; Rom 1:5–6, 13; 11:13. See discussion in Johnson Hodge, *If Sons, Then Heirs,* 55–56; Garroway, *Paul's Gentile-Jews;* and Concannon, *When You Were Gentiles.*

61. See Acts 4:27; 9:15; 10:45; 11:1, 18; 13:46–48; 14:2, 5, 27; 15:3, 7, 12, 14, 17, 19, 23; 18:6; 21:11, 25; 22:21; 26:17, 20, 23; 28:28.

62. Concannon, *When You Were Gentiles,* xi.

63. Some, like Valentinus (fl. 130 CE) and in a different way Marcion (fl. 140 CE), contended that *Ioudaioi* worshipped an inferior deity while Christians worshipped the one high God. Others, like Justin Martyr and Irenaeus, asserted that Jews misunderstand their own scriptures: Christians interpret Jewish scriptures more accurately than *Ioudaioi* through allegory. See Fredriksen and Irshai, "Christian Anti-Judaism," 979–83.

64. Justin, *Dial* 11.5. Cf. also *Dial.* 26.1: τὰ δὲ ἔθνη τὰ πιστεύσαντα εἰς αὐτὸν καὶ μετανοήσαντα ἐφ' οἷς ἥμαρτον, αὐτοὶ κληρονομήσουσι μετὰ τῶν πατριαρχῶν καὶ τῶν προφητῶν καὶ τῶν δικαίων ὅσοι ἀπὸ Ἰακὼβ γεγέννηνται· εἰ καὶ μὴ σαββατίζουσι μηδὲ περιτέμνονται μηδὲ τὰς ἑορτὰς φυλάσσουσι, πάντως κληρονομήσουσι τὴν ἁγίαν τοῦ θεοῦ κληρονομίαν ("But the ἔθνη, who have trusted in him [Christ], and have repented of the sins which they committed, they will receive the inheritance along with the patriarchs and the prophets and the just ones who have descended from Jacob, even though they neither keep the Sabbath, nor are circumcised, nor observe the feasts, they will in every way receive the holy inheritance of God").

Denise Buell argues that for Justin, Christianness and Jewishness are both flexible and fixed categories (*Why This New Race?*, 94–115). Similarly, Knust, *Abandoned to Lust*, 143–63.

65. See, for example, Justin, *Dial.* 26, 28–29. Fredriksen and Irshai, "Christian Anti-Judaism," 981–82. In the next chapter, I suggest that though Luke does present nonbelieving Jews in a negative light, his rhetoric is not one that presents Christians as "true Israel." Rather, he seeks to identify non-Jewish Christians as Jewish.

66. On Christian anti-Judaism, see Efroymson, "Patristic Connection"; Fredriksen and Irshai, "Christian Anti-Judaism."

67. See discussion in Buell, "Christian Universalism"; Buell, *Why This New Race?*, 1; and Concannon, *When You Were Gentiles*, xi.

68. A host of scholars have opposed such dichotomous readings in the study of Jesus and Paul. Krister Stendahl famously proposed that Paul did not "convert" to Christianity but was "called" by God ("Apostle Paul," 199–215). E. P. Sanders (*Jesus and Judaism*) (and others) shifted the discussion about the historical Jesus toward a Jewish context. Cf. also the work of Paula Fredriksen on both fronts ("Judaism" and *Jesus of Nazareth*).

69. See, for example, Craig Keener, who makes the connection between a gentile mission and universalism explicit. Keener writes, "Most scholars recognize that the Gentile mission (i.e., more accurately, a 'universal' mission) is one of the central themes (if not *the* central theme) in the book of Acts" (*Acts*, 1:505, emphasis original). See also Cadbury, *Making of Luke-Acts*, 316; and Wilson, *Gentiles and the Gentile Mission*.

70. See, for example, Thomas Phillips ("Prophets, Priests"), who writes: "In Luke-Acts, [Godfearers, i.e., gentiles attracted to Judaism] could find all the themes that drew them to Judaism—monotheism, a rejection of idolatry, a just ethic, and an alternative to the Roman Empire—without any of the practices that repelled them from Judaism—circumcision, dietary and ritual laws, and *Jewish exclusivism*. Luke-Acts offered reflective Godfearers an opportunity to locate everything they admired about Judaism within the prophetic (and Christian) tradition and to locate everything they disdained about Judaism within the priestly (and Jewish) tradition" (238, emphasis mine). On the implication of such readings, see Buell, "Christian Universalism." See also Gary Gilbert ("Disappearance"), who understands the Godfearers as literary characters in Acts that are contrasted with Jews.

71. As is already clear, I have chosen to use the term "Christian" to describe the members of the Jesus communities that the author of Acts most frequently identifies with the phrase ἡ ὁδός ("the Way"; 9:2; 19:9, 23; 22:4; 24:14, 22).

The term Χριστιανός does appear two times in Acts (11:26, 26:28), but the author uses it only in the mouth of outsiders, indicating that he knows of the term but may not be entirely comfortable with its use. I recognize the limitations of the term "Christian" but have decided to use it in this book because it remains a heuristically useful shorthand for those individuals who honored Jesus as Christ.

Chapter 1. Recontextualizing Acts

1. On the title of Acts, see Fitzmyer, *Acts*, 47–49; and Jervell, *Apostelgeschichte*, 56–58. The transmission history of Acts is complicated. Luke Timothy Johnson notes that "Acts presents a particularly acute form of a problem found everywhere in the New Testament, namely establishing the Greek text that is the basis for any interpretation" (*Acts of the Apostles*, 2). For a list of papyri and manuscript of Acts, see Fitzmyer, *Acts*, 65. To Fitzmyer's list of papyri add the small fragment p[112] (P.Oxy. 4496) and the fifth-century p[127] (P.Oxy. 4968), which contains portions of Acts 10–17. See Head, "P127 = POxy 4968."

2. The Gospel of Luke is also anonymous. See also the thorough discussion of the literature on the authorship of Acts in Keener, *Acts*, 1:402–16. Keener contends that Luke "may have been a Gentile God-fearer who spent time with Paul especially during part of all of his Roman custody" (1:403). See also Pervo, who argues that the author was not a companion of Paul and wrote after the end of the first century CE (*Acts*, 5–7).

3. On the identity of Theophilus, see Barrett, *Critical and Exegetical Commentary*, 1:65–66. On the literary character of the preface, see Alexander, *Preface to Luke's Gospel*, who argues that Luke's prefaces were similar to Hellenistic scientific and technical manuals.

4. A majority of scholars take this connection as proof of shared authorship. See Keener (*Acts*), who claims that "almost all scholars acknowledge that Luke and Acts share the same author" (1:402).

5. Irenaeus (130–202 CE) is the first known author to identify Luke as the author of Acts. He based his assessment largely on the "we" passages in the latter half of Acts. See *Haer.* 3.14.1.

6. For views emphasizing the difference between the two works, see Parsons and Pervo, eds., *Rethinking;* and Walters, *Assumed Authorial Unity.* See also the discussion of scholarship in Bird, "Unity of Luke-Acts."

7. There is, however, value in reading these texts together for other themes. As Ward Gasque points out, one of the primary contributions of scholarship on

Acts during the first half of the last century was the continuity of themes (*History*, 308). See also Tannehill, *Narrative Unity;* and Holladay, *Acts,* 50–52.

8. See Luke 7:3; 23:3 (// Mark 15:2), 37–38 (// Mark 15:26), 51. See discussion of the uses of Ἰουδαῖος below.

9. See discussion in Barreto, *Ethnic Negotiations,* 80–93.

10. Harnack, *Acts of the Apostles,* 290–97; Haenchen, *Acts,* 86; Dunn, *Acts of the Apostles,* xi; Fitzmyer, *Acts,* 54–55; Holladay, *Acts,* 4–7; Jervell, *Apostelgeschichte,* 86.

11. One reason for the shift in date of Acts is a claim that Luke knew of a Pauline corpus and/or had knowledge of Josephus. For knowledge of a Pauline corpus, see Pervo, *Acts,* 12. For knowledge of Josephus, scholars point to Acts 5:36–37 (Theudas and Judas); 11:28–29 (famine during Claudius's reign); 12:21–23 (death of Agrippa I); 25:13, 23; 26:30 (marriage of Agrippa II and Bernice); and 24:24–26 (Drusilla). See Mason, *Josephus and the New Testament,* 251–296; Pervo, *Dating Acts,* 149–200, 347–358. See Townsend, who dates Acts to the 140s ("The Date of Luke-Acts," 47–62). Nasrallah ("Acts") reads Acts in light of Hadrian's early-second-century Panhellenion. Also supporting a late date are Matthews, *Perfect Martyr;* and Wills, "Depiction of the Jews."

12. So Pervo, "Acts in the Suburbs"; and Pervo, *Acts,* 7. Cf. Pervo, *Dating Acts.*

13. Tyson, *Marcion and Luke-Acts,* xi, 76–77; Knox, *Marcion and the New Testament.* This view is also followed by Matthews, *Perfect Martyr.*

14. Gasque, *History,* 308. In his introduction to scholarship on Acts, Mark Allan Powell groups previous scholarship on the purpose of Acts under six general headings: irenic, polemical, apologetic, evangelistic, pastoral, and theological (*What Are They Saying?,* 13–14). For a bibliography of previous studies on the purpose of Acts, see Mattill and Mattill, *Classified Bibliography,* 152–57.

15. The view that Acts creates a synthesis is most famously associated with the Hegelian views of F. C. Baur and the so-called Tübingen school. Some scholars thought that Acts was a defense against "Gnosticism" (Talbert, *Luke and the Gnostics*). More recently scholars have understood Acts to be a defense against outsiders, including Jewish Christians (Sanders, *Jews in Luke-Acts*) and Marcion (Knox, *Marcion and the New Testament;* Tyson, *Marcion and Luke-Acts*). See discussion below. Ernst Haenchen (*Acts*) thought that Acts offered a legal defense before Rome. See also Tajra, *Trial;* and Walaskay, *And So We Came to Rome.* Marianne Palmer Bonz (*Past as Legacy*) argues that Acts mimics Virgil's *Aeneid* in order to give Christianity social legitimacy with Romans.

16. Esler, *Community and Gospel;* cf. Brawley, *Luke-Acts.* See also Malina and Pilch (*Social-Science Commentary*), who write Luke and Acts "are not

documents for outsiders. They were not composed to be shared with non-Jesus group members to read. . . . On the contrary, they are documents to be read within specific groups to maintain those groups in their loyalty to the God of Israel as revealed in the experience of Jesus and those change agents commissioned by him" (10).

17. Given the length and complexity of the narrative, Acts was likely written and edited from multiple locations over a period of time. On writing and publication in the Roman era, see Johnson, *Readers and Reading,* who argues that writing and publication were activities of (elite) communities and involved multiple drafts and presentations of works in preparation. See also Mason, "Of Audience and Meaning," who argues that Josephus's elite Roman audience influenced the way that he retold the story of the war in Judea.

18. Pervo (*Acts,* 6) observes that Acts discusses a significant amount of Ephesian local flavor, and he points out that seventy verses (approximately 7 percent of the narrative of Acts) take place in Ephesus; the city that receives the next most discussion, Pisidian Antioch, receives only a third as much as attention Ephesus. A similar assumption guides those who assume that the Greek novelist Longus was from Lesbos because his tale Daphnis and Chloe was set on the island. See as a counterexample Chariton's *Callirhoe.* Chariton was from Aphrodisias, yet a majority of his novel is set in Syracuse. But see also *An Ephesian Tale* by Xenophon of Ephesus, which is set in Ephesus.

19. See, for example, Acts 9:2 (Damascus), 13:1 (Antioch), 13:5 (Paphos), 14:6 (Derbe), 16:1 (Lystra), 16:12 (Philippi), 17:1 (Thessalonica), 17:10 (Berea), 17:16 (Athens), 18:1 (Corinth), 19:1 (Ephesus), 20:15 (Miletus), and 28:16 (Rome). Jerusalem, of course, plays a central role in Acts. Though not a traditional "Greek" city, Jerusalem was a Hellenizing city. See also discussion in Nasrallah, "Acts," of the how the cities depicted in Acts contribute to the construction of a unified Christian identity.

20. The juxtaposition of Rome's narrative absence and rhetorical presence is a significant feature of the Greek novels. See Whitmarsh, *Greek Literature.*

21. See, for example, the frequency that Paul and other Christians interact with Greco-Roman civic authorities (including those in Jerusalem): Acts 4:1 (Sadducees and temple guards in Jerusalem; cf. 5:17, 6:12, 7:1, 12:2–3), 13:7 (Roman proconsul on Cyprus), 13:50 (devout women and leading men in Antioch), 14:13 (priest of Zeus in Lystra), 16:22 (chief magistrates in Philippi), 17:22 (philosophers in Athens), 18:12 (Roman proconsul in Corinth), and 19:35 (town clerk in Ephesus).

22. The connection between Christians and Jewish civic associations from Greek cities spills into Jerusalem as well. See Acts 2:5–13, 6:9, and 21:27, where some Jews are explicitly identified as from diaspora locations.

23. Nasrallah, "Acts," 534; see also Alexander, "Mapping Early Christianity"; and Scott, "Luke's Geographical Horizon."

24. See, for example, the essays collected in Balch, *Contested Ethnicities and Images,* esp. "Part One: Luke-Acts."

25. On this phenomenon more generally, see the essays collected in Goldhill, ed., *Being Greek Under Rome.*

26. Greekness was viewed as a quality of proper, elite education or *paideia.* Some Romans, however, viewed Greek *paideia* as effeminate; it made Romans soft. See this and other claims in Benjamin Isaac's illuminating discussion in *The Invention of Racism in Classical Antiquity,* 381–405.

27. For this and the following discussion, see Fredriksen, "Judaizing the Nations," 235. See also Fox, *Pagans and Christians,* esp. ch. 2, "Pagans and Their Cities."

28. Richard Lim writes, "The Romans were not always victorious on the battlefield and, given their belief that each community had its own protective gods, they saw defeat as a sign that the enemy's patron deities were simply too powerful" ("Gods of the Empire," 262–63).

29. Jews, including those who were citizens of various cities, were famously exempt from venerating non-Jewish gods, but as long as they lived in the Greek πόλις, they still interacted with gods on a regular basis. See discussion below and S. Schwartz, "Rabbi in Aphrodite's Bath." Exemptions for Jews from participation in civic cults continued into the fifth century. See, for example, *Code of Theodosius* 16.8.3–4 in Linder, *Jews in Roman Imperial Legislation,* 120–24.

30. On civic aspects of "religion," see Rives, *Religion in the Roman Empire,* 105–131; and Rogers, *Mysteries,* 18–32. See also Rives, "Graeco-Roman Religion"; Woolf, "Polis-Religion and Its Alternatives"; and Elsner, "Origins of the Icon."

31. Bowie, "Greeks and Their Past." See also Whitmarsh, "Reading Power"; and Swain, *Hellenism and Empire,* esp., 65–100. On the use of the past in Acts, see Bonz, *Past as Legacy,* who contends that Acts used Virgil's *Aeneid* as a model for crafting his narrative.

32. Nasrallah, *Christian Responses,* 89. For the concept of "memory theater," see Alcock, *Archaeologies of the Greek Past,* 54 n. 29, cited in Nasrallah, *Christian Responses,* 89. Alcock proposes that the Roman-era Greeks used the buildings and images of the reconstructed Athenian agora to "conjure up specific and controlled memories of the past." The agora thus served as a type of civic museum or "memory theater."

33. See Goldhill, ed., *Being Greek Under Rome.*

34. For a review of scholarship on Jews and Judaism in Acts, see Tyson, *Luke, Judaism, and the Scholars.* See also Weatherly, *Jewish Responsibility,* 13–49; and Bovon, *Luke the Theologian,* 364–86.

35. These two general interpretations developed during a flurry of scholarship on "the Jews" in Acts that appeared from the mid-eighties to the early nineties. Important for this discussion are the essays collected in Tyson, ed., *Luke-Acts and the Jewish People;* Sanders, *Jews in Luke-Acts;* Brawley, *Luke-Acts;* Wills, "Depiction of the Jews"; and Tyson, "Jews and Judaism in Luke-Acts." On this resurgence of interest in Jews in Luke-Acts, see Tyson, *Luke, Judaism, and the Scholars,* 110–33. See also the discussion in Bovon, "Studies in Luke-Acts," 186–90.

36. This is not to minimize the anti-Jewish interpretations of Acts perpetuated by Christians and others. See discussion in Tyson, *Luke, Judaism, and the Scholars,* 1–12.

37. That Acts is anti-Jewish is early and pervasive in scholarship. See Adolf von Harnack (*Acts*), who views the rejection of the gospel by Jews as indicative of the divine rejection of Jews: "The Jew is in a sense the villain in this dramatic history, yet not—as in the Gospel of St. John and the Apocalypse—the Jew in the abstract who has almost become an incarnation of the evil principle. But the real Jew without generalisation and exaggeration in his manifold gradations of Pharisee, Sadducee, aristocrat, Jew of Palestine or of the Dispersion. Where St. Luke knows anything more favourable concerning particular sections or persons among the Jews he does not keep silence, and so sacrifice the truth to his theology of history" (xxiv; cf. Tyson, *Luke, Judaism, and the Scholars,* 41–42).

38. Conzelmann, *Theology of St. Luke.* The original German title, *Die Mitte der Zeit* (The Middle of Time), highlights Conzelmann's emphasis on redemptive history.

39. See Conzelmann, *Theology of St. Luke,* 16–17. On the problems with this model, see Minear, "Luke's Use of the Birth Stories." Minear points out that Conzelmann does not address the image of Judaism presented in Luke 1–2. If he had, Minear argues, Conzelmann would have needed significant changes to his model of redemptive history.

40. Conzelmann, *Theology of St. Luke,* 146. Conzelmann writes, "Both the outline of the attitude of the Jews to the Christian mission and also the thesis of Luke xxi, that the judgement of history has fallen upon the Jews, are based on an understanding of the principles involved in the problem of the Jews" (145 n. 1).

41. Conzelmann, *Theology of St. Luke,* 145. See also Gutbrod, "Ἰουδαῖος," 3:379–80.

42. Conzelmann acknowledges that Luke does not use the term "true Israel" but implies that Luke does have this concept (*Theology of St. Luke,* 146 n. 6).

43. See the early critiques of Conzelmann's model of redemptive history in Oliver, "Lucan Birth Stories"; and Minear, "Luke's Use of the Birth Stories." More recently, see Tyson, *Luke, Judaism, and the Scholars,* 84–85.

44. Quotations from Haenchen, *Acts,* 100 (emphasis original), 100, 116, and 100–101, respectively.

45. Martin Dibelius (*Studies,* 149–50) sees the threefold renunciation of "the Jews" by Luke in Acts as a conscious redaction of the author. David Tiede ("'Glory to Thy People Israel'") and David Moessner ("Ironic Fulfillment") understand them as a (temporary) rejection of "Israel" in order to offer salvation to non-Jews.

46. Haenchen, *Acts,* 101.

47. Haenchen, "Book of Acts as Source Material," 278.

48. Haenchen, *Acts,* 100.

49. Haenchen does not use *religio licita* in the later editions of his commentary; however, he does support, without critique, those who do. See Haenchen, *Acts,* 100 n. 12.

50. Haenchen, *Acts,* 692–93.

51. Haenchen writes that by solving the theological problem Luke "had also at the same time done most of the work necessary for the solution of the political problem" (*Acts,* 102).

52. The concept of *religio licita* likely derives from the third-century CE author Tertullian. See *Apol.* 4.4, 21.1. This observation was made in Cadbury, "Some Foibles," 215–16; see further discussion in Esler, *Community and Gospel,* 205–214 (esp. 211–14). Esler writes: "We may begin by scotching the idea that Rome had some process for licensing foreign religions. There is no historical support for this whatsoever; it was always the Roman way to treat foreign religions on an *ad hoc* basis, and there never was a juridical category of *religio licita*" (211). Cf. Rajak, "Was There a Roman Charter?"

53. Esler, *Community and Gospel,* 212–15. Ancestral practices commonly shaped veneration of deities. Summing up the situation nicely, the second-century Christian apologist Athenagoras writes, οἰκουμένη ἄλλος ἄλλοις ἔθεσι χρῶνται καὶ νόμοις, καὶ οὐδεὶς αὐτῶν νόμῳ καὶ φόβῳ δίκης, κἂν γελοῖα ᾖ, μὴ στέργειν τὰ πάτρια εἴργεται ("different inhabitants have different customs and laws; and no one is hindered by law or fear of punishment from following his ancestral usages, however amusing these may be") (*Legato,* 1). Greek text from *TLG;* quoted in Fredriksen, "Judaizing the Nations," 235.

54. Paula Fredriksen writes: "Mediterranean empires, whether Hellenistic or Roman, were in consequence extremely commodious in terms of what we think of as 'religion.' To label all of this religious breathing space as 'religious

tolerance' is to misdescribe it with a word drawn from our own later civil societies. *Ancient empire embodied pragmatic pluralism*" ("Paul, Practical Pluralism," 90, emphasis original).

55. Fredriksen, "Paul, Practical Pluralism," quotation from 90 (emphasis original). Roman practical pluralism did have its limits. Tiberius is said to have expelled the Druids from Rome (Pliny, *Nat.* 30.13). See also Suetonius, *Claud.* 25.5. Jews were expelled from Rome multiple times. Evidence for the earliest expulsion of Jews from Rome in 139 BCE is late. See Valerius Maximus, *Facta et Dicta Memorabilia* 1.3.3 epitome of Nepotianus (Stern, *Greek and Latin Authors,* no. 147a). See also epitome of Iulius Paris (*Greek and Latin Authors,* no. 147b). More secure is an expulsion in 19 CE (Josephus, *Ant.* 18.81–84; Suetonius, *Tib.,* 36; Dio Cassius, *Hist. Rom.* 57.18.5a; Tacitus, *Ann.* 2.85.4). Another occurred under Claudius in either 41 or 49 CE. See Suetonius, *Claudius* 25.4; Dio Cassius, *Hist. Rom.* 60.6.6; Acts 18:2. See also discussion in Barclay, *Jews,* 303–6.

56. The view that Acts is anti-Jewish throughout is also supported by Augusto Barbi, "Use and Meaning."

57. Sanders, "Jewish People," 73. Cf. Sanders, *Jews in Luke-Acts;* Sanders, "Salvation"; and Sanders, "Who Is a Jew."

58. Sanders, "Jewish People," 72. The fact that Paul is not actually "done in" at the end of Acts creates problems for this interpretation. Elsewhere, Sanders takes his argument even further. He states that the conclusion of Acts indicates the arrival at a "final solution of the Jewish problem" (Sanders, "Salvation," 115). Sanders's rhetoric situates Luke's perspective on Jews as comparable to Nazi Germany's concept of *die Endlösung der Judenfrage* ("the final solution of the Jewish question"). On uses of the New Testament in Nazi Germany, see Heschel, *Aryan Jesus.*

59. Sanders, "Jewish People," 72.

60. Sanders, "Jewish People," 70.

61. Sanders, "Jewish People," 73, emphasis original.

62. At the end of his monograph on "the Jews" in Luke-Acts, Sanders writes, "The modern reader of Luke-Acts is now forced to ask whether Luke's polemic against 'Jews' has not become the leaven within Christianity—and within Western society—against which we must all and eternally be on guard" (*Jews in Luke-Acts,* 317).

63. See Sanders, "Jewish People," 72.

64. Brawley, *Luke-Acts.* On Brawley's views, see discussion below.

65. Barbi, "Use and Meaning," 125; see Blass, Debrunner, and Funk, *Greek Grammar,* §262 (1). See, for example, the ways that scholars have emphasized the

uses the phrase: the "Jews" (Barbi), "the Jews" (Conzelmann), *THE JEWS* (Sanders), and *the Jews* (M. Smith) (see below).

66. Barbi, "Use and Meaning," 126.

67. Barbi, "Use and Meaning," 134. Barbi observes five ways that Ἰουδαῖοι is used that indicate sites of interaction: the phrase "synagogue of the Jews," the phrase "Jews and Hellenes," Paul's activity in relation to the "Jews," activity of the "Jews" in relation to preachers of the gospel, and interactions in direct discourse (126–33).

68. Barbi, "Use and Meaning," 134. See also Sanders, *Jews in Luke-Acts,* 258–59.

69. Barbi's conclusion that Acts offers a tragic picture of the "Jews" is similar to that in Tannehill, "Israel in Luke-Acts." Quotation from Barbi, "Use and Meaning," 140.

70. Smith, *Literary Construction.* For a fuller treatment of the literary and narrative structure of Acts, see Tannehill, *Narrative Unity of Luke-Acts.* As the title of his multivolume work indicates, Tannehill uses the narrative features of the Gospel of Luke and Acts to argue that the texts are two volumes of a single work. For Tannehill, Luke and Acts present the rejection of the gospel by Jews as a "tragic" turn of events in the history of Israel ("Israel in Luke-Acts").

71. Smith, *Literary Construction,* 61.

72. Smith uses a theory of transitivity analysis to better understand *the Jews* in Acts. Transitivity analysis looks at the subject and objects of verbal actions to determine "active" and "passive" actors in narratives. Smith observes that Luke usually represents *the Jews* as the subjects (active) and Christians as objects (passive). See discussion in Smith, *Literary Construction,* 8–9.

73. Quotations from Smith, *Literary Construction,* 93–94, 71, 63–64 (emphasis original), and 94, respectively. At some points Smith differentiates the literary representation of these Jews as *the Jews* and other Jews, but at other points she seems to combine the uses of οἱ Ἰουδαῖοι with other uses of Ἰουδαῖος in Acts. In a footnote Smith states, "From this point forward, when the term *the Jews* refers to the presence of the Greek plural with the definite article of *ho Ioudaios (hoi Ioudaioi)* in Acts, it is italicized (*Literary Construction,* 58 n. 2); however, two pages later she claims, "The expression *the Jews (hoi Ioudaioi)* occurs seventy-nine times in Acts" (60). The Greek word Ἰουδαῖος, in all its forms, occurs seventy-nine times in Acts, but the articular plural use of Ἰουδαῖος occurs forty-two times in Acts.

74. Smith does not historically contextualize Acts but prefers to focus on the texts as a literary whole (*Literary Construction,* 8–9).

75. Tyson, "Problem of Jewish Rejection," 127; cf. Tyson, "Jews and Judaism in Luke-Acts"; Tyson, "Jewish Public in Luke-Acts."

76. Tyson, *Marcion and Luke-Acts,* 32, 137. Marcion—as he is reconstructed from the writings of his opponents—offers an interesting interlocutor for Luke and places more emphasis on theological discussions from the first quarter of the second century CE than previous works. However, the push to read Acts in light of Marcion or "marcionite thinking" assumes that Luke begins with a developed theology of salvation history and then constructs a narrative of the spread of the Christian message to fit that message. That is to say, these views assume that a theologically robust "Christianity" exists outside of the narrative.

77. Tyson, *Images;* cf. Lieu, *Image and Reality.*

78. Matthews, *Perfect Martyr.* Matthews's work builds on Knox, *Marcion and the New Testament;* and Tyson, *Marcion and Luke-Acts.*

79. Matthews, *Perfect Martyr,* 36, emphasis original. On the *Adversus Judaeos* tradition, see Fredriksen and Irshai, "Christian Anti-Judaism"; and Efroymson, "Patristic Connection."

80. Matthews, *Perfect Martyr,* 34.

81. Cf. the claim by Knust (*Abandoned to Lust*) that Justin, Irenaeus, and others "thought with" their opponents. She argues that early Christians used sexual accusations to challenge those who opposed them and define their own movement(s).

82. Jervell, *Luke and the People of God.* Jervell published four of the essays between 1962 and 1971. The programmatic essay in this collection was originally published as Jervell, "Das Gespaltene Israel und die Heidenvölker." Cf. discussion in Tyson, *Luke, Judaism, and the Scholars,* 93–109. See also Lohfink (*Die Sammlung Israels*), who argues that Luke views Jews and Judaism positively but that after Acts 5:42 the "Jerusalem springtime" ends and "Israel that still persists in rejecting Jesus loses any claim to be the true people of God—it becomes Judaism" (55; quoted and translated in Tyson, *Luke, Judaism, and the Scholars,* 110).

83. Jervell writes: "One usually understands the situation to imply that only when the Jews have rejected the gospel is the way opened to gentiles. It is more correct to say that only when Israel has accepted the gospel can the way to gentiles be opened. The acceptance of the message took place primarily through the Jewish Christian community in Jerusalem" (*Luke and the People of God,* 55).

84. Jervell, *Luke and the People of God,* 43.

85. Brawley, *Luke-Acts.* For Brawley, "The Jews in Luke-Acts play out their roles enmeshed in an intricate pattern of theme and plot development" (155).

86. Brawley, *Luke-Acts,* 83. See the more recent statements in Brawley, "Ethical Borderlines," where he sees the stand of Luke toward the Jews as "open-ended" (415).

87. This is the view of Bovon, "Studies in Luke-Acts," 190. See also Hakola, "'Friendly' Pharisees."

88. Jervell, *Luke and the People of God*, 46, emphasis mine. "Belief" and "believer" are problematic categories for describing the relations between ancient peoples and their gods. See below and discussion in Fredriksen, "Judaizing the Nations," 235–36.

89. Brawley, *Luke-Acts*, 159, emphasis mine. Brawley does not distinguish between Jewish and non-Jewish Christians.

90. Salmon, "Insider or Outsider?"

91. See also Donaldson, *Jews and Anti-Judaism*, 55–80, who acknowledges that understanding Acts as either pro- or anti-Jewish depends upon the author's relationship with Judaism.

92. Salmon, "Insider or Outsider?," 79–80.

93. Bovon correctly observes a shift from theological methods to social-cultural approaches in many recent works ("Studies in Luke-Acts," 186).

94. Esler, *Community and Gospel*.

95. Esler, *Community and Gospel*, 17–21, quotation from 17, emphasis mine. Cf. Berger and Luckmann, *Social Construction of Reality*. See also the work of Coleman Baker, who uses social theory to argue that "the narrative of Acts attempts the recategorization of Judean and non-Judean Christ-followers and those on either side of the debate over non-Judean inclusion in the Christ movement into a common ingroup" (*Identity, Memory, and Narrative*, xv).

96. Esler, *Community and Gospel*, 2.

97. See Esler, *Community and Gospel*, 46–70, esp. 65–70.

98. Esler, *Community and Gospel*, 30–70, quotation from 69. Esler contends that Luke wrote so that he "could console his fellow-Christians with the message that it was not they but Jews still attending the synagogue who had abandoned the God of Abraham, Isaac and Jacob, of Moses and of David" (*Community and Gospel*, 70).

99. For Esler, legitimating table fellowship between Jews and non-Jews is a central concern of Acts: "One issue in Luke-Acts towers above all others as significant for the emergence and subsequent sectarian identity of the type of community for whom Luke wrote: namely, table-fellowship between Jews and Gentiles" (*Community and Gospel*, 71–109, quotation from 71).

100. Wills, "Depiction of the Jews."

101. Wills, *Not God's People*, 199.

102. Wills, "Depiction of the Jews," 653.

103. See the recent works Barreto, *Ethnic Negotiations*; Hakola, "'Friendly' Pharisees"; and Baker, *Identity, Memory, and Narrative*.

104. See Barreto, *Ethnic Negotiations*, 81, 83, 97–98.

105. Barreto's seven categories are naming individuals, Ἰουδαῖοι specified by place, references to the prerogatives and/or possessions of the Ἰουδαῖοι, pairings between Ἰουδαῖος and other groups, Ἰουδαῖος and the political powers, sites of contestation, and wide ethnic appeals. See discussion in Barreto, *Ethnic Negotiations*, 88–91.

106. Barreto notes three verses that are "wide ethnic appeals" (2:5; 10:22, 28). He contends that these verses use Ἰουδαῖος generically ("the Jews") but they remain limited by their immediate context (*Ethnic Negotiations*, 90–91). See my discussion of Acts 2:5–13 in chapter 2.

107. Barreto, *Ethnic Negotiations*, 98.

108. Barreto's view is also supported by Chrupcała, *Everyone Will See*.

109. See Barreto, *Ethnic Negotiations*, 158–160.

110. The Jews who accuse Paul contend that he persuades people to worship God in ways that are contrary to "the law" (19:13). Gallio responds that Jews, not Romans, should tend to questions about a word, names, and laws (19:14–15). See my discussion of Acts 18:12–17 in chapter 4.

111. See my discussion of "proselyte" in chapter 2. On Jewish proselytes generally, see Donaldson, *Judaism and the Gentiles*, 482–94. For an exhaustive study of the primary evidence for "Godfearers" and "proselytes," see Wander, *Gottesfürchtige und Sympathisanten*. For additional discussion, see Levinskaya, *Book of Acts*. See also discussion in Fredriksen, "Judaizing the Nations," 235–40, esp. 238–39. A still valuable collection on the topic of the Jewish identity of non-Jews is Cohen, *Beginnings*, esp. "Part 2: The Boundary Crossed: Becoming a Jew."

112. This was apparently the view of ancient non-Jews. See discussion in Cohen, *Beginnings*, 159–60. See *Gospel of Philip* (*NHC* 2.2–7) and *Acts of Pilate* 2.4; and primary texts in Stern, *Greek and Latin Authors*, nos. 254 (Epictetus) and 515 (Life of Severus). Cf. Jdt 14:10; Josephus, *Ant.* 20.17–48.

113. See Cohen, *Beginnings*, 109–39; Cohen sees proselytes as participating in a larger shift in Jewish identity from an ethnic and geographic identity to a cultural and religious one during the Hasmonean period. For other examples, see Cohen, "Crossing the Boundary,"; repr. in *Beginnings*, 140–74. Cohen sees three elements necessary to "become" Jewish: practice of Jewish laws, exclusive devotion to God, and integration into the Jewish community (see Jth 14:10; Tacitus, *Histories* 5.5.2; Juvenal, *Satires* 14.96–106). However, he notes that most "conversion" stories do not entail each of these elements (e.g., Philo, *Vir.* 20.102–21.208). Matthew Thiessen ("Revisiting the προσήλυτος") has persuasively argued that in the LXX προσήλυτος does not usually mean "convert"; rather, the term covers a range of ways of af-

filiating with the Jewish people. See also Malina and Pilch (*Social-Science Commentary*, 30), who contend that proselytes are merely "respectful" outsiders who "would be supportive of a forthcoming Israelite theocracy" but did not necessarily follow Jewish customs. As I argue in chapter 3, Luke uses the distinction between the translated meaning of προσήλυτος in the LXX and the contemporaneous concept of the proselyte (also προσήλυτος in Greek) to identify Christian non-Jews as proselytes according to the LXX.

114. See Fredriksen, who identifies proselytes as "Jews of a special kind" ("Judaizing the Nations," 242).

115. In an authorial aside, Luke makes it clear that he refers to Paul's proclamation of Jesus and resurrection (Acts 17:19).

116. See, for example, Philo, *Creation* 2; Aristobulous, frag. 2 on God as creator and Isa. 66:1–2; Josephus, *Ant.* 8.227–28; and *Sib Or.* 4.8–11 on God and the temple.

117. Luke's Paul takes both of these claims from Greek authors. Scholars dispute exactly who Luke's Paul is quoting. The first may be based on the sixth-century BCE poet Epimendies. Cadbury views this as uncertain (*Book of Acts*, 49). See also the discussion in Keener, *Acts*, 3:2657–59. The second is likely from the third-century poet Aratus (so Pervo, *Acts*, 439).

118. Cf. Acts 14:8–18 where Acts also presents the God of the Jews as the god who made heaven and earth and everything in them.

119. For discussion of the approach to Pharisees in Acts, see Hakola, "'Friendly' Pharisees." Acts opposes the view of some Pharisees that non-Jews should be circumcised and follow the Mosaic law (15:5). See my discussion of Acts 15 in chapter 3.

Chapter 2. Collecting *Ethnē* in Aphrodisias and Acts 2:5–13

1. I use the transliterated terms *ethnos* and *ethnē* throughout to highlight that though similar, modern "ethnic groups" and ancient ἔθνη are not the same. See the discussion of the term ἔθνη in Acts below.

2. I have chosen to emphasize the word "proselyte" here in order to highlight its origin as a transliterated Greek word in a similar way that I have chosen to emphasize *polis* and *ethnos*. See discussion of this category below.

3. Zanker, *Power of Images*, 335–38.

4. Pliny, *Nat.* 36.4, 36.39. According to Suetonius, Nero was tormented in a nightmare by these images of various people groups (*Nero* 46); Severius, *Ad. Aen.* 8.721. See discussion in Smith, "Simulacra Gentium," 72; Nasrallah,

Christian Responses, 76; and Velleius, *Hist.* 2.39.2. Velleius Paterculus (19 BCE–31 CE) wrote an abridged version of Roman history from the Trojan War until 29 CE; Dio Cassius, *Hist. Rom.* 56.34.3. According to Tacitus, only the names of the conquered peoples were presented (*Ann.* 1.8.4). See discussion in Nasrallah, *Christian Responses,* 76–77.

5. Nasrallah, *Christian Responses,* 77.
6. See, for example, Price, *Rituals and Power.* On the naturalization of ethnic rhetoric, see Zanker, *Power of Images,* 335–38.
7. Scholars continue to read Virgil's *Aeneid* as both a pro-Augustus text and an anti-Augustus text (the so-called Harvard school). For discussion of these views, see Schmidt, "Meaning of Vergil's Aeneid." See also Francesco Sforza, "Problem of Virgil," who in 1935 asked whether Virgil was sincere in his praise of Augustus and whether there was a second, more sinister meaning of the *Aeneid.*
8. For example, Sabine Grebe ("Augustus' Divine Authority," esp. 53) argues that since the *Aeneid* locates the origin of authority in the divine, Virgil legitimates Augustus's role as emperor.
9. Josephus, *J.W.* 2.178–82. Acts identifies this Agrippa as "Herod" (12:20–23).
10. Text and translation (adapted) from Colson, *Philo,* 142–43.
11. Cf. Philo, *Flaccus* 46.
12. Baker, "'From Every Nation,'" 89.
13. Cf. Josephus, *Ant.* 15.315.
14. Josephus, *J.W.* 2.345–401. See discussion in Rajak, "Friends, Romans, Subjects"; and Baker, "'From Every Nation,'" 86–91.
15. Josephus, *J.W.* 2.390–91.
16. The example of the reliefs from the Sebasteion deserves further evaluation in part because it has become a common example in scholarship on ancient Christian identity. See, for example, Nasrallah, *Christian Responses,* 76–83; Lopez, *Apostle to the Conquered,* 44–48; and Friesen, *Imperial Cults,* 148–50.
17. Called the Sebasteion because of the connection between the Latin "Augustus" and Greek "Sebastos." On the modern discovery and excavation of the Sebasteion, see Erim, *Aphrodisias,* 106–12. The construction probably began under Tiberius (14–37 CE), but it is possible that the project was only decided upon during his reign, with construction beginning later. Erim, *Aphrodisias,* 112; see also Smith, "Imperial Reliefs," 90. On the imperial cult in Asia Minor, see Price, *Rituals and Power;* Rives, "Graeco-Roman Religion"; and Brodd and Reed, eds., *Rome and Religion.*
18. Joyce Reynolds ("New Evidence") dates the complex to the Julio-Claudian period; see also Smith, "Imperial Reliefs"; Smith, "Simulacra Gentium"; and discussion of the Sebasteion's discovery in Erim, *Aphrodisias,* 106–23.

19. See Smith, "Imperial Reliefs," 90. As Paul Zanker observed, "the physical setting of the cult of the emperor was usually in the middle of the city, integrated into the center of religious, political, and economic life" (*Power of Images,* 298). Contra Hal Taussig, who claims that the Sebasteion was not in a central location in the city ("Melancholy, Colonialism, and Complicity," 284).

20. See Reynolds, Roueché, and Bodard, *Inscriptions of Aphrodisias,* 107.

21. Reynolds, "New Evidence," 319–22.

22. Erim, *Aphrodisias,* 107. The "porticos" are not like any known porticos in antiquity. For discussion, see Friesen, *Imperial Cults,* 83.

23. The steps from the paved walkway between the porticos led to the temple stylobate, which was at the second-story level of the porticos. Smith, "Imperial Reliefs," 92–93; Hueber, "Der Baukomplex," 102.

24. Smith, "Myth and Allegory in the Sebasteion," 89.

25. See Hueber, "Der Baukomplex," 102. On the number of reliefs, see Smith, "Imperial Reliefs," 93. Friesen says that there were originally 190 panels (*Imperial Cults,* 85). For discussion and images, see Erim, *Aphrodisias,* 112–18. Romans often depicted conquered enemies as females. See also the *Judaea capta* coins from the period after the Jewish revolt. See discussion in Smallwood, *Jews Under Roman Rule,* 353.

26. R. R. R. Smith has also included the Ethiopians on the basis of the physical features of a female image without an inscribed base. Other *ethnē* likely were represented on the basis of the space available in the complex. See discussion in Smith, "Simulacra Gentium."

27. Reynolds, "New Evidence," 326–27. Roman imperial rule included Sicilians, Cypriots, Cretans, and Jews before the time of Augustus. See Smith, "Simulacra Gentium," 58–59. Trajan conquered the Arabians and the Dacians, and the Bosporans were never incorporated into the empire.

28. Smith, "Simulacra Gentium," 59.

29. See also discussion of how the images of the Sebasteion were a means of "extolling Rome's universal rule" in Gilbert, "List of Nations in Acts 2," 516.

30. See discussion in Reynolds, *Aphrodisias and Rome,* 2–4. It was common for cities to represent themselves as unconquered allies of Rome. See, for example, *ITroas* 573, *IDidyma* 151, and *ISmyrn* 697. For inscriptions, see Packard Humanities Institute, "Searchable Greek Inscriptions."

31. Aeneas's divine birth and trek from the fallen Troy (a city in western Asia Minor) to Rome appear in relief. Irad Malkin perceptively notes, "The Romans probably used Aeneas to attach 'Greek' validity to their origins, yet at the same time marked their difference within the same Greek construct by insisting on

Trojan identity" ("Introduction," 10). See further discussion in Smith, "Imperial Reliefs," 97.

32. This position as ally to Rome is asserted and maintained a few centuries later in a collection of inscriptions on the so-called Archival Wall of the city theater. For documents, see Reynolds, *Aphrodisias and Rome.*

33. On the mockery of the new wine see Fitzmyer, *Acts,* 235.

34. Some manuscripts of the Vulgate (vg^ms) and Syriac Peshitta (sy^p) omit Ἰουδαῖοι as well. Codex Ephraemi (C 04; fifth century) reads ἄνδρες Ἰουδαῖοι; Codex Basiliensis (E 08; eighth century) reads Ἰουδαῖοι κατοικοῦντες; and Codex Bezae (D 05; fifth century) reads Ἰουδαῖοι εὐλαβεῖς ἄνδρες. For other possible readings, see Swanson, ed., *New Testament Greek Manuscripts,* 16; Nestle et al., eds., *Novum Testamentum Graece,* ad loc.; Barrett, *Critical and Exegetical Commentary,* 1:117–19; and discussion in Pervo, *Acts,* 65.

35. Lake, "Gift of the Spirit," 113. Lake suggests that "Jews" were probably added to 2:5 based on the audience of Peter's speech in 2:14 (Ἰουδαῖοι).

36. Pervo, *Acts,* 65.

37. Bonz, *Past as Legacy,* 97.

38. Metzger, *Textual Commentary,* 251. Metzger does think that Ἰουδαῖοι was part of the earliest attainable text, but only because it is the *lectio difficilior.*

39. Codex Vaticanus (B 03; fourth century), Codex Alexandrinus (A 02; fifth century), Codex Athous Laurae (Ψ 044; eighth/ninth century), and the majority text (𝔐) include Ἰουδαῖοι.

40. Swanson, *New Testament Greek Manuscripts,* 376.

41. Commenting on these two verses, Jack Sanders writes, "What we have uncovered here, therefore, is an anti-Semitic tendency in ℵ, whose scribe did not want to write that Jews were either 'reverent' or 'believers' and so simply omitted the word 'Jews' in both cases" (*Jews in Luke-Acts,* 232–33). Sanders contends that Jews must be included in the list because Luke wishes to implicate all Jews everywhere in the death of Jesus.

42. So Fitzmyer, *Acts,* 234; Nasrallah, *Christian Responses,* 107.

43. On the relation between diaspora and homeland, see Barclay, "Introduction."

44. See Acts 1:19–20; 2:5, 9, 14; 4:16; 7:2, 4, 48; 9:22, 32, 35; 11:29; 13:27; 17:24, 26; 19:10, 17; 22:12. Cf. Luke 11:26, 13:4; Josephus, *Ant.* 1.239, 2.6, 3.40, 13.67; IG XIV 830 (text in Ascough, Harland, and Kloppenborg, eds., *Associations in the Greco-Roman World,* no. 317). See also Johnson, *Acts,* 43; Holladay, *Acts,* 93; and Kuecker, *Spirit and the "Other."* Contra Fitzmyer, *Acts,* 234; and Nasrallah, *Christian Responses,* 107. Bonz sees κατοικέω as an ambiguous term (*Past as Legacy,* 98–99).

45. Εὐλαβής appears one time in the Gospel of Luke and describes the δίκαιος Simeon (2:25). See Fitzmyer, *Acts,* 239; and Holladay, *Acts,* 93.

46. Luke tells the story of Paul's "call" three times in Acts (9:1–19, 22:4–16, 26:9–18). On (the historical) Paul's "call" rather than "conversion," see Stendahl, "Apostle Paul."; and Gager, *Reinventing Paul.*

47. This is the first of eleven times that Luke uses the singular form of the term ἔθνος (Generic [Acts 2:5, 10:35, 17:26], Egyptians [7:7], Samaritans [8:9], and Jews [10:22; 24:2, 10, 17; 26:4; 28:19]).

48. See my discussion in chapter 4. On Paul's speech more generally, see Dibelius, *Studies,* 26–77 ("Paul on the Areopagus"); and Rothschild, *Paul in Athens.*

49. In the narrative sequence of Acts, Peter has not yet proclaimed the gospel to Cornelius, implying that the God of Israel accepts Cornelius before the proclamation of the gospel or his baptism.

50. Metzger, *Textual Commentary,* 251. About Acts 2:5, Holladay writes: "That they represent 'every people under heaven' underscores the universal character of the audience. Here 'people' translates *ethnos,* which is often rendered 'nation' or even 'race.' Because modern notions of 'nationhood' and 'race' are often read back into the first-century situation, 'people' is a preferable translation. It signifies those with a distinctive ethnic identity connected with a land, country, city, or geographical area, such as Egyptians, Scythians, and Romans" (*Acts,* 93–94). Holladay does not here address the fact that these gathered people are Jews as well.

51. Pervo, *Acts,* 65, emphasis mine.

52. Malina and Pilch, *Social-Science Commentary,* 29. Malina and Pilch identify those whom scholars usually term "Jews" as "Judeans."

53. Conzelmann is probably right in his observation that the inclusion of the Medes and Elamites indicates that Luke's list is an archaizing reflection of a previous time. Cf. Curtius Rufus 6.3.3. See discussion in Conzelmann, *Acts,* 14. Cf. Pervo (*Acts*), who calls these three "an obscure and archaic trio not otherwise encountered" (66).

54. A number of earlier scholars pointed to astrological lists. In a creative attempt to make sense of the list of *ethnē* in Act 2, Stefan Weinstock ("Geographical Catalogue") argues that Luke's list compares with astrological lists that use geographical regions to represent the zodiac. Weinstock compared the list in Acts 2 with a list compiled by the fourth-century author Paul of Alexandria. This Paul mapped a catalogue of twelve geographic locations onto the signs of the zodiac in order to represent the inhabited world from these twelve locations (cf. Ptolemy, *Apotelesmatica,* 2.4.73, and Strabo, *Geogr.* 5.15.1–7). In

his article, Weinstock contends that the list in Acts served a similar function (cf. Artapanus *apud* Eusebius, *Praep. ev.* 9.18.1; Ps. Eupolemus *apud* Eusebius, *Praep. ev.* 9.17.9; Philo, *Creation* 112–13; Josephus, *Ant.* 1.68. See also the condemnation of astrology in Jub. 8.1–4, 11.8, 12.16–21). On this interpretation, Luke used representatives from around the known world as exemplars of the unmentioned regions. As Weinstock and many others note, however, this model has one crucial problem: Luke did not use twelve *ethnē* in his list. Weinstock found an offprint of an article on astrological geography by Franz Cumont with notations from F. C. Burkitt that initially made this comparison (Cumont, "La plus ancienne géographie astrologique"). This view is also supported in Brinkman, "Literary Background"; Bonz, *Past as Legacy,* 98.

55. Scholars have tried to understand the list a number of other ways as well. For example, Dupont, "La première pentecôte chrétienne," associates Acts 2 with the theophany on Sinai and reestablishes the covenant with all people. See Butticaz, *L'identité de l'église,* 97: "Pour Dupont en effet, évoquant la grande théophanie du Sinaï, l'épisode d'Ac 2 élargit la nouvelle alliance à l'ensemble des nations établies sous le ciel."

56. For example, Eduard Lohse views Acts 2 as a "grand portal" of the early church that allows the reader to enter the global church: "Das Pfingstereignis steht nach Lukas als ein großes Portal am Anfang der Kirchengeschichte, durch das der Leser schreiten und Eingang in die Weltkirche finden soll" ("Die Bedeutung des Pfingstberichtes," 434; supported by Butticaz, *L'identité de l'église,* 90).

57. See Scott, "Luke's Geographical Horizon." See also Scott, *Paul and the Nations;* Scott, "Acts 2:9–11 as an Anticipation."

58. For example, Scott tries to read the whole of Acts through the lens of Noah's three sons, Shem, Ham, and Japheth ("Geographical Horizon," 531–41).

59. For example, Goulder, *Type and History,* 158. Cf. Scott, "Luke's Geographical Horizon," 528–30.

60. Scott points out that the list in Acts only has a 50 percent correspondence with Josephus's updated list from Genesis 10 ("Geographical Horizon," 529). Beyond the surface parallels between Genesis 10–11 and Acts 2, significant differences exist with such comparisons. See a critique of the relation between Acts 2 and Babel in Wedderburn, "Traditions and Redaction," 34. Dupont also questioned this view by contending that if this were a reversal of Babel, one would expect a single language as the outcome ("Première Pentecôte"; cited in Wedderburn, "Traditions," 34 n. 14).

61. So Johnson, *Acts,* 45; Jervell, *Apostelgeschichte,* 136; see discussion in Gilbert, "List of Nations," 505–7.

62. Translation mine. On the ingathering of the remnant of Israel, see Jer 23:3; Tobit 13:15; 1 *En.* 90:33; 2 Macc 2:18; *Ps. Sol.* 17:31; 4 *Ezra* 13:39–40. 2 Macc 2:18 is striking because it describes the gathering as ἐκ τῆς [γῆς] ὑπὸ τὸν οὐρανὸν ("from the land under the heaven"). Cf. Joel 3:1–5 (4:1–5 LXX), where it is the non-Jews who are gathered to face judgment by God. See also Donaldson, *Judaism and the Gentiles,* 493–98.

63. Gilbert, "List of Nations," 524–29, quotation from 524. The "early readers" Gilbert has in mind are those like the third-century author Tertullian (*Adv. Jud.* 7), but he allows for the possibility of a similar thinking of first-century readers as well.

64. Gilbert, "List of Nations," 516.

65. Gilbert, "List of Nations," 523. Gilbert minimizes the fact that the list is only of Jews and not of "all persons."

66. Gilbert, "List of Nations," 499. Gilbert writes, "Luke, inspired by the geographical catalogues that celebrated Rome's imperial power, wrote his own list of nations to critique this ideology and present an alternative vision of universal authority" (518–19). Cf. Jervell, who downplays the anticipatory element: "Die Völkerliste zeigt auch deutlich, dass es um das Weltjudentum, nicht um die Welt geht" (*Apostelgeschichte,* 134–35).

67. Cf. Lohse, "Bedeutung," 434; Butticaz, *L'identité de l'église,* 90.

68. Gilbert, "List of Nations," 518. Tertullian's proposition is interesting because it remaps the Roman world in Christian terms.

69. The strongest of Gilbert's claims for such a political reading is the fact that the most politically charged *ethnos,* the rebellious Parthians, is listed first ("List of Nations," 528–29). This does not undermine the fact that the list is of Jews, not conquered peoples. See Matthews, *Perfect Martyr,* 37. See also discussion below.

70. Gilbert, "List of Nations," 524. Cf. Nasrallah, "Acts"; reprinted in *Christian Responses,* 51–84.

71. Bonz, *Past as Legacy,* 108–10. The comparison of Aeneas's shield and Luke's list is part of Bonz's larger project of reading Luke-Acts as an epic presentation of Christian origins comparable to Vergil's *Aeneid.* See the critique in Butticaz, *L'identité de l'église,* 97–98.

72. Bonz, *Past as Legacy,* 109–10, quotations from 109 and 110, respectively.

73. See Isaac, *Invention of Racism,* esp. 55–168, 169–224.

74. Smith, "Simulacra Gentium," esp. 70–71.

75. See Goldhill, "Introduction." One way ancients did this was by depicting other ἔθνη or cities as deficient or deviant in some way. Presenting others as captives was an especially effective means of constructing the deficiencies or

deviances of others, as Benjamin Isaac has made imminently clear (*Invention of Racism*, 55–168).

76. Baker, "'From Every Nation.'"
77. Baker, "'From Every Nation,'" 87–95, quotation from 92.
78. καὶ πῶς ἡμεῖς ἀκούομεν ἕκαστος τῇ ἰδίᾳ διαλέκτῳ ἡμῶν ἐν ᾗ ἐγεννήθημεν; ("And how is it that we hear, each of us, in our own language into which we were born?") (Acts 2:8).
79. Cf. Acts 10:28, where Peter is identified as a Jew.
80. This section focuses on the Jewishness of Luke's list rather than the specific ἔθνη included in the list. For a full discussion of the various ἔθνη, see Fitzmyer, *Acts*, 240.
81. See discussion above. Cf. Güting ("Geographische Horizont"), who views the list as random. The listing of Parthians and Medes first is interesting because Parthia was the only empire that withstood assaults by Rome. In 116, Trajan defeated the Parthian king Osroes, but the Parthian Empire would not fall until 227 CE (Dio Cassius, *Hist. Rom.* 68.17). It is worth noting that in 68, Dio Cassius also records that Trajan conquered those in Mesopotamia and Arabia, as well as squelching a Jewish revolt in Cyrene, Cyprus, and Egypt. He also built a stone road through the marshes in Pontus. In the context of the early second century, the inclusion of Parthians (from a region not directly under Roman control) still supports Roman dominance. Contra Gilbert ("List of Nations," 527–28), who views the inclusion of the Parthians as subversive of Roman authority because they were unconquered. See also discussion in Isaac, *Invention of Racism*, 371–80, esp. 375–76. Isaac notes that the Parthians are often conflated with the Medes.
82. See discussion in Fitzmyer, *Acts*, 240.
83. Eusebius, *Comm. Isa.* 1.63.54. Cf. Eusebius, *Vit. Const.* 3.8.1 and *Comm. Ps.* (in Migne, *Patrologiae cursus completus*, vol. 23, 717). In both places Eusebius includes Ἰουδαίαν. Fitzmyer lists other options (*Acts*, 241).
84. According to Acts, the native language of Judea and Jerusalem is Hebrew (Ἑβραΐς διάλεκτος). See Acts 21:40, 22:2, 26:14.
85. Luke's claim that Jews need not be from Judea was, of course, not his own creation. He used this historical fact rhetorically. On Jewish communities in the Greek and Roman world, see Barclay, *Jews*.
86. See discussion of proselytes in the next chapter. On full assimilation in Second Temple Judaism, see Cohen, *Beginnings*, 140–74. Cohen does not think that ancient Jews viewed proselytes as Jews, but Luke apparently did. See Cohen, *Beginnings*, 57–62. Commentators vary on whether to take Luke's ref-

erence to Jews and proselytes as referring specifically to those from Rome or as describing the whole list. See Fitzmyer, *Acts*, 243. Contextually, it makes sense that Ἰουδαῖοί τε καὶ προσήλυτοι modifies Ῥωμαῖοι, as the only city listed in the catalogue, but grammatically the phrase could modify the whole catalogue.

87. See discussion in chapter 3 and Thiessen, *Contesting Conversion*. Josephus states that kinship comes not only through birth but also through adherence to the Jewish law. Speaking about the laws established by Moses, Josephus writes, ὅσοι μὲν γὰρ θέλουσιν ὑπὸ τοὺς αὐτοὺς ἡμῖν νόμους ζῆν ὑπελθόντες δέχεται φιλοφρόνως οὐ τῷ γένει μόνον ἀλλὰ καὶ τῇ προαιρέσει τοῦ βίου νομίζων εἶναι τὴν οἰκειότητα τοὺς δ' ἐκ παρέργου προσιόντας ἀναμίγνυσθαι τῇ συνηθείᾳ οὐκ (Josephus, *Ag. Ap.*, 2.210). The author of Jubilees limits the value of "conversion" through circumcision, one of the common stipulations in Jewish ancestral customs. See Jub. 15:25–26. See discussion of this passage in Thiessen, *Contesting Conversion*, 26–28.

88. Contra Thiessen, *Contesting Conversion*, 35. Thiessen does not take the larger context of Acts 2:5–13 into account when he states: "Regardless of what the term [proselytes] came to mean at a later point, the evidence of Acts suggests that Luke does not believe that προσήλυτοι are Jews." Acts 2:5 indicates that *all* of the ones in the list are *Jews*. See the other uses of προσήλυτος in Acts 6:5 and 13:43. Acts 13:43 appears to equate proselytes with Godfearers. Cf. Matt. 23:15. See also Malina and Pilch (*Social-Science Commentary*, 30), who wrongly interpret Acts as understanding proselytes to be "outside residents of the Israelite section of the city" and inaccurately claim that Luke did not indicate whether they follow "the customs of Judea" or not. Luke has identified these proselytes as Jews and called them devout, a term used in Acts to describe devotion with regard to Jewish customs.

89. Some non-Jews also recognized the ethnicity-changing power of proselytism as well. See, for example, Horace, *Sat.* 1.9.68–70; Petronius, *Sat.* 102.14; Epictetus, *Discourses* 2.9.19–21; Juvenal, *Sat.* 14.96–106; Tacitus, *Hist.* 5.5.1–2; and Suetonius, *Domitian* 12.2. See discussion in Cohen, *Beginnings*, 29–49.

90. See Donaldson, *Judaism and the Gentiles*, esp. chapter 11, "Conversion."

Chapter 3. The Jerusalem Council and the Foundation of Salutaris

1. *IGLSkythia* II 153. Translation available in Ascough, Harland, and Kloppenborg, eds., *Associations in the Greco-Roman World*, no. 82. See also Harland, *Associations*, 34.

2. *IG* XIV 830. The inscription is dated to 174 CE. Translation from Ascough, Harland, and Kloppenborg, eds., *Associations in the Greco-Roman World,* no. 317.

3. For the preceding paragraph, see discussion in Fredriksen, "Question of Worship," 177–79. Fredriksen also observes that "cult is an ethnic designation/ ethnicity is a cultic designation; cult makes gods happy; unhappy gods make for unhappy humans" ("Mandatory Retirement," 232). See also Steve Mason, who writes, "An ancient *ethnos* normally had a national cult . . . , involving priests, temples, and animal sacrifice. This cannot be isolated from the *ethnos* itself, since temples, priesthood, and cultic practices were part and parcel of a people's founding stories, traditions, and civic structures" ("Jews," 484). See also Richard Lim, who writes, "The Romans were not always victorious on the battlefield and, given their belief that each community had its own protective gods, they saw defeat as a sign that the enemy's patron deities were simply too powerful ("Gods of Empire," 122–23); Rives, *Religion in the Roman Empire,* 122–23; Ascough, Harland, and Kloppenborg, eds., *Associations in the Greco-Roman World;* and Harland, *Associations.* For primary evidence, see, for example, Williams, *Jews Among the Greeks and Romans;* for discussion, see Gruen, *Diaspora;* Barclay, *Jews;* Rutgers, *Hidden Heritage;* Rutgers, *Jews in Late Ancient Rome;* and Leon, *Jews of Ancient Rome.*

4. Buell, *Why This New Race?,* 49. Louise Revell persuasively argues that with regard to Roman identity, "any uniformity in meaning was constantly slipping, to create a multiplicity of possible meanings" (*Roman Imperialism,* 191). On the development of Roman identity, see Dench, *Romulus' Asylum;* and Farney, *Ethnic Identity and Aristocratic Competition.*

5. Scholars such as Oliver "try to avoid the term 'council' as it projects an anachronistic notion of higher ecclesiological structures and organization upon the burgeoning Jesus movement of the first century" (*Torah Praxis,* 365 n. 1). In this book I use the term "council" in relation to the Greek city council rather than the later ecclesiastical councils.

6. Chapter 4 develops these themes in relation to movement through civic space.

7. According to Rogers, διάταξις is a technical term "to describe a bequest made while the founder was still alive, which was intended to be perpetual" (*Sacred Identity,* 25 and 36 n. 87). More generally the term means "arrangement" or even "imperial constitution." See Liddell et al., *Greek-English Lexicon,* s.v. διάταξις, esp., A. II. 2. Διάταξις also appears on a statue base dedication by Salutaris for Artemis and the Ephesian *ephebes* (*IEph* 34; cf. *IEph* 28, *IEph* 29, *IEph* 30, *IEph* 35). In 1866, archeologist J. T. Wood discovered a monumental inscription near the south *parodos* of the colossal Ephesian city the-

ater. The inscription indicates that it was to be placed on the south parodos and "in a suitable place" in the Artemision. We do not have evidence of the location of the inscription in the Artemision or whether it was ever completed. See discussion Rogers, *Sacred Identity*, 19.

8. Artemis's birthday was on the sixth of Thargelion (late April/early May). See Rogers, *Mysteries*, 184 and 394 n. 73. On the frequency of the processions, see Rogers, *Sacred Identity*, 83. On the lotteries, see Rogers, *Sacred Identity*, 20–21, 39–79. For Greek text and translation, see Rogers, *Sacred Identity*, 152–83. See also the discussion in Elsner, *Roman Eyes*, 228–34; and Tilborg, *Reading John in Ephesus*, 179–81.

9. This is the central argument of Rogers, *Sacred Identity*. See the critique of Rogers's interpretation in Walbank, "Review."

10. See Rogers, *Sacred Identity*, 44–45.

11. Rogers, *Sacred Identity*, 52.

12. Rogers writes that the inscription and the Foundation were "non-verbal means of communication, by which the Ephesians negotiated their personal and social identities over space and time" (*Sacred Identity*, 26–27 and 80–82, quote from 82). See also Reynolds, *Aphrodisias and Rome*. On the related use of images to negotiate identities, see Nasrallah, *Christian Responses;* Elsner, *Roman Eyes;* Elsner, *Art and the Roman Viewer;* and Zanker, *Power of Images*.

13. Another version of the foundation of the city is recorded in Athenaeus, *Deipnosophistae* 8.361; quoted in Rogers, *Sacred Identity*, 106. See also the founding story in Pausanias, *Descr.* 7.2.7.

14. Other Hellenistic myths place their birth on the island of Delos.

15. On the Kouretes, see Thomas, "Greek Heritage," 125–31.

16. According to Pausanias, the inhabitants were "partly Leleges, a branch of the Carians, but a greater number were Lydians" (Λέλεγες δὲ τοῦ Καρικοῦ μοῖρα καὶ Λυδῶν τὸ πολὺ οἱ νεμόμενοι τὴν χώραν ἦσαν) (*Descr.* 7.2.8). Texts and translation from Pausanias, *Description of Greece*, 176–77.

17. In the Hellenistic period, see, for example, *IEph* 1449, 1459, 3111; for the Roman period, see discussion below.

18. Knibbe, "Via Sacra," 144.

19. Strabo calls this harbor Πάνορμος (*Geogr.* 14.1.20). Dieter Knibbe argues that Lysimachus did this, not to found a new city, but to found his own city, Arsinoeia, so that it would be outside of the control of the Artemision priests ("Via Sacra," 144–45). See also Scherrer, "City of Ephesos," 3.

20. Knibbe, "Via Sacra," 145.

21. Writing a little less than a century before Salutaris, Strabo states that "the city, because of its advantageous situation in other respects, grows daily, and is the

largest emporium in Asia this side of the Taurus" (ἡ δὲ πόλις τῇ πρὸς τὰ ἄλλα εὐκαιρίᾳ τῶν τόπων αὔξεται καθ' ἑκάστην ἡμέραν, ἐμπόριον οὖσα μέγιστον τῶν κατὰ τὴν Ἀσίαν τὴν ἐντὸς τοῦ Ταύρου). Text and translation from Strabo, *Geogr.* 14.1.24.

22. By the first century CE, the Kouretes became an Ephesian civic position. An office of Kouretes was established and hosted in the Artemision but later moved to the Prytaneion located in upper Ephesus. According to Strabo, each year a special συμπόσια τῶν Κουρήτων ("college of the Kouretes") performed sacrifices and participated in a festival (*Geogr.* 14.1.20). On the Kouretes, see Rogers, *Mysteries,* esp. 162–71. For a list of Roman-era building projects, see White, "Urban Development," 52–54, Table 2. For excavation information, see Knibbe, *Der Staatsmarkt.*

23. See discussion in White, "Urban Development."

24. *IEph* 27–35 are related to the Foundation. *IEph* 36A–D are four identical statue base inscriptions that are dedicated by Salutaris to Ephesian Artemis, the Sebastoi (τῷ Σεβαστῶν οἴκῳ), the pious city council (τῇ ἱερωτάτῃ Ἐφεσίων βουλῇ), and the temple-keeping people (τῷ νεωκόρῳ δήμῳ). Cf. *IEph* 640, an inscription for M. Arruntius Claudianus by Salutaris, his friend and benefactor (φίλωι καὶ εὐεργέτηι ἰδίωι). For Salutaris's *cursus* see Rogers, *Sacred Identity,* 16–19. See also Devijver, *Prosopographia Militiarum Equestrium,* 3:870–72, no. 106.

25. Scheidel and Friesen ("Size of the Economy," 77) estimate that there were approximately ten individuals of equestrian wealth in each city. A wealthy city like Ephesus would likely have at least a few more.

26. The Oufentina were a rural Italian tribe originating south of Rome, along the Appian Way. See Taylor, *Voting Districts,* 55–56.

27. The Latin portion of this inscription seems to indicate that Salutaris's position as grain authority was in Sicily (*item promagister frumenti mancipalis eiusdem provinciae*), while the Greek adds for the *dēmos* of the Romans. P. A. Brunt contends that the Latin portion indicates that he was "the local manager of publican companies" (*Roman Imperial Themes,* 391). Brunt's conclusion is supported by Rogers, *Sacred Identity,* 32 n. 52.

28. See discussion in Rogers, *Sacred Identity,* 17, 32–33 n. 53. Cf. Devijver, *Prosopographia Militiarum Equestrium,* 3:871.

29. Rogers, *Sacred Identity,* 17.

30. It is possible that Salutaris had a prior association with Ephesus through his father, however. The Foundation inscription states that some of the Ephesian council knew about the good character of his father (27.17–18). This does not mean that his father's character was well known in the city, as Rogers argues,

but does indicate that the Ephesian council, at least, knew about his father. See Rogers, *Sacred Identity*, 16. Citing Rogers, Thomas states that "he owned estates in the vicinity of Ephesos" ("Greek Heritage," 133). This must be inferred from the inscription or his wealth. Archeologists have discovered another connection between Salutaris and the city in the so-called Terrace Houses near the Embolos: a graffito in an *insula* latrine mentions the name Salutaris. The graffito, located in Dwelling Unit 2 of Slope House 2, reads "Salutaris cun(n)um li(n)ge Libetr(a)e" ("Salutaris licks the vulva of Libetra"). For texts, see Taeuber, "C. Vibius Salutaris," 350. According to some archeologists, this graffito, when combined with an ivory freeze of Trajan's campaigns found in Slope House 2, Unit 2, could indicate that Salutaris lived in the *insula*. See discussion in Taeuber, "C. Vibius Salutaris"; Rogers, *Mysteries*, 389 n. 7.

31. Cf. the language of citizenship is used of Aquillius Proculus and Afranius Flavianus (*IEph* 27.80–81). They are "as our legitimate citizens themselves" (ὡς γνήσιοι πολεῖται ἡμῶν αὐτοί).

32. White, "Urban Development," 63–64, quotation from 63.

33. *IEph* 27.23–31. The twenty silver statues include a statue of Trajan, his wife Plotina, the Roman Senate (ἱερός συνκλήτου), the Roman equestrian order (τὸ Ῥωμαίων ἱππικόν τάγμα), the Roman people (δῆμος), the Ephesian people (δῆμος), the six Ephesian tribes (φυλαί) (Sebaste, Ephesians, Karenaeans, Teians, Euonumoi, and Bembinaeans), the city council (βουλή), city elders (γερουσία), city youths (ἐφηβεία), Augustus, Androklos[?], Lysimachus (restored from *IEph* 29.9), Euonumos[?], and Pion (restored from *IEph* 31.8; cited as 38.8 in Rogers, *Sacred Identity*, 117 n. 16). For lines in the inscription, see Rogers, *Sacred Identity*, 84–85, Table 9; Salutaris subsequently donated two additional images (*IEph* 27.465–73), bringing the total to thirty-one. For discussion of restoration possibilities, see Rogers, *Sacred Identity*, 83 and 117 n. 16. All inscriptions are available at Packard Humanities Institute, "Searchable Greek Inscriptions." See Rogers, *Sacred Identity*, 83–86, esp. Table 9 (84–85). One type-statue of Artemis was made of gold with two silver stags (ἔλαφοι) overlaid with gold. The rest were silver (*IEph* 27.157–59). On the importance of archive, see Stoler, *Along the Archival Grain;* and Foucault, *Order of Things*.

34. Βουλή (*IEph* 27.158–60), γερουσία (*IEph* 27.164–65), ἐφηβεία (*IEph* 27.168–69), φυλαί (*IEph* 27.173–74, 177–78, 182–83, 186–87, 189–91, 194–95). Cf. the image Salutaris dedicated to Artemis and the βουλή between 107 and 110 CE; *IEph* 36), γερουσία (*IEph* 35), ἐφηβεία (*IEph* 34), Sebaste (*IEph* 28), Karenaeans (*IEph* 30), Teians (*IEph* 29), Bembaiaeans (*IEph* 31). Cf. Rogers, *Sacred Identity*, 84, Table 9.

35. According to Stephen of Byzantium (fl. sixth century CE), Ephorus (a Greek historian from the fourth century CE) connects the tribes to the founding of the city by Androklos (*Ethnica*, s.v. Βέννα, 2; cited in Rogers, *Sacred Identity*, 60, 77 n. 123). However, Ephorus includes the Βεννιᾶοι in the list of Ephesian tribes and excludes the Βεμβειναίων.

36. Usually the identity of the φυλή is followed by the identity of the χιλιαστύς, a term used for tribal subdivisions in Ephesus, Samos, and Cos. See *LSJ*, s.v. φυλή. For φυλή of Ephesians (*IEph* 1420, 1447, 1458, 1460, 1578; *JÖAI* 59: nos. 23, 26), Karenaeans (*IEph* 534, 965, 1443, 1459, 2083d), Teians (*IEph* 963, 1421, 1588b; *JÖAI* 59: nos. 20, 22, 24, 28), Euonumoi (*IEph* 956a, 1412, 1419, 1441; *JÖAI* 53: no. 137; 59: nos. 16, 27), and Bembinaeans (*IEph* 941, 954, 1450).

37. Cf. *JÖAI* 53: no. 137. A list of tribes including the tribe of Hadrian and Antoninus appears in the middle of the second century (*IEph* 2050, 2083g; cf. *IEph* 4331). φυ(λῆς) Τηΐων· Μενεκράτης Διαδο[χιανοῦ] Ἀρτεμίδωρος Ἐπα[—] Μ(ᾶρκος)· Ὅσιος Μ(άρκου)· Ὀσίο τοῦ στρώματ[ος—] βυβλιοθήκη[—] υἱοῦ Πομ[—] (*JÖAI* 55: 114–15, no. 4180).

38. *IEph* 2083d, 2083g, 2084, 2085. It is unclear how the *neopoios,* Neikon Eisidoros, changed his φυλή. The reconstructed inscription reads Εἰσίδωρος Εἰδιδώρου τοῦ [—] μου Νείκων χι(λιαστὺν) Ἰουλιεὺς [γραμ]ματικὸς ἀλειτούργητος [βουλευ]τής· οὗτος ὢν ἐκ τῆς Εὐ[ωνύμων] / φυλῆς εἰς ταύτην [μετέβη].

39. Cf. Davies ("Phylai"), who notes on the tribes of Athens, "Though the vitality of the tribes diminished with time, the system gave the Athenian citizen body a stable and effective internal articulation throughout antiquity." On the "tribal" system, see Davies, "Phylai." On such civic groups see Harland, *Associations,* 25–53.

40. The Sebaste "tribe" likely formed sometime in the early first century (cf. *IEph* 949a, 2050). The Salutaris Foundation is the earliest securely datable occurrence of the tribe of the Sebaste according to a search of the Packard Humanities Institute, "Searchable Greek Inscriptions." On the cult of the Sebastoi in Asia Minor, see Price, *Rituals and Power.* For Ephesus, see Friesen, *Twice Neokoros.* On worship of the emperors more generally, see Gradel, *Emperor Worship.*

41. For the use of similar kinship language to form civic alliances, see Jones, *Kinship Diplomacy,* 51–65.

42. The ancient Greek novelists responded to Rome by looking to a Hellenistic past where Rome did not matter and was not in control. See Swain, *Hellenism and Empire,* 101–31; and Whitmarsh, *Narrative and Identity.*

43. Iulianus is from the Quirina tribe and is the secretary of the Ephesian *dēmos* (γραμματεὺς τοῦ δήμου; *IEph* 27.)
44. Greek text and translation (adapted) from Rogers, *Sacred Identity*, 152–53.
45. He is called an Artemis-lover (φιλάρτεμις; 27.89–90). *IEph* 695 is the only extant evidence of someone else identified as an Artemis-lover. In this inscription, dated to 80/81 CE, L. Herennios Peregrinos is identified as "pure and Artemis-lover" (ἁγνός καὶ φιλαρτέμις).
46. *IEph* 27.75–81. Both Aquillius Proculus and Afranius Flavianus filled these roles in 103/104 CE. On Aquillius Proculus, see *IEph* 34, *IEph* 509, and *IMilet* 226. Afranius Flavianus later became proconsul (ἀνθυπάτος; *IEph* 430). See also Rogers, *Sacred Identity*, 18, 33 n. 59. On monumental inscriptions, see Woolf, "Monumental Writing."
47. Flavianus writes: "[Salutaris] has appeared to be a most intimate and kindred friend to us, it has been recognized on many occasions, if the majority have overlooked it, how he maintains goodwill and purpose toward you" (*IEph* 27.378). Rogers, *Sacred Identity*, 25, 36 n. 85.
48. The letter from Flavianus was included in the inscription and is identified as *IEph* 27D.
49. Rogers views this as evidence that the foundation was rejected by the *boulē* on the first vote (*Sacred Identity*, 25).
50. Thomas notes that Salutaris is actually a counter-patron because he does not offer any sacrifices for public consumption ("Greek Heritage," 136). Cf. *IEph* 27.366–688. Aquillius Proculus states that Salutaris's "goodwill toward the city in the theater [will] now become clear to all." Translation from Rogers, *Sacred Identity*, 173.
51. Flavianus was later given Ephesian citizenship and was proconsul of Asia around 130 CE. See *IEph* 430.28–29 and discussion in Rogers, *Sacred Identity*, 18.
52. Elsner, *Roman Eyes*, 232. Knibbe downplays the present value of the Foundation, writing "Salutaris [and his Foundation] revealed the Greek nostalgia that still existed in a world that had become Roman" ("Via Sacra," 124).
53. "Acts 15 is difficult" (Pervo, *Acts*, 367). Holladay correctly notes that the Jerusalem council is reported as a "watershed event" by Luke (*Acts*, 294).
54. Pervo writes that Acts 15 is "central in that it brings together the various threads of the plot" but cautions: "Although the chapter deals with the central issue of Acts—legitimacy of the gentile mission—and occurs in the center of the book, it is not the basic structural pivot, nor does it break new ground" (*Acts*, 368). Barrett observes that Acts 15 "is the best example of a pattern that occurs several times in Acts and represents the way in which Luke conceived

the progress of Christianity" (*Critical and Exegetical Commentary,* 2:709). Tannehill points out that the "narrator demonstrates an active interest in the so-called apostolic decree by the attention it receives in the narrative [15:20, 29; 21:25] and the indications of the positive response by the Antioch church and Paul" (*Narrative Unity,* 2:191). Acosta Valle ("Acts 10,1–11:18") has argued that the author of Acts did not include references to the Jewish scriptures in Acts 10:1–11:18 in order to defer the provision of a scriptural foundation for the acceptance of non-Jews until Acts 15. On the centrality of this passage see, for example, Barrett, *Critical and Exegetical Commentary,* 2:709; and Jervell, *Apostelgeschichte,* 403. Conzelmann remarks that it "is not by chance that the Apostolic Council occupies the middle of the book" (*Acts of the Apostles,* 115).

55. Because the focus of this book is on how Acts uses ethnic reasoning in the depiction of Jewish identity and thus the literary, rather than the historical, features, I do not address in this chapter discussions of the historicity of Acts 15 and its relationship with Galatians 2. For opposite sides of the discussion, see Haenchen, *Acts,* 455–68; and Keener, *Acts* 3:2195–2206.

56. Though see the Ethiopian eunuch, who Luke apparently takes to be a Jew (Acts 8:26–40). See Plunkett, "Ethnocentricity," 465. On the Cornelius episode, see also Garroway, "Pharisee Heresy"; and Oliver, *Torah Praxis,* 230–64.

57. On the cleansing of non-Jews in Acts, see Shellberg, *Cleansed Lepers,* esp. 95–147.

58. Wilson observes that Peter's assessment of Cornelius is "remarkably similar to Jewish summaries of the law and, although presented as part of Peter's Christian experience, expresses what we might call a 'liberal' Jewish position" (*Luke and the Law,* 70).

59. The "witness" of the disciples spreads sequentially from Jerusalem all the while indicating the spread to non-Jews. See, for example, Acts 2:5–11 (Jews from every *ethnos*), 2:17 (the spirit will be poured out on all flesh), 6:1–7 (Hellenists), 8:4–25 (Samaritans), and 8:26–40 (the Ethiopian eunuch).

60. As Garroway ("Pharisee Heresy") points out, the Cornelius episode does not address circumcision but deals with table fellowship. Willie James Jennings observes that "Acts 15 confronts us with the difference between Jew and Gentile, and between the people of God and the Gentile peoples. This difference is crucial because it illumines a God who creates all peoples and through the Spirit issues an invitation to life together. . . . Acts 15 brings us to the interface of creaturely difference and divine desire where God exposes both bound toward each other in ways never before seen in Israel and among the Gentiles" (*Acts,* 145).

61. Members of "the Way" were first called "Christians" in Antioch according to Acts 11:26.

62. Acts does not indicate whether these Judeans were Christians or not.

63. The Judeans' message that non-Jews required circumcision causes στάσις—the great Roman fear. See Acts 19:40.

64. On the portrayal of Pharisees in Acts, see Marshall, *Portrayals*, esp. 159–62. Marshall observes that the Pharisees' view "is problematic and causes dissension because they are *Christians*" rather than because they are Pharisees (161).

65. Barrett, *Critical and Exegetical Commentary*, 2:699.

66. Joshua Garroway ("Pharisee Heresy") has argued convincingly that Luke deliberately placed the Cornelius episode before the Jerusalem council in order to depict the Pharisees' claim that Christian non-Jews should be circumcised and follow the Jewish law as a secondary, late claim. By first indicating that God accepted Cornelius, the non-Jew, and his household without circumcision or the Mosaic law, Luke belies the result of the dispute with both the Judeans and the Pharisees. As Garroway maintains, "numerous details in Luke's presentation of the Jerusalem Council vis-à-vis the Cornelius affair combine to depict the movement to circumcise [Christian non-Jews] as belated, extrinsic, and pernicious" ("Pharisee Heresy," 27). On this reading, Luke intentionally clarifies the religious identity of the Christian non-Jews before he addresses their ethnic identity.

67. Barreto concludes, "At least in Judith, circumcision is capable of shifting one's ethnic identity: Achior the Ammonite is now Achior the Israelite" (*Ethnic Negotiations*, 106).

68. In her discussion of 1 Maccabees, Livesey highlights this political affiliation by identifying circumcision as "a mark of political allegiance to the Hasmonean rule" (*Circumcision*, 32). On the centrality of Jewish identity in the Jewish novellas, see Wills, "Jewish Novellas." He persuasively argues that such negotiations of identity are a central feature of the Jewish novellas, concluding, "Identity in the Jewish novellas is not so much *made* as deconstructed and *re-made*" (165, emphasis original).

69. On the ways non-Jews affiliate with the God of Israel in the ancient world, see Fredriksen, *Augustine and the Jews*, 3–15.

70. On Idumeans, see Josephus, *Ant.* 13.257–58; *J.W.* 1.63, 4.272–81; Strabo, *Geogr.* 16.2.34; and Ptolemy (via Ammonios and cited in Stern, *Greek and Latin Authors*, no. 146). See discussion in Thiessen, *Contesting Conversion*, 88–110; Appelbaum, "Idumaeans in Josephus' *The Jewish War.*" Appelbaum views the Idumeans as victims of Josephus's racial rhetoric. Cf. the forced

circumcision of the Itureans (Josephus, *Ant.* 13.318 and Strabo [via Josephus *Ant.* 13.319]). For other ancient perspectives on the Idumeans' relationship to Jews, see *Animal Apocalypse* (*1 En.* 85–90) and 1 Esdras. See discussion in Thiessen, *Contesting Conversion*, 88–96.

71. The Idumean general, Simon, displays the complexity of Idumean identity as well (Josephus, *J.W.* 4.272–81). When barred from entering Jerusalem during the Roman siege, Simon claims Jerusalem as a "common *polis*" (ἡ κοινὴ πόλις) and the Idumeans as "kinsmen" (συγγενής, ὁμόφυλος) of Jews. See also Cohen, *Beginnings*, 112 n. 5.

72. Cf. the complicated relationship between Galileans and Jews. See, for example, Josephus, *J.W.* 2.323; and *Ant.* 20.118. See discussion of other views of Herod in Thiessen, *Contesting Conversion*, 96–103.

73. See discussion in Livesey, *Circumcision*, 35–40. For a recent bibliography, see Thiessen, *Contesting Conversion*, 157–58 n. 22. See also Nanos, "Question of Conceptualization." For a different view, see also Gilbert, "Making of a Jew." Gilbert contends that Izates became a Jew before he was circumcised.

74. Collins, "Symbolic Otherness," 164.

75. Following Cohen, *Beginnings*, 79. Contra Barreto, who observes that both tutors are concerned with identity issues rather than religious ones and thus creates an unnecessary distinction between "identity" and "religion" (*Ethnic Negotiations*, 109).

76. Collins, "Symbolic Otherness," 179. On the possible existence of uncircumcised proselytes in Jewish literature, see Nolland, "Uncircumcised Proselytes?" Nolland argues that Jews did not think such a category existed. For Nolland an instance that does posit uncircumcised proselytes is a hypothetical construction rather than an actual example (b. Yeb. 46b). Nolland's article responds to the claim in McEleney, "Conversion, Circumcision and the Law," that uncircumcised proselytes did exist.

77. Paul and Barnabas differ from Ananias as well. Ananias, according to Josephus, affirms that adherence to Jewish ancestral customs (except for circumcision) was needed.

78. Tib. Cl. Iulianus calls Salutaris a "true Ephesian" who should be honored like other great Ephesians from the past (*IEph* 27.8–14). See discussion above.

79. Συμεὼν in 15:14 clearly refers to Peter (Πέτρος; 15:7). See discussion in Pervo, *Acts*, 375.

80. Although Luke's quotation of Amos does not align with the LXX text, it is from a Greek text. Cf. the use of πάντα τὰ ἔθνη in Acts 15:17/LXX Amos 9:12. For discussion of the Greek text of Amos upon which Luke draws and its differences from Hebrew texts, see Barrett, *Critical and Exegetical Commentary*,

2:725–29; Fitzmyer, *Acts,* 555–56; and Holladay, *Acts,* 300–302. Amos 9:11 was also used for different purposes in CD 7:16 and 4QFlor 1–2 I, 12–13.

81. Greek text from Ziegler, ed., *Duodecim prophetae,* 204.

82. On the meaning of ἐκζητλησωσιν with and without an object, see BDAG, s.v. ἐκζητέω, 1, 3.

83. 4QFlor 1–2 I, 12–13 connects Amos 9:11 to the Davidic messiah. See discussion in Barrett, *Critical and Exegetical Commentary,* 2:726; Jervell, *Apostelgeschichte,* 395–96.

84. The Masoretic text of Amos 9:12 reads "Edom," which the LXX translates as ἀνθρώπωος.

85. On the prohibition of eating blood, see Gen 9:4; Deut 12:23; Lev 17:11, 14; *Aramaic Levi* 55; Jub. 6:7, 21:18. Hanneken argues that Jubilees presents those eating blood as "anyone who eats meat not processed by a Levite" ("Sin of the Gentiles," 4). The textual transmission of these four prohibitions is complicated. See discussion in Pervo, *Acts,* 376–78, who lists six possible options.

86. Barrett observes that description of the Christian non-Jews as τοῖς ἀπὸ ἐθνῶν ἐπιστρέφοθσιν ἐπὶ τὸν θεόν could be said by a Jew of proselytes (*Critical and Exegetical Commentary,* 2:729).

87. Wilson calls Acts 15:21 "the notoriously obscure verse" (*Luke and the Law,* 83).

88. Haenchen, *Acts,* 469; Conzelmann, *Acts of the Apostles,* 119; Malina and Pilch, *Social-Science Commentary,* 109. See discussion of scholarship in Wilson, *Luke and the Law,* 84–101.

89. Witherington, *Acts of the Apostles,* 463; Dibelius, *Studies,* 97. See also Conzelmann, *Acts of the Apostles,* 118; and Barrett, *Critical and Exegetical Commentary,* 2:734–35.

90. For example, Mary Marshall writes, "The decree requires them, as Gentiles, to keep those commandments which are laid down for Gentile sojourners in the land of Israel" (*Portrayals,* 160). See also Haenchen, *Acts,* 469; Conzelmann, *Acts of the Apostles,* 118–19; Barrett, *Critical and Exegetical Commentary,* 2:734; Fitzmyer, *Acts,* 557–58; and Holladay, *Acts,* 303–4. For others who hold this view, see Wedderburn, "'Apostolic Decree,'" 362 n. 2. On the problems with this view, see Wilson's challenge (*Luke and the Law,* 84–94). See, for example, Jub. 6:4–16. The rabbinic literature lists seven precepts for the children of Noah. See, for example, t. 'Abod. Zar. 8.4; b. Sanh. 56a–b. See discussion in Bockmuehl, "Noachide Commandments." Cf. also Bockmuehl, *Jewish Law in Gentile Churches,* 145–73; and discussion in Fitzmyer, *Acts,* 557. For a more general discussion of the Noahide commandments, see Novak, *Image of the Non-Jew,* esp. 3–51, 107–65.

91. Barrett, *Critical and Exegetical Commentary,* 2:733. See also Taylor, "Jeru-salem Decrees." Wedderburn ("'Apostolic Decree'") tentatively proposes a "demonological" influence that connects strangling with unreleased souls.

92. Quoted in Taylor, "Jerusalem Decrees," 377.

93. Taylor, "Jerusalem Decrees," 377.

94. See Holladay (*Acts*), who writes that 15:21, "which asserts the ancient and universal practice of weekly synagogal reading of Torah, is often read as a non sequitur, yet it may have its own logic: If we include gentiles within the people of God, and especially if we require of them only what Torah requires, this decision cannot threaten the synagogue as a long-standing institution or the visibility of torah as life-giving instructions for the Jewish people" (303–4).

95. On the specific problems with connecting Acts 15:19–21 with Leviticus 17–18, see Wilson, *Luke and the Law,* 85–87. Wilson's specific problems do not, however, negate the general connections between the two texts.

96. See Elsner, *Roman Eyes,* 232.

97. Oliver, *Torah Praxis,* 370–93. Cf. Holladay, *Acts,* 303 n. 21.

98. Oliver, *Torah Praxis,* 372. Oliver concludes discussion of the prohibition against idolatry by contending that the demand "in the Apostles Decree to refrain from 'things polluted by idols' would require Gentile followers of Jesus to distance themselves from meat, wine, and other food items offered to idols, while also exhorting them to avoid polytheistic rituals and idola-trous practices in general" (375).

99. Oliver, *Torah Praxis,* 375–80 (*pornea*), 380–90 (strangled meat), 390–93 (blood). Fitzmyer connects the prohibition of blood with Lev 17:15 and takes these as three "dietary taboos" and one, fornication, as moral (*Acts,* 557). For other views, see Wedderburn, "'Apostolic Decree,'" 362–70.

100. Oliver, *Torah Praxis,* 370.

101. Oliver, *Torah Praxis,* 394.

102. Wilson also critiqued views such as Oliver's by claiming that "we have vir-tually no evidence of how Lev 17–18 was understood in first-century Juda-ism" (*Luke and the Law,* 86). Oliver claims that this view is no longer tenable because of studies on "certain passages from the Dead Sea Scrolls" (*Torah Praxis,* 392 n. 99).

103. Wilson, *Luke and the Law,* 86.

104. Wilson, *Luke and the Law,* 86.

105. It was likely assumed that these former non-Jews followed the laws of Moses, if they were willing to commit to the Jewish custom of circumcision. See, for example, the story of Izates, discussed above.

106. The letter written by the council is addressed to the brothers ἐξ ἐθνῶν (15:23).

Chapter 4. Moving Through the *Polis*,
Asserting Christian Jewishness

1. The processions regulated by the Salutaris Foundation and the movement of Paul in Acts do not represent the same type of movement. The Salutaris Foundation describes "actual" processions that (likely) took place in Ephesus, whereas Acts depicts Paul's literary movement through the Roman world. The processions of the Salutaris Foundation are reenacted ritual movements through a single *polis*, whereas Acts provides a literary description of unrepeated movements through various Roman cities. Though different in their mode of movement, I argue that both participate in a geographical way of thinking that rhetorically employs the movement of gods and of particular figures in ways that make and mask ethnic identifications. The comparison in this chapter emphasizes how the movement and representation of movement through space legitimates ethnic changes while also constructing unified ethnic identities and marginalizing others.

2. Paul does not face direct opposition from Jews in Lystra, but Jews from that region are identified as the reason why Paul circumcises Timothy. Cf. Acts 14:8–20, esp. 14:19. See discussion below.

3. Philip Harland defines associations as "small, unofficial ('private') groups, usually consisting of about ten to fifty members (but sometimes with larger memberships into the hundreds), that met together on a regular basis to socialize with one another and to honour both earthly and divine benefactors, which entailed a variety of internal and external activities. . . . All associations were in some sense religious" (*Dynamics of Identity*, 25–26). Throughout this chapter, I continue the strategic use of the term "association" as group identification for local Jewish communities rather than the standard "synagogue." The modern term "synagogue," which is a transliteration of the Greek term συναγωγή, can mean both the building where a Jewish community gathers and the Jewish community itself. I use "association" in part to distinguish Jewish communities from their places of meeting and in part to highlight the similarities between Jewish communities and other associations that gathered in the ancient *polis*. In antiquity other associations also used the Greek term συναγωγή. Harland concludes his discussion of relevant inscriptions with the observation that "designating one's group a 'synagogue' was a relatively common practice in some areas, a practice that also happened to be adopted by some Judean gatherings, ultimately becoming the prominent term" (*Dynamics of Identity*, 40).

4. On a theoretical framework for processions in the Roman world, see Stavrianopoulou, "Archaeology of Processions," who observes that processions are

"communicative events that involve a sequential structuring of a wider variety of actions. They join the performance of these actions to their interpretation and thus create meaning" (349). Stavrianopoulou depends upon Geertz's understanding of procession as both models of and models for constituting and validating social institutions and practices (see Geertz, "Religion as a Cultural System," esp. 93).

5. Quotation from Rogers, *Sacred Identity*, 82. Rogers's work on the procession is still the most detailed analysis of the Salutaris Foundation (*Sacred Identity*, 80–126). On festivals and processions in the ancient city see Price, *Rituals and Power*, 101–14. See also Graf ("Pompai in Greece"), who concludes his discussion of processions in the Greek *polis* stating that a procession "is not just a journey from A to B: undoubtedly, it matters where A and B are, and who is doing the journeying. In the final analysis, the differences . . . must be linked back to different religious aims and religious experiences, from the display and confirmation of civic order . . . to the quest for individual blessing" (64).

6. Quotation from Rogers, *Mysteries*, 4. About Ortygia, Strabo notes, "A general festival (πανήγυρις) is held there annually; and by a certain custom the youths vie for honor, particularly in the splendor of their banquets there. At that time, also, a special college of the Kouretes holds symposiums and performs certain mystic sacrifices" (*Geogr.* 14.1.20). See discussion in Rogers, *Mysteries*, 171. Another version of the foundation of the city is recorded in Athenaeus, *Deipnosophistae* 8.361; quoted in Rogers, *Sacred Identity*, 106. See also the founding story in Pausanias, *Descr.* 7.2.7. On the Kouretes, see Thomas, "Greek Heritage," 125–31.

7. Quotation from Oster, "Ephesus as a Religious Center," 1711. In Ephesus, according to Rogers, Artemis's birthday "was the Fourth of July and Christmas rolled into one general festival" (*Mysteries*, 7). See discussion of the "sacred way" in Knibbe, "Via Sacra." Rogers notes that at the beginning of the first century CE, the Ephesians altered the processional route by moving the Palateia and building a new altar to Artemis (*Mysteries*, 135–40).

8. Rogers observes that "piety and careful accounting go hand in hand" and divides the recipients of Salutaris's largess into three groups. The first consisted of those who cared for the statues; the second, those who were directed to spend their allotments on the celebrations of the mysteries of Artemis; and the third, those who were not required to perform any known tasks (e.g., citizens, members of the *boulē*, elders, *ephebes*). See discussion in Rogers, *Sacred Identity*, 39–79. See also the discussion in Knibbe and Langmann, *Via Sacra Ephesiaca I*, 18–32; cf. Thomas, "Greek Heritage," 134.

9. As discussed in the previous chapter, the center of the city of Ephesus had moved away from the Artemision through successive resettlements. On the archeology of the upper part of the city, see Knibbe, *Der Staatsmarkt.*

10. *IEph* 27.49–52. See Rogers, *Sacred Identity,* 68.

11. An accessible and accurate description of the city's layout can be found in Scherrer, ed., *Ephesus.*

12. On this complex, see Friesen, *Twice Neokoros,* 29–75.

13. See *IEph* 404 for the dedication of the Ephesian Stoa Basilica. C. Sextilius Pollio also dedicated an aqueduct for the city and after his death was buried in the heart of Ephesus on the Embolos (*IEph* 402, 407). See discussion in Scherrer, "City of Ephesos," 6–7. The *bouleuterion* was first built in the first century BCE and underwent extensive renovations (dedicated by P. Vedius Antonius) in the middle of the second century CE. See *IEph* 460 and discussion in Rogers, *Sacred Identity,* 87. The double temple has been identified as either dedicated to Dea Roma and Divius Iulius or to Artemis and Augustus. See discussion and literature in Scherrer, ed., "Temenos (Rhodian Peristyle)" in *Ephesus,* 84. On the development of the college of Kouretes, see Rogers, *Mysteries,* esp. 162–71. Knibbe notes that in the second century deities other than Artemis begin appearing in the Prytaneion ("Via Sacra," 146–47). This is also the location of the discovery of two large statues of Artemis that are now located in the Ephesus museum in Selçuk, Turkey. The chalcidicum is dated to the reign of Nero (43–68 CE). On the chalcidicum, see Bammer, "Chalcidicum," 88–90. *IEph* 1300 identifies the street that is now called "Kouretes Street" as ἐμβολός. Scholars have called the street Kouretes since a reused stone with an inscribed list of Kouretes was discovered in the paving. See Scherrer, ed., *Ephesus,* 114.

14. Scherrer, "City of Ephesos," 6–7. See also Hueber, "Der Embolos." There is little evidence for what existed before these monuments were built, but because of the street's role in other processions from the temple of Artemis to Ortygia, its off-set alignment with the rest of the city's Hippodamian grid, and its placement between two *agorai,* we can be sure that the area surrounding the Embolos was prime Ephesian real estate at the beginning of the second century. On buildings lining the Embolos during the Hellenistic period, see Thür, "Processional Way," 157–63. On the identification of the tombs and date of the Slope Houses, see Thür, "Processional Way," 171–83. Arisonë's death was considered a sacrilege because she was murdered while in the precincts of the temple of Artemis. See Josephus, *Ant.,* 15.89; Appian, *Bell. civ.* 5.9; Dio Cassius, *Hist. Rom.* 43.19.

15. For a more thorough description of the cityscape, see Rogers, *Sacred Identity*, 86–111. The Gate of Hadrian and the Celsus Library were built in the middle of the second century CE, a few decades after the Salutaris Foundation processions began. On the south *parados* as the location of the Salutaris Foundation inscription, see *IEph* 27.123–25.

16. The procession associated with Salutaris and those associated with Artemis's birthday celebration were by no means the only processions in Ephesus. Knibbe notes that processions from the temple of Artemis through the *polis* occurred on certain days, unknown to modern scholars ("Via Sacra," 153–54). Two other examples of the challenge to Artemis's dominance are the movement of the Kouretes from the Artemision to the Prytaneion during the time of Augustus and the addition of other deities to the Prytaneion in the middle of the second century. See Knibbe, "Via Sacra," 146.

17. On the frequency of the processions, see Rogers, *Sacred Identity*, 83.

18. On the pedagogical function of the processions, see Rogers, *Sacred Identity*, 136–37.

19. Rogers, *Sacred Identity*, 145. See discussion of the absence of the Kouretes in Rogers, *Sacred Identity*, 144–46.

20. See Thomas, "Greek Heritage," 134; Rogers, *Sacred Identity*, 65; and Knibbe, *Der Staatsmarkt*, esp. 96–105. Knibbe highlights the importance of the Prytaneion for holding the Greek *polis* together. Christine Thomas has argued that during this period the location of the Prytaneion and the Latin names on the list of Kouretes reveal that the Kouretes were being Romanized ("Greek Heritage," 129–36). On the present reading, the Salutaris Foundation offers an alternate way of being Roman in Ephesus, a way that works around the Prytaneion. The exclusion from the lotteries of members of the civic guilds is striking. Civic guilds typically held an important place in the city's structure. See Harland, *Associations*, 38–44. In Ephesus, we know that the silversmiths held a prominent place in the city (*IEph* 425, 457, 586, 2441; cf. Acts 19:23–41). One silversmith was a temple-keeper (νεοποιός; *IEph* 2212) and would have received money from Salutaris's distributions—but as a νεοποιός.

21. Geography is, of course, important for understanding Acts. See, for example, Nasrallah, *Christian Responses*, 87; and Alexander, "Mapping." See also John Moles, who argues that "the road" is the master metaphor for all of Luke-Acts ("Time and Space Travel"), and Sleeman, *Geography*.

22. The title "Second Sophistic" is based on the designation of the third-century author Flavius Philostratus (see *Lives of the Sophists*, 481 and 507, for its uses). Tim Whitmarsh notes that though "Second Sophistic" is "catchy, alliterative, urbane-sounding, and not a little arcane," it is analytically problematic because

there is no clear consensus about what the Second Sophistic was (*Second Sophistic*, 4–10, quotation from 4).

23. Nasrallah, "Acts," 534, 535, 565, 566. A revised version of this article appears in Nasrallah, *Christian Responses*, 87–118.

24. Wills, "Depiction of the Jews"; an adapted and updated version of the article appears in Wills, *Not God's People*, 195–209.

25. Wills, "Depiction of the Jews," 634.

26. Wills lists seventeen examples of the pattern of action, opposition, and expansion in Acts 13:1–28:31 ("Depiction of the Jews," 640–42, Table 1).

27. Quotations from Wills, *Not God's People*, 198, 199, 202. The claim that Acts is focused on the formation of a new *politeia* is the central argument in Balch, "ΜΕΤΑΒΟΛΗ ΠΟΛΙΤΕΙΩΝ."

28. Alan F. Segal calls the circumcision of Timothy a "puzzling" report (*Paul the Convert*, 218). Cf. Fitzmyer, *Acts*, 574. Joseph B. Tyson comments that this passage "constitutes a surprise, perhaps an anomaly" (*Images*, 150).

29. In Jewish literature of this period, there are relatively few mentions of the offspring of mixed marriages like Timothy. Josephus mentions a child of Felix and Drusilla named Agrippa, but he does not discuss the child's ethnicity (*Ant.* 20.143). Similarly, Eupolemus, a Hellenistic Jewish author from the middle of the second century BCE, describes a "Tyrian architect from a Jewish mother from the tribe of David" (ἀρχιτέκτων Τυρίος ἐκ μητρὸς Ἰουδαίας ἐκ τῆς φυλῆς Δαβίδ) (Frag. 2 = Clement, *Strom.*, 1.21.130.3; Greek text from Holladay, *Fragments*, 1:109).

30. F. C. Baur notes that Acts 16:3 "belongs undoubtedly to the simply incredible side of the Acts of the Apostles" (*Paul the Apostle*, 1:135n). See discussion of this view of Tübingen scholars in Gasque, *History*, 66–67. See also Segal, *Paul the Convert*, 218. Hans Conzelmann interpreted Acts 16:1–4 in relation to Luke's salvation history: the message of the gospel must first go to Jews before it is preached to non-Jews (*Acts of the Apostles*, 125). This is similar to the position developed by Jacob Jervell and collected in *Luke and the People of God*. The so-called gentile mission in Luke and Acts is possible, according to Jervell, only after the successful proclamation of the gospel to Jews. See also Jervell, *Apostelgeschichte*, 412–13. Along similar lines, Richard Pervo states, "To enhance Timothy's fitness for mission, Paul circumcised him" (*Acts*, 388). Joseph Tyson views this as a further example of Lukan "ambivalence" toward Judaism (*Images*, 149–50).

31. See, for example, Fitzmyer, *Acts*, 574; and Hvalvik, "Paul as a Jewish Believer," 135–39. For ancient views, see Cohen, "Was Timothy Jewish?," esp. 254–63. For modern views, see Gasque, *History*, 66; and Barreto, *Ethnic Negotiations*,

63–71. Barreto states, "the passage has intrigued scholars looking for coher-
ent theological positions on the part of Paul, but it has also precipitated a great
deal of confusion and uncertainty, even something resembling benign neglect"
(*Ethnic Negotiations,* 61). According to Fitzmyer, even though Timothy's
father was a "heathen," circumcision was a religious necessity for bringing him
into alignment with Jewish norms. Cf. Tyson, *Images,* 150; and Foakes-Jackson
and Cadbury, *English Translation and Commentary,* 184. For a more complete list of those holding this view, see Bryan, "Further Look," esp. 292 n. 1.
Similarly, Luke Timothy Johnson views Timothy as a "Jewish Christian"
whose circumcision is "not a condition for discipleship but rather a means of
assuring acceptability among the Jews with whom he will work" (Johnson,
Acts, 284). Cf. Parsons (*Acts*), who writes, "[Timothy's] circumcision is an attempt on Paul's part to accommodate Jewish sensitivity and to ensure Timothy's *acceptability among the Jews with whom he will work*" (222, emphasis
mine). Cf. Baker, *Identity, Memory, and Narrative,* 159. Richard Pervo has
questioned this perceived benefit by pointing out that Timothy's circumcision
was not likely to provide more advantage to Timothy in the Jewish community than circumcision had for Paul (*Acts,* 388). See discussion in Cohen, "Was
Timothy Jewish?," 252–54; and Slingerland, "'The Jews,'" 309–11. Slingerland presents possible scenarios in which Paul might circumcise Timothy and
persuasively argues that Timothy's circumcision was not an indication of Paul
becoming a "Jew to Jews" (1 Cor 9:20).

32. Cohen, "Was Timothy Jewish?," 254, 263.

33. Responding to Cohen, Christopher Bryan ("Further Look," 294) contends
that though Timothy may not technically be Jewish, the context of the passage suggests that the Jewishness of Timothy's mother was significant; and
Alan Segal (*Paul the Convert,* 218) argues that the point of the story is to show
that Timothy was Jewish, in spite of being regarded as a non-Jew and having
a non-Jewish father.

34. Barreto, *Ethnic Negotiations,* 63. Cf. C. Clifton Black's comment that Timothy's "mixed parentage symbolizes the ethnic alliance of Jews and Gentiles
that, in Luke's judgment, should be the way of Christianity's future" ("John
Mark," 117).

35. Barreto, *Ethnic Negotiations,* 63. So for Barreto, by asking whether Timothy
was Jewish, Cohen and others exclude "an additional and fitting alternative:
that ethnicities are not either/or propositions but pliable constructions" (*Ethnic Negotiations,* 71).

36. Barreto, *Ethnic Negotiations,* 99.

37. Barreto, *Ethnic Negotiations,* 99.

38. Corollary to the absence of a matrilineal principle of lineage is the dominance of a patrilineal principle of lineage for both Jews and non-Jews. On this, see Johnson Hodge, *If Sons, Then Heirs*, 22–26.

39. Not all scholars consider circumcision a clear means for non-Jews to become Jews. Barreto comments, "from an emic perspective, there is no evidence that circumcision was a useful marker of ethnic identity" (*Ethnic Negotiations*, 110). Livesey writes, "the Jewish practice of circumcision . . . has no single monovalent meaning" (*Circumcision*, 1). Similarly, Thiessen argues that lineage takes precedent over circumcision in many cases and writes, "There were no established criteria held by all Jews to define Jewishness. Jewish identity was, therefore, a matter of debate" (*Contesting Conversion*, 4). He argues that Luke refers positively to circumcision throughout Luke and Acts and emphasizes the importance of eighth-day circumcision as the only legitimate form. Because of this emphasis on eighth-day circumcision, Thiessen calls Timothy's circumcision an "anomaly" (*Contesting Conversion*, 120). He writes, "in Luke's mind, these Jews [who knew Timothy's father was Greek and wanted him circumcised] might have concluded that Timothy was a Jew, and so Paul circumcised him to avoid any appearance of laxity toward the law—even though he did not agree with their interpretation of the law's requirements" (*Contesting Conversion*, 122).

40. Schäfer, *Judeophobia*, 97–98. On the positive side, if one is a male circumcised for any reason associated with the Jewish practices, one is considered a Jewish man. On the negative side, if one is an uncircumcised male, one was either not a Jew or an apostate Jew. Cf. 1 Macc 1:11–15. There, "renegades" (υἱοὶ παράνομοι) arranged for the construction of a gymnasium, thus observing "the ordinances of the non-Jews" (τὰ δικαιώματα τῶν ἐθνῶν) and "removed the marks of circumcision, and abandoned the holy covenant. They joined with the non-Jews and sold themselves to do evil" (ἐποίησαν ἑαυτοῖς ἀκροβυστίας καὶ ἀπέστησαν ἀπὸ διαθήκης ἁγίας καὶ ἐζευγίσθησαν τοῖς ἔθνεσιν καὶ ἐπράθησαν τοῦ ποιῆσαι τὸ πονηρόν) (1 Macc 1:14–15).

41. Barreto, *Ethnic Negotiations*, 63.

42. After Timothy's circumcision, his name does not appear in Acts until he mysteriously shows up in Berea where he stays behind with Silas while Paul goes to Athens (17:14). Though not mentioned by name, it is probable that the author of Acts includes him in the "they" who went through Phrygia and Galatia (16:6) and the "we" who traveled to Philippi (16:11). His inclusion with Paul and Silas in Berea suggests that he was also with them in Thessalonica.

43. The first example of this pattern occurs when Saul/Paul leaves Jerusalem to persecute Christians in Damascus and returns to Jerusalem as a member of

the Christian community (9:1–30). See also 12:25–15:2, 15:30–18:22, and 18:23–21:17. Paul's final departure from Jerusalem, notably, ends in Rome (21:17–28:31).

44. This pattern, though interesting, is beyond the scope of this book. On the implications of this incomplete pattern, see, for example, Walaskay, *And So We Came to Rome*.

45. Wills, "Depiction of the Jews."

46. Cf. the linguistic parallel between 16:20b–21 and 16:37–38. The accuser creates a contrast between Jews and Romans (Ἰουδαῖοι ὑπάρχοντες, Ῥωμαίοις οὖσιν) while Luke marks the two Jews as Romans (Ῥωμαίοις ὑπάρχοντες, Ῥωμαίοις εἰσιν). On the ethnic rhetoric of this passage, see Barreto, *Ethnic Negotiations*, 139–80.

47. Following Sherwin-White, who contends that Jason gives a security for the good behavior of Paul and Silas (*Roman Society and Roman Law*, 95).

48. About the authority of the Jewish sacred texts in Luke and Acts generally, Tyson observes that "the authority of the Hebrew Scriptures is assumed throughout Luke-Acts, where, with proper interpretation, they provide support for a wide variety of events and concepts" (*Images*, 185).

49. On Godfearers as a category, see Donaldson, *Judaism and the Gentiles*, 469–82; Schürer, *History of the Jewish People*, 3:150–76; and Fredriksen, "Judaism," 540–43; for bibliography, see Pervo, *Acts*, 332 n. 12; for primary texts and discussion, see Levinskaya, *Book of Acts*, 51–126. The Greek terms usually translated "Godfearers" could merely mean "pious." Pervo understands Godfearers as a general term of support for Jews, "whether for political, humanitarian, religious, or other motives" (*Acts*, 333).

50. Acts 13:17 and 26 could also refer to Jews. See Pervo, *Acts*, 332. Pervo follows Fitzmyer and others who understand these two terms to be roughly equivalent. See Fitzmyer, *Acts*, 449. A. Thomas Kraabel thought that Luke invented the category ("Disappearance of the God-Fearers," 113–26). Subsequent archeological discoveries call this thesis into question. See, for example, Reynolds and Tannenbaum, *Jews and God-Fearers*; and Bonz, "Jewish Donor Inscriptions from Aphrodisias." On the literary role of Jews in Acts, see Tyson, "Jews and Judaism"; Phillips, "Prophets, Priests"; and Lake, "Proselytes and Godfearers."

51. Cornelius (10:2); Titius Justus (18:7); cf. Lydia (16:14). What remains unclear is whether Acts imagines Godfearers as continuing to honor ancestral and other deities.

52. Pervo, *Acts*, 420.

53. So Rowe, *World Upside Down*, 93.

54. Since Paul does not face opposition from Jews in Athens, his trip there is beyond the scope of this chapter. On Paul in Athens, see Rothschild, *Paul in Athens,* who persuasively argues that Paul's speech is explained by the traditions that formed around Epimenides as a cult transfer figure in the second century CE.

55. Paul's dismay at the sight of idols is odd, since *poleis,* and the ancient world in general, were full of statues of deities. Pervo comments, "the verb παρωξύνετο could imply anger or mere pity for the failings of polytheism. Athens was famous for its religious monuments and piety, but the other cities in which Paul had labored were scarcely less contaminated with the physical excretions of polytheism" (*Acts,* 426).

56. For bibliography on Paul's speech, see Pervo, *Acts,* 429–30 n. 45; and Barrett, *Critical and Exegetical Commentary,* 2:823–24.

57. Quotation from Nasrallah, *Christian Responses,* 114. On the style of the speech, Pervo writes, "A cultured Greek would dismiss these brief words as a stylistically inadequate and muddled collection of clichés with an unexpected and improbable conclusion" (*Acts,* 429–30).

58. The historical Corinth was sacked by the Roman consul, L. Mummius, in 146 BCE and refounded as a Roman colony around 44 BCE. On the refounding of Corinth, see Millis, "Social and Ethnic Origins."

59. It is unclear whether Aquila and Priscilla were Christians before Paul's arrival. Luke does give the impression that they were. So Sanders, *Jews in Luke-Acts,* 275. See also Holladay, *Acts,* 348.

60. Many commentators take the phrase διελέγετο δὲ ἐν τῇ συναγωγῇ ("he was reasoning in the [Jewish] synagogue") as a locative description of the place where Paul reasoned. So, for example, Fitzmyer, *Acts,* 626; and Malina and Pilch, *Social-Science Commentary,* 130. Cf. the NRSV: "Paul argued in the synagogue." However, the deponent verb, διαλέγομαι, is followed by a dative of *person* rather than dative of *location.* See *LSJ,* s.v., B. On this reading, Luke indicates that Paul reasons with those gathered during the weekly [Jewish] assemblies. Cf. Rajak and Noy, "Archisynagogoi," 76.

61. Cf. 17:3. On συνέχω as "wholly absorbed," see BDAG, s.v., 6.

62. On the title ἀρχισυνάγωγος, see Rajak and Noy, "Archisynagogoi." They note that an ἀρχισυνάγωγος was not necessarily a Jew but could be a benefactor of the Jewish community ("Archisynagogoi," Appendix I).

63. On the translation of εἶναι with the dative and predicate noun, see BDF §190(1).

64. In Luke and Acts the phrase ἀπὸ τοῦ νῦν is used with future tense verbs to convey a distinction between a future and present action. See Luke 1:48; 5:10;

12:52; 22:18, 69. On the basis of the LXX use, the phrase is best understood
as "now" rather than "from now on." To indicate continuation, authors used
qualifying phrases such as εἰς τὸν ἅπαντα χρόνον (1 Macc 11:36) or καὶ ἕως
τοῦ αἰῶνος (Ps 112:2). Cf. Gen 46:30; 1 Kgs 18:29; 2 Chr 16:9; Tob 7:12, 11:9;
1 Macc 10:41, 11:35, 15:8; Pss 113:26, 120:8, 124:2, 130:3; Odes Sol. 9:48; Sir
11:23–24; Mic 4:7; Isa 9:6, 18:7, 48:6, 59:21; John 8:11; 2 Cor 5:16. See also Josephus, *Ant.* 13.50, 128. On the ellipsis of the verb, see *BDF* §480.5.

65. Fitzmyer, *Acts,* 627; see also Pervo, *Acts,* 453. Cf. Acts 13:51, Matt 10:14, Mark
6:11. See Cadbury, "Dust and Garments." Cadbury finds no clear parallels to
Paul's actions. Fitzmyer associates this with Neh 5:13. There, Nehemiah shakes
out his ἀναβολήν ("cloak") as a prophetic symbol of God "shaking out" those
who οὐ στήσει τὸν λόγον τοῦτον ("will not stand in this word"). See *LSJ,*
s.v., II. 2.

66. Sanders, *Jews in Luke-Acts,* 276.

67. Pervo, *Acts,* 453.

68. So Tannehill, "Rejection by Jews," 90. Contra Sanders, *Jews in Luke-Acts,*
276; Jervell, *Apostelgeschichte,* 459. This interpretation does not alleviate the
anti-Jewish readings of this text that continue to haunt Acts.

69. Cf. the similar juxtaposition of "blood" passages (Matt 26:28, 27:25) in Nicklas, "Versöhnung mit Israel?" Nicklas contends that you cannot understand
Matt 27:25 ("his blood be on us and on our children") without reading Matt 26:28
("blood of the covenant").

70. Brawley, *Luke-Acts,* 73.

71. Acts 18:6 is the second time that Luke's Paul has preached in a Jewish association, faced opposition, and "turned" to non-Jews. See Acts 13:44–47. Many
scholars view this as part of a pattern in Acts that culminates in 28:28 with
Paul's proclamation that the salvation of God has been sent to the non-Jews
because they will listen. See, for example, Pervo's comments on Acts 13:13–
52: "This lengthy episode may stand for all of the Pauline mission that follows" (*Acts,* 344). Cf. Jervell, *Apostelgeschichte,* 459; and Tyson, *Images,* 142.
Cf. Rowe, *World Upside Down,* 57: "Paul's response to his Jewish opposition . . . is intentionally more provocative than programmatic."

72. Contra Sanders, *Jews in Luke-Acts;* cf. Conzelmann, *Theology of St. Luke;*
Haenchen, *Acts.*

73. Brawley, *Luke-Acts,* 68–83.

74. According to BDAG, the verb συνομορέω ("border upon"/"be next door to")
occurs for the first time in Acts 18:7.

75. The only other person identified as a venerator of the God of the Jewish people
(σεβομένη τὸν θεόν) with this exact syntax is Lydia, who is from the city of

the Thyatirans (πόλεως Θυατείρων; 16:14). See discussion of Lydia's ambiguous identity in Barreto, *Ethnic Negotiations*, 133–35. Cf. Acts 13:43. Titius Justus is not identified as "trusting" or joining Paul, the two phrases that Luke has used to identify "Christians" in Acts 15:30–18:23.

76. Cf. m. ʾAbod. Zar. 3.8, which describes the Jewish ritual purity issues involved with rebuilding a house next to a temple. The implication being that Jewish homes (theoretically) existed next to temples. There is, of course, historical evidence for the existence of multiple Jewish associations in single cities throughout the Greek and Roman world. In Rome, for example, the inscriptions from the so-called Jewish catacombs indicate that between eleven and fourteen Jewish associations were in the city. Following Mary Smallwood, the Jewish associations in Rome are thought to be independent structures that jointly form the Jewish community in Rome (*Jews*, 133–34). See Margaret Williams, who contends that there was a "supra-synagogal" structure that governed the entirety of the Jewish community in Rome (*Jews Among Greeks and Romans*, 224–26). On the Jewish communities in Rome, see Leon, *Jews of Ancient Rome*. See also Rutgers, *Jews in Late Ancient Rome*. Elsewhere in Acts, Luke depicts multiple Jewish associations existing in single cities as well (cf. 6:9; 9:2, 20; 13:5). The Greek term translated as "Jewish association" (συναγωγή) occurs nineteen times in Acts (6:9; 9:2, 20; 13:5, 14, 43; 14:1; 15:21; 17:1, 10, 17; 18:4, 7, 19, 26; 19:8; 22:19; 24:12; 26:11). Cf. Josephus, who uses συναγωγή only eight times in his entire corpus (*Ant.* 1:10; 15:346; 19:300, 305 (two times); *J.W.* 2:285, 289; 7:44).

77. Cf. Mark 5:22, 35–36, 38; Luke 8:49, 13:14; Acts 13:15; 14:2 (D-Text); 18:8, 17; Justin, *Dial.* 137.2. Cf. Irenaeus, *Haer.* 1.1.16; Origen, *Cels.* 2.48. On the literary shift in uses of *archisynagōgos* that occurred after Constantine, see Rajak and Noy, "Archisynagogoi," 80–81. Cf. the rabbinic use of the Hebrew phrase r'š hknst ("head of the congregation"; m. Yoma 7.1, m. Sota 7.7, t. Meg. 4.21). See *CIJ* 714 for the mention of a Ἰουδαῖα ἀρχισυνάγωγος named Rufina. See discussion in Kraemer, *Unreliable Witnesses*, 179–241. Rajak and Noy list thirty-eight occurrences in epigraphic sources dating from the first to sixth centuries CE ("Archisynagogoi," Appendices I and II). A search on Packard Humanities Institute, "Searchable Greek Inscriptions," includes fifty occurrences. When examining titles in Greek and Roman associations, Rajak and Noy point out that outsiders, women, nongroup members, children, deceased, and deities could be given titles ("Archisynagogoi," 85).

78. Rajak and Noy, "Archisynagogoi." Previous scholars identified *archisynagōgoi* as "people who made prayer their business and who were assigned to the

sphere of the sacred" ("Archisynagogoi," 83). For a critique of Rajak and Noy, see Kraemer, *Unreliable Witnesses*, 234–38.

79. *Archisynagōgoi* are listed as donors of buildings/repairs (*CIJ* 722, 744, 766, 1404), mosaics (*CIJ* 803, 804; *SEG* 20.462), columns (*Salamine XIII* 200), and chancel screens (*CIJ* 756). See quotation and discussion in Rajak and Noy, "Archisynagogoi," 87.

80. Cf. 1 Cor 1:14, where (the historical) Paul indicates that he baptized Crispus. Acts does not indicate that Crispus was baptized. The shift in verb tense from the first half of 18:8 to the second and the repetition πιστεύω, first in the aorist and then in the imperfect, indicates that it is only the multitude of Corinthians who are baptized.

81. Cf. Acts 18:4.

82. See, for example, the negotiated civic identity of Favorinus, the mid-second-century CE sophist, in Corinth. Gleason, "Semiotics of Gender"; Concannon, *When You Were Gentiles.*

83. Contra Pervo, who states that Luke "made Crispus a Jew" (*Acts,* 448).

84. Cf. the similar charges in Acts 16:21 and 17:7.

85. On Acts 18:12–17 as the narrative climax, see Haenchen, *Acts,* 538; cf. Rowe, *World Upside Down,* 57. Steve Walton understands these issues as intra-Jewish issues ("Trying Paul," 129). On Paul's silence before Gallio, see Smith, *Rhetoric of Interruption,* esp. chapter 6, "Interrupted Speech in the Acts of the Apostles."

86. Much is made of Luke's mention of Junius Annaeus Gallio, a well-connected Roman *equites* who lived during the middle of the first century CE. Gallio, born as Marcus Annaeus Novotus, was adopted by Lucius Junius Gallio and was proconsul of Asia in 51 CE (Tajra, *Trial,* 51). The date of Gallio's service as proconsul appears in an inscription from Delphi (SIG 2, 801d; translated in Murphy-O'Connor, *St. Paul's Corinth,* 149–50). See Deissmann, *Light from the Ancient East,* 5 n. 1. On Gallio and his family, see Tacitus, *Ann.* 12.8, 14.53, 15.73, 16.17; Pliny, *Nat. Hist.* 31.33; and Dio Cassius, *Hist. Rom.* 41.20, 62.25. Lake, Foakes-Jackson, and Cadbury provide discussion of Gallio's family and career (*Beginnings of Christianity,* 4:226). Notably, he is the brother of the orator Seneca and the uncle of the satirist Lucian.

Because of Luke's inclusion of Gallio, scholars have focused on two aspects when interpreting this passage: describing the historical Gallio and examining Luke's presentation of Gallio to detect whether it is pro-Roman or anti-Roman. See Tajra, *Trial,* 45–61. See also discussion in Fitzmyer, *Acts,* 630–31. Scholars evoke Luke's Gallio in order to date (the historical) Paul's time in Corinth and to lend historical credibility to the narrative of Acts and have interpreted Luke's depiction of Gallio in both positive and negative ways. For a more positive view, see Hubbard, "Urban Uprisings"; and Walton, "Trying Paul"; for more negative views, see Rowe, *World Upside Down,* 57–62; Tajra, *Trial,* 56, 59, 61; and Murphy-O'Connor, *St. Paul's Corinth,* 168–69. See discussion of Luke's stance toward Rome in Pickett, "Luke and Empire"; Rowe, *World Upside Down,* 1–2. Many interpret the passage as Luke's attempt to situate "Christianity" as a legal entity before Rome. See, for example, Haenchen, *Acts,* 541; and Winter, "Gallio's Ruling."

Steve Walton offers a slightly different perspective. He finds the key to understanding this passage in Paul's dream in Acts 18:9–10. In the dream, the Lord says that no one will harm Paul. This sets the stage for the trial scene in 18:12–15 by foreshadowing the resolution between Jews and a Roman. Walton concludes, "Luke's literary focus in presenting this incident appears less on the role of the Roman proconsul and more on God's action in taking the mission forward, and thus in protecting his servants. Gallio is one chess piece in God's hands" ("Trying Paul," 131).

87. Walton, "Trying Paul," 129. Walton echoes Winter, "Gallio's Ruling," 217.

88. Cf. Winter, "Gallio's Ruling," 217–18. Elsewhere, Winter writes, "Whether Jewish Christian or Gentile Christians, Roman citizens, or provincials, they [Christians] were all seen as 'a party' operating under the Jewish umbrella. Therefore being a Christian in the province of Achaea was not a criminal offence, according to Gallio" ("Gallio's Ruling," 222).

89. Rowe, *World Upside Down,* 58.

90. Some manuscripts include the qualifier Ἕλληνες, but the earliest leave the referent open. The D-Text includes "Greeks," while 𝔓⁷⁴, ℵ 01, A 02, and B 03 do not. See full list in Swanson, *New Testament Greek Manuscripts,* 321.

91. Many scholars take the depiction of Sosthenes's mobbing as an example of Greco-Roman anti-Jewish bias. For the tendency to interpret this verse as an example of anti-Jewish bias, see discussion in Hubbard, "Urban Uprisings," 416–17. Cf. Jervell (*Apostelgeschichte*), who sees the mobbing against all of the Jewish accusers; he concludes, "Was Lukas mit dieser Szene beabsichtigt, lässt sich nicht sagen" ("What Luke intends with this scene can not be said") (462).

92. Fitzmyer, *Acts,* 630; Pervo, *Acts,* 454–55; Malina and Pilch, *Social-Science Commentary,* 132; cf. Tajra, *Trial,* 58.

93. Malina and Pilch, *Social-Science Commentary,* 132.

94. Quotations from Hubbard, "Urban Uprisings," 418, 427. However, Hubbard and others unnecessarily limit the referents of πάντες with reference to Jews and Greeks and thereby exonerate Paul and his community from participation in the violence. Cf. Pervo, *Acts,* 455. Pervo remarks that the beating of

Sosthenes is the point in the story where "Christians" hearing it told would have jumped up and cheered.

95. There is no contextual reason to think that Luke's Paul himself is not involved in the public beating. In fact, given Paul's proclivity for violence and the strong opposition he inspires throughout Acts, it is possible that Luke imagines Paul's involvement.

96. This Lukan rhetoric identifies Christians as Jews, but in doing so it appropriates and manipulates Jewishness in ways that have had significant historical consequences. I have argued that an internal distinction among Jewish civic associations quickly became anti-Jewish rhetoric and was leveraged by later interpreters to condemn Jews and promote violence.

Conclusion. Christian Non-Jews and the *Polis*

1. See Denise Buell, who contends, "Claims of peoplehood in texts *re-membered* as Christian are resources from which hegemonic religious, ethnic, national, and racial belonging have subsequently been constructed." She posits "haunting" as a powerful way to speak about forces that affect us yet remain "invisible and elusive" ("God's Own People," 159, 166–67).

Bibliography

Acosta Valle, Martha M. "Acts 10,1–11:18: Une intertextualié différée pour un lecteur davantage impliqué." *Science et Esprit* 66 (2014): 417–31.

Alcock, Susan E. *Archaeologies of the Greek Past: Landscape, Monuments, and Memories.* Cambridge: Cambridge University Press, 2002.

Alexander, Loveday. "Mapping Early Christianity: Acts and the Shape of Early Church History." *Int* 57 (2003): 163–73.

———. *The Preface to Luke's Gospel: Literary Convention and Social Context in Luke 1.1–4 and Acts 1.1.* Cambridge: Cambridge University Press, 1993.

Anderson, Benedict. *Imagined Communities: Reflections on the Origin and Spread of Nationalism.* Rev. ed. New York: Verso, 2006.

Appelbaum, Alan. "The Idumaeans in Josephus' *The Jewish War.*" *JSJ* 40 (2009): 1–22.

Ascough, Richard S., Philip A. Harland, and John S. Kloppenborg, eds. *Associations in the Greco-Roman World: A Sourcebook.* Waco, TX: Baylor University Press, 2012.

Ashton, John. "The Identity and Function of the Ἰουδαῖοι in the Fourth Gospel." *NT* 27 (1985): 40–75.

Baker, Coleman A. "Early Christian Identity Formation: From Ethnicity and Theology to Socio-Narrative Criticism." *CBR* 9 (2011): 228–37.

———. *Identity, Memory, and Narrative in Early Christianity: Peter, Paul, and Recategorization in the Book of Acts.* Eugene, OR: Pickwick, 2011.

Baker, Cynthia M. "'From Every Nation Under Heaven': Jewish Ethnicities in the Greco-Roman World." Pages 79–99 in *Prejudice and Christian Beginnings: Investigating Race, Gender, and Ethnicity in Early Christian Studies.* Edited by Laura Nasrallah and Elizabeth Schüssler Fiorenza. Philadelphia: Fortress, 2009.

Balch, David L. *Contested Ethnicities and Images: Studies in Acts and Art.* WUNT 345. Tübingen: Mohr Siebeck, 2015.

———. "ΜΕΤΑΒΟΛΗ ΠΟΛΙΤΕΙΩΝ: Jesus as Founder of the Church in Luke-Acts: Form and Function." Pages 139–88 in *Contextualizing Acts: Lukan Narrative and Greco-Roman Discourse.* Edited by Todd C. Penner and Caroline Vander Stichele. Leiden: Brill, 2004.

Bammer, A. "Chalcidicum on the Basilica Stoa." Pages 88–90 in *Ephesus: The New Guide*. Edited by Peter Scherrer. Istanbul: Ege Yayınları, 2000.

Barbi, Augusto. "The Use and Meaning of (Hoi) Ioudaioi in Acts." Pages 123–42 in *Luke and Acts*. Edited by Gerald O'Collins and Gilberto Marconi. New York: Paulist, 1993.

Barclay, John M. G. "Introduction: Diaspora Negotiations." Pages 1–6 in *Negotiating Diaspora: Jewish Strategies in the Roman Empire*. Edited by John M. G. Barclay. Library of Second Temple Studies 45. London: T&T Clark International, 2004.

———. *Jews in the Mediterranean Diaspora: From Alexander to Trajan (323 BCE–117 CE)*. Edinburgh: T&T Clark, 1996.

Barreto, Eric. *Ethnic Negotiations: The Function of Race and Ethnicity in Acts 16*. WUNT 2/294. Tübingen: Mohr Siebeck, 2010.

Barrett, C. K. *A Critical and Exegetical Commentary on the Acts of the Apostles*. 2 vols. ICC. Edinburgh: Clark, 1994.

Barth, Fredrik, ed. *Ethnic Groups and Boundaries: The Social Organization of Culture Difference*. Bergen: Universitetsforlaget, 1969.

Baur, Ferdinand Christian. *Paul the Apostle of Jesus Christ: His Life and Works, His Epistles and Teachings*. Translated by Allan Menzies. 2 vols. London: Williams & Norgate, 1873.

Berger, Peter L., and Thomas Luckmann. *The Social Construction of Reality: A Treatise in the Sociology of Knowledge*. Garden City, NY: Doubleday, 1966.

Bhabha, Homi. "Signs Taken as Wonders: Questions of Ambivalence and Authority Under a Tree Outside Delhi, May 1817." *Critical Inquiry* 12 (1985): 144–65.

Billings, Drew W. *Acts of the Apostles and the Rhetoric of Roman Imperialism*. Cambridge: Cambridge University Press, 2017.

Bird, Michael F. "The Unity of Luke—Acts in Recent Discussion." *JSNT* 29 (2007): 425–48.

Black, C. Clifton. "John Mark in the Acts of the Apostles." Pages 101–20 in *Literary Studies in Luke-Acts: Essays in Honor of Joseph B. Tyson*. Edited by Richard P. Thompson and Thomas E. Phillips. Ithaca, NY: Mercer University Press, 1998.

Blass, Friedrich, Albert Debrunner, and Robert Walter Funk. *A Greek Grammar of the New Testament and Other Early Christian Literature*. Chicago: University of Chicago Press, 1961.

Bockmuehl, Markus. *Jewish Law in Gentile Churches: Halakhah and the Beginning of Christian Public Ethics*. London: Continuum, 2000.

———. "The Noachide Commandments and New Testament Ethics with Special Reference to Acts 15 and Pauline Halakhah." *RB* 102 (1995): 72–101.

Bonz, Marianne Palmer. "The Jewish Donor Inscriptions from Aphrodisias: Are They Both Third-Century, and Who Are the Theosebeis?" *Harvard Studies in Classical Philology* 96 (1994): 281–99.

———. *The Past as Legacy: Luke-Acts and Ancient Epic.* Minneapolis: Fortress, 2000.

Bovon, François. *Luke the Theologian: Fifty-Five Years of Research (1950–2005).* Waco, TX: Baylor University Press, 2006.

———. "Studies in Luke-Acts: Retrospect and Prospect." *HTR* 85 (1992): 175–96.

Bowie, E. L. "Greeks and Their Past in the Second Sophistic." Pages 166–209 in *Studies in Ancient Society.* Past and Present. London: Routledge, 1974.

Brawley, Robert L. "Ethical Borderlines Between Rejection and Hope: Interpreting the Jews in Luke-Acts." *CurTM* 27 (2000): 415–23.

———. *Luke-Acts and the Jews: Conflict, Apology, and Conciliation.* SBLMS 33. Atlanta: Scholars Press, 1987.

Brinkman, J. A. "The Literary Background of the 'Catalogue of the Nations' (Acts 2:9–11)." *CBQ* 25 (1963): 418–27.

Brodd, Jeffery, and Jonathan L. Reed, eds. *Rome and Religion: A Cross-Disciplinary Dialogue on the Imperial Cult.* Writings from the Greco-Roman World Supplement Series 5. Atlanta: Society of Biblical Literature, 2011.

Brubaker, Rogers. *Ethnicity Without Groups.* Cambridge, MA: Harvard University Press, 2004.

Bruce, F. F. *The Book of the Acts.* NICNT. Grand Rapids: Eerdmans, 1988.

Brunt, P. A. *Roman Imperial Themes.* Oxford: Oxford University Press, 1990.

Bryan, Christopher. "A Further Look at Acts 16:1–3." *JBL* 107 (1988): 292–94.

Buell, Denise Kimber. "Challenges and Strategies for Speaking About Ethnicity in the New Testament and New Testament Studies." *SEÅ* 49 (2014): 33–51.

———. "Early Christian Universalism and Modern Forms of Racism." Pages 109–31 in *The Origins of Racism in the West.* Edited by Miriam Eliav-Feldon, Benjamin H. Isaac, and Joseph Ziegler. Cambridge: Cambridge University Press, 2009.

———. "God's Own People: Specters of Race, Ethnicity, and Gender in Early Christian Studies." Pages 159–90 in *Prejudice and Christian Beginnings: Investigating Race, Gender, and Ethnicity in Early Christian Studies.* Edited by Elisabeth Schüssler Fiorenza and Laura Nasrallah. Minneapolis: Fortress, 2009.

———. "Producing Descent/Dissent: Clement of Alexandria's Use of Filial Metaphors as Intra-Christian Polemic." *HTR* 90 (1997): 89–104.

———. "Rethinking the Relevance of Race for Early Christian Self-Definition." *HTR* 94 (2001): 449–76.

————. *Why This New Race? Ethnic Reasoning in Early Christianity.* Gender, Theory, and Religion. New York: Columbia University Press, 2005.

Buell, Denise Kimber, and Caroline E. Johnson Hodge. "The Politics of Interpretation: The Rhetoric of Race and Ethnicity in Paul." *JBL* 123 (2004): 235–51.

Butticaz, Simon. *L'identité de l'église dans les actes des apôtres: de la restauration d'Israël à la conquête universelle.* Berlin: de Gruyter, 2010.

Cadbury, Henry J. *The Book of Acts in History.* London: A. & C. Black, 1955.

————. "Dust and Garments." Pages 269–77 in *The Beginnings of Christianity. Part 1: The Acts of the Apostles.* Edited by Kirsopp Lake and F. J. Foakes-Jackson. Vol. 5. New York: Macmillan, 1933.

————. *The Making of Luke-Acts.* New York: Macmillan, 1927.

————. "Some Foibles of New Testament Scholarship." *JBR* 26 (1958): 213–16.

Chrupcała, L. Daniel. *Everyone Will See the Salvation of God: Studies in Lukan Theology.* Studium Biblicum Franciscanum Analecta 83. Milan: Edizioni Terra Santa, 2015.

Cohen, Shaye J. D. *The Beginnings of Jewishness: Boundaries, Varieties, Uncertainties.* Berkeley: University of California Press, 2000.

————. "Crossing the Boundary and Becoming a Jew." *HTR* 82 (1989): 13–33.

————. "Was Timothy Jewish (Acts 16:1–3)? Patristic Exegesis, Rabbinic Law, and Matrilineal Descent." *JBL* 105 (1986): 251–68.

Collins, John J. "Symbolic Otherness." Pages 163–86 in *"To See Ourselves as Others See Us": Christians, Jews, "Others" in Late Antiquity.* Edited by Jacob Neusner and Ernest S. Frerichs. Chico, CA: Scholars Press, 1985.

Colson, F. H. *Philo.* Vol. 10. LCL. Cambridge, MA: Harvard University Press, 1971.

Concannon, Cavan W. *When You Were Gentiles: Specters of Ethnicity in Roman Corinth and Paul's Corinthian Correspondence.* New Haven: Yale University Press, 2014.

Conzelmann, Hans. *Acts of the Apostles: A Commentary on the Acts of the Apostles.* Translated by James Limburg, A. Thomas Kraabel, and Donald H. Juel. Hermeneia. Philadelphia: Fortress, 1987.

————. *The Theology of St. Luke.* Translated by Geoffrey Buswell. Philadelphia: Fortress, 1961.

Cumont, Franz. "La plus ancienne géographie astrologique." *Klio* 9 (1909): 263–73.

Davies, John Kenyon. "Phylai." In *The Oxford Classical Dictionary.* Edited by Simon Hornblower, Antony Spawforth, and Esther Eidinow. New York: Oxford University Press, 2012.

Deissmann, Adolf. *Light from the Ancient East: The New Testament Illustrated by Recently Discovered Texts of the Graeco-Roman World.* Translated by Lionel R. M. Strachan. New York: George H. Doran, 1927.

Dench, Emma. *Romulus' Asylum: Roman Identities from the Age of Alexander to the Age of Hadrian.* Oxford: Oxford University Press, 2005.

Devijver, H. *Prosopographia Militiarum Equestrium quae fuerunt ab Augusto ad Gallienum.* 3 vols. Symbolae Facultatis Litterarum et Philsophiae Lovaniensis A. Leuven: Universitaire Pers Leuven, 1976.

Dibelius, Martin. *Studies in the Acts of the Apostles.* Edited by Heinrich Greeven. Translated by Mary Ling. London: SCM, 1956.

Donaldson, Terence L. *Jews and Anti-Judaism in the New Testament: Decision Points and Divergent Interpretations.* Waco, TX: Baylor University Press, 2010.

———. *Judaism and the Gentiles: Jewish Patterns of Universalism (to 135 CE).* Waco, TX: Baylor University Press, 2008.

Dunn, James D. G. *The Acts of the Apostles.* Narrative Commentaries. Valley Forge, PA: Trinity Press International, 1996.

Dupont, Jacques. "La première pentecôte chrétienne (Actes 2, 1–11)." Pages 481–501 in *Études sur les Actes des Apôtres.* LD 45. Paris: Cerf, 1967.

Efroymson, David P. "The Patristic Connection." Pages 98–117 in *Antisemitism and the Foundations of Christianity.* Edited by Alan T. Davies. New York: Paulist, 1979.

Elsner, Jaś. *Art and the Roman Viewer: The Transformation of Art from the Pagan World to Christianity.* Cambridge: Cambridge University Press, 1995.

———. "The Origins of the Icon: Pilgrimage, Religion and Visual Culture in the Roman East as 'Resistance' to the Centre." Pages 178–199 in *The Early Roman Empire in the East.* Edited by Susan E. Alcock. Oxford: Oxbrow, 1997.

———. *Roman Eyes: Visuality and Subjectivity in Art and Text.* Princeton, NJ: Princeton University Press, 2007.

Erim, Kenan T. *Aphrodisias: City of Venus Aphrodite.* London: Muller, Bond & White, 1986.

Esler, Philip F. *Community and Gospel in Luke-Acts: The Social and Political Motivations of Lucan Theology.* SNTSMS 57. Cambridge: Cambridge University Press, 1987.

Farney, Gary D. *Ethnic Identity and Aristocratic Competition in Republican Rome.* Cambridge: Cambridge University Press, 2007.

Fitzmyer, Joseph A. *The Acts of the Apostles: A New Translation with Introduction and Commentary.* AB (Anchor Yale Bible) 31. New York: Doubleday, 1998.

Foakes-Jackson, F. J., and Henry J. Cadbury. *English Translation and Commentary*. Vol. 4. 5 vols. The Beginnings of Christianity. Part 1: Acts of the Apostles. London: Macmillan, 1933.

Foucault, Michel. *The Order of Things: An Archaeology of the Human Sciences*. New York: Pantheon, 1971.

Fredriksen, Paula. *Augustine and the Jews: A Christian Defense of Jews and Judaism*. New York: Doubleday, 2008.

——. *Jesus of Nazareth, King of the Jews: A Jewish Life and the Emergence of Christianity*. New York: Knopf, 1999.

——. "Judaism, the Circumcision of Gentiles, and Apocalyptic Hope: Another Look at Galatians 1 and 2." *JTS* 42 (1991): 532–64.

——. "Judaizing the Nations: The Ritual Demands of Paul's Gospel." *NTS* 56 (2010): 232–52.

——. "'Mandatory Retirement': Ideas in the Study of Christian Origins Whose Time Has Come to Go." *SR* 35 (2006): 231–46.

——. *Paul: The Pagans' Apostle*. New Haven, CT: Yale University Press, 2017.

——. "Paul, Practical Pluralism, and the Invention of Religious Persecution in Roman Antiquity." Pages 87–113 in *Understanding Religious Pluralism: Perspectives from Religious Studies and Theology*. Edited by Peter C. Phan and Jonathan Ray. Eugene, OR: Pickwick, 2014.

——. "The Question of Worship: Gods, Pagans, and the Redemption of Israel." Pages 175–201 in *Paul Within Judaism: Restoring the First-Century Context to the Apostle*. Edited by Mark D. Nanos and Magnus Zetterholm. Minneapolis: Fortress, 2015.

Fredriksen, Paula, and Oded Irshai. "Christian Anti-Judaism: Polemics and Policies." Pages 997–1034 in *The Late Roman-Rabbinic Period*. Edited by Steven T. Katz. Vol. 4. Cambridge: Cambridge University Press, 2006.

Friesen, Steven J. *Imperial Cults and the Apocalypse of John: Reading Revelation in the Ruins*. Oxford: Oxford University Press, 2006.

——. *Twice Neokoros: Ephesus, Asia, and the Cult of the Flavian Imperial Family*. Religions in the Graeco-Roman World 116. Leiden: Brill, 1993.

Gager, John G. *Reinventing Paul*. Oxford: Oxford University Press, 2000.

Garroway, Joshua D. *Paul's Gentile-Jews: Neither Jew nor Gentile, but Both*. New York: Palgrave Macmillan, 2012.

——. "The Pharisee Heresy: Circumcision for Gentiles in the Acts of the Apostles." *NTS* 60 (2014): 20–36.

Gasque, W. Ward. *A History of the Criticism of the Acts of the Apostles*. Grand Rapids: Eerdmans, 1975.

Geertz, Clifford. *The Interpretation of Cultures*. New York: Basic Books, 1973.

———. "Religion as a Cultural System." Pages 87–125 in *The Interpretation of Cultures*. New York: Basic Books, 1973.

"Gentile, adj. and n." *OED Online*. Oxford: Oxford University Press, 2015. http://www.oed.com/view/Entry/77647.

Gilbert, Gary. "The Disappearance of the Gentiles: God-fearers and the Image of the Jews in Luke-Acts." Pages 172–184 in *Putting Body and Soul Together: Essays in Honor of Robin Scroggs*. Edited by Virginia Wiles, Alexandra Brown, and Graydon F. Snyder. Valley Forge, PA: Trinity Press International, 1997.

———. "The List of Nations in Acts 2: Roman Propaganda and the Lukan Response." *JBL* 121 (2002): 497–529.

———. "The Making of a Jew: 'God-fearer' or Convert in the Story of Izates." *USQR* 44 (1991): 299–313.

Gleason, Maud W. "The Semiotics of Gender: Physiognomy and Self-Fashioning in the Second Century C.E." Pages 389–413 in *Before Sexuality: The Construction of Erotic Experience in the Ancient Greek World*. Edited by David M. Halperin, Froma I. Zeitlin, and John J. Winkler. Princeton: Princeton University Press, 1990.

Goldhill, Simon, ed. *Being Greek Under Rome: Cultural Identity, the Second Sophistic and the Development of Empire*. Cambridge: Cambridge University Press, 2001.

———. "Introduction: Setting the Agenda: 'Everything Is Greece to the Wise.'" Pages 1–29 in *Being Greek Under Rome: Cultural Identity, the Second Sophistic and the Development of Empire*. Edited by Simon Goldhill. Cambridge: Cambridge University Press, 2001.

Goulder, M. D. *Type and History in Acts*. London: SPCK, 1964.

Gradel, Ittai. *Emperor Worship and Roman Religion*. Oxford Classical Monographs. Oxford: Clarendon, 2002.

Graf, Fritz. "Pompai in Greece: Some Considerations About Space and Ritual in the Greek Polis." Pages 55–65 in *The Role of Religion in the Early Greek Polis: Proceedings of the Third International Seminar on Ancient Greek Cult, Organized by the Swedish Institute at Athens, 16–18 October 1992*. Edited by Robin Hägg. Skrifter Utgivna av Svenska Institutet I Athen, 8° 14. Stockholm: Paul Åströms, 1996.

Grebe, Sabine. "Augustus' Divine Authority and Vergil's 'Aeneid.'" *Vergilius* 50 (2004): 35–62.

Gruen, Erich S. *Diaspora: Jews Amidst Greeks and Romans*. Cambridge, MA: Harvard University Press, 2002.

Güting, Eberhard. "Der geographische Horizont der sogenannten Völkerliste des Lukas (Acta 2.9–11)." *ZNW* 66 (1975): 149–69.

Haenchen, Ernst. *The Acts of the Apostles: A Commentary*. Philadelphia: Westminster, 1971.

———. "The Book of Acts as Source Material for the History of Early Christianity." Pages 258–78 in *Studies in Luke-Acts: Essays Presented in Honor of Paul Schubert*. Edited by Leander E. Keck and J. Louis Martyn. Nashville: Abingdon, 1966.

Hakola, Raimo. "'Friendly' Pharisees and Social Identity in Acts." Pages 181–200 in *Contemporary Studies in Acts*. Edited by Thomas E. Phillips. Macon, GA: Mercer University Press, 2009.

Hall, Edith. *Inventing the Barbarian: Greek Self-Definition Through Tragedy*. Oxford: Oxford University Press, 1989.

Hall, Jonathan M. *Ethnic Identity in Greek Antiquity*. Cambridge: Cambridge University Press, 1997.

Hanneken, Todd R. "The Sin of the Gentiles: The Prohibition of Eating Blood in the Book of Jubilees." *JSJ* 46 (2015): 1–27.

Harland, Philip A. *Associations, Synagogues, and Congregations: Claiming a Place in Ancient Mediterranean Society*. Minneapolis: Fortress, 2003.

———. *Dynamics of Identity in the World of the Early Christians: Associations, Judeans, and Cultural Minorities*. New York: T&T Clark, 2009.

Harnack, Adolf von. *The Acts of the Apostles*. New York: Putnam, 1909.

Head, Peter M. "P127 = POxy 4968." Evangelical Textual Criticism, December 16, 2009. http://evangelicaltextualcriticism.blogspot.com/2009/12/p127-poxy -4968.html.

Heberdey, Rudolf, Wilhelm Wilberg, and G. Niemann. *Das Theater in Ephesos*. Vienna: A. Hölder, 1912.

Heschel, Susannah. *The Aryan Jesus: Christian Theologians and the Bible in Nazi Germany*. Princeton: Princeton University Press, 2008.

Holladay, Carl R. *Acts: A Commentary*. New Testament Library. Louisville: Westminster John Knox, 2016.

———. *Fragments from Hellenistic Jewish Authors*. 4 vols. SBL Texts and Translations: Pseudepigrapha. Chico, CA: Scholars Press, 1983.

Hubbard, Moyer V. "Urban Uprisings in the Roman World: The Social Setting of the Mobbing of Sosthenes." *NTS* 51 (2005): 416–28.

Hueber, F. "Der Embolos, ein urbanes Zentrum von Ephesos." *Antike Welt* 15 (1984): 3–23.

Hueber, Friedmund. "Der Baukomplex einer Julio-Claudischen Kaiserkultanlage in Aphrodisias: Ein Zwischenbericht zur Theoretischen Rekonstruktion des Baubestandes." Pages 101–22 in *Aphrodisias de Carie, colloque de l'Université de Lille III, 13 November 1985*. Edited by J. de la Genière and Kenan T. Erim. Paris: Recherche sur les civilisations, 1987.

Hutchinson, John, and Anthony D. Smith. "Introduction." Pages 3–16 in *Ethnicity*. Edited by John Hutchinson and Anthony D. Smith. Oxford: Oxford University Press, 1996.

Hvalvik, Reidar. "Paul as a Jewish Believer: According to the Book of Acts." Pages 121–53 in *Jewish Believers in Jesus: The Early Centuries*. Peabody, MA: Hendrickson, 2007.

Isaac, Benjamin H. *The Invention of Racism in Classical Antiquity*. Princeton: Princeton University Press, 2004.

Jenkins, Richard. *Rethinking Ethnicity: Arguments and Explorations*. Thousand Oaks, CA: Sage, 1997.

Jennings, Willie James. *Acts*. Belief: A Theological Commentary on the Bible. Louisville: Westminster John Knox, 2017.

Jervell, Jacob. "Das Gespaltene Israel und die Heidenvölker." *Studia Theologica* 19 (1965): 68–96.

———. *Die Apostelgeschichte: Übersetzt und erklärt*. 17th ed. KEK 3. Göttingen: Vandenhoeck & Ruprecht, 1998.

———. *Luke and the People of God: A New Look at Luke-Acts*. Minneapolis: Augsburg, 1972.

Johnson, Aaron P. *Ethnicity and Argument in Eusebius' Praeparatio Evangelica*. Oxford Early Christian Studies. Oxford: Oxford University Press, 2006.

Johnson Hodge, Caroline E. "Apostle to the Gentiles: Constructions of Paul's Identity." *BibInt* 13 (2005): 270–88.

———. *If Sons, Then Heirs: A Study of Kinship and Ethnicity in the Letters of Paul*. Oxford: Oxford University Press, 2007.

Johnson, Luke Timothy. *The Acts of the Apostles*. SP 5. Collegeville, MN: Liturgical Press, 2006.

Johnson, William A. *Readers and Reading Culture in the High Roman Empire: A Study of Elite Communities*. New York: Oxford University Press, 2010.

Jones, Christopher P. *Kinship Diplomacy in the Ancient World*. Cambridge, MA: Harvard University Press, 1999.

Keener, Craig S. *Acts: An Exegetical Commentary*. Vol. 1. Grand Rapids: Baker Academic, 2012.

———. *Acts: An Exegetical Commentary: 15:1–23:35*. Vol. 3. Grand Rapids: Baker Academic, 2014.

Kittel, Gerhard, and Gerhard Friedrich, eds. *Theological Dictionary of the New Testament*. Translated by Geoffrey W. Bromiley. 10 vols. Grand Rapids: Eerdmans, 1964–1976.

Klawans, Jonathan. *Impurity and Sin in Ancient Judaism*. New York: Oxford University Press, 2000.

————. *Josephus and the Theologies of Ancient Judaism.* Oxford: Oxford University Press, 2012.

————. "Josephus on Fate, Free Will, and Ancient Jewish Types of Compatibilism." *Numen* 56 (2009): 44–90.

————. "Josephus, the Rabbis, and Responses to Catastrophes Ancient and Modern." *Jewish Quarterly Review* 100 (2010): 278–309.

————. *Purity, Sacrifice, and the Temple: Symbolism and Supersessionism in the Study of Ancient Judaism.* Oxford: Oxford University Press, 2006.

Knibbe, Dieter. *Der Staatsmarkt: die Inschriften des Prytaneions: die Kureteninschriften und sonstige religiöse Texte.* Vienna: Österreichischen Akademie der Wissenschaften, 1981.

————. "Via Sacra Ephesiaca: New Aspects of the Cult of Artemis Ephesia." Pages 141–54 in *Ephesos: Metropolis of Asia. An Interdisciplinary Approach to Its Archaeology, Religion, and Culture.* Edited by Helmut Koester. Harvard Theological Studies 41. Cambridge, MA: Harvard University Press, 2004.

Knibbe, Dieter, and Gerhard Langmann. *Via Sacra Ephesiaca I.* Österreichisches Archäologisches Institut Berichte und Materialien 3. Vienna: Schindler, 1993.

Knox, John. *Marcion and the New Testament.* New York: AMS Press, 1980.

Knust, Jennifer Wright. *Abandoned to Lust: Sexual Slander and Ancient Christianity.* New York: Columbia University Press, 2006.

Kok, Michael. "The True Covenant People: Ethnic Reasoning in the Epistle of Barnabas." *SR* 40 (2011): 81–97.

Kraabel, A. Thomas. "The Disappearance of the God-Fearers." *Numen* 28 (1981): 113–26.

Kraemer, Ross Shepard. *Unreliable Witnesses: Religion, Gender, and History in the Greco-Roman Mediterranean.* Oxford: Oxford University Press, 2011.

Kuecker, Aaron. *Spirit and the "Other": Social Identity, Ethnicity and Intergroup Reconciliation in Luke-Acts.* Library of New Testament Studies 444. New York: T&T Clark, 2011.

Lake, Kirsopp. "The Gift of the Spirit on the Day of Pentecost." Pages 111–21 in *Additional Notes to the Commentary.* Edited by Kirsopp Lake and Henry J. Cadbury. Vol. 5. The Beginnings of Christianity. New York: Macmillan, 1933.

————. "Proselytes and Godfearers." Pages 74–96 in *The Beginnings of Christianity. Part 1: The Acts of the Apostles.* Vol. 5. New York: Macmillan, 1933.

Lake, Kirsopp, F. J. Foakes-Jackson, and Henry J. Cadbury. *The Beginnings of Christianity. Part 1: The Acts of the Apostles.* Vol. 5. New York: Macmillan, 1933.

Lane Fox, Robin. *Pagans and Christians.* New York: HarperCollins, 1988.

Leon, Harry J. *The Jews of Ancient Rome.* Updated ed. Peabody, MA: Hendrickson, 1995.

Levine, Amy-Jill. *The Misunderstood Jew: The Church and the Scandal of the Jewish Jesus.* San Francisco: Harper, 2006.

Levinskaya, I. A. *The Book of Acts in Its Diaspora Setting.* The Book of Acts in Its First Century Setting 5. Grand Rapids: Eerdmans, 1996.

Liddell, Henry George, Robert Scott, Henry Stuart Jones, and Roderick McKenzie. *A Greek-English Lexicon.* Oxford: Oxford University Press, 1996.

Lieu, Judith. *Image and Reality: The Jews in the World of the Christians in the Second Century.* Edinburgh: T&T Clark, 1996.

Lim, Richard. "The Gods of the Empire." Pages 260–89 in *The Cambridge Illustrated History of the Roman World.* Edited by Greg Woolf. Cambridge: Cambridge University Press, 2003.

Linder, Amnon. *The Jews in Roman Imperial Legislation.* Detroit: Wayne State University Press, 1987.

Livesey, Nina E. *Circumcision as a Malleable Symbol.* WUNT 2/295. Tübingen: Mohr Siebeck, 2010.

Lohfink, Gerhard. *Die Sammlung Israels: Eine Untersuchung zur lukanischen Ekklesiologie.* SANT 39. Munich: Kösel, 1975.

Lohse, Eduard. "Die Bedeutung des Pfingstberichtes im Rahmen des lukanischen Geschichtswerkes." *EvT* 13 (1953): 422–36.

Lopez, Davina C. *Apostle to the Conquered: Reimagining Paul's Mission.* Paul in Critical Contexts. Minneapolis: Fortress, 2008.

Malina, Bruce J., and John J. Pilch. *Social-Science Commentary on the Book of Acts.* Minneapolis: Fortress, 2008.

Malkin, Irad. "Introduction." Pages 1–28 in *Ancient Perceptions of Greek Ethnicity.* Edited by Irad Malkin. Cambridge, MA: Harvard University Press, 2001.

Marshall, Mary. *The Portrayals of the Pharisees in the Gospels and Acts.* Forschungen zur Religion und Literatur des Alten und Neuen Testaments 254. Göttingen: Vandenhoeck & Ruprecht, 2015.

Mason, Steve. "Jews, Judaeans, Judaizing, Judaism: Problems of Categorization in Ancient History." *JSJ* 38 (2007): 457–512.

———. *Josephus and the New Testament.* 2nd ed. Peabody, MA: Hendrickson, 2003.

———. "Of Audience and Meaning: Reading Josephus' Bellum Judaicum in the Context of a Flavian Audience." Pages 71–100 in *Josephus and Jewish History in Flavian Rome and Beyond.* Edited by Joseph Sievers and Gaia Lembi. Boston: Brill, 2005.

———. "Series Preface." *Judean Antiquities.* Flavius Josephus: Translation and Commentary. Leiden: Brill, 2000.

Matthews, Shelly. *Perfect Martyr: The Stoning of Stephen and the Construction of Christian Identity.* Oxford: Oxford University Press, 2010.

Mattill, Mary, and A. J. Mattill. *A Classified Bibliography of Literature on the Acts of the Apostles.* Leiden: Brill, 1966.

McEleney, Neil J. "Conversion, Circumcision and the Law." *NTS* 20 (1974): 328–33.

McRay, John. "Archaeology and the Book of Acts." *CTR* 5 (1990): 69–82.

Metzger, Bruce M. *A Textual Commentary on the Greek New Testament: A Companion Volume to the United Bible Societies' Greek New Testament.* 3rd ed. New York: United Bible Societies, 1975.

Migne, J.-P. *Patrologiae cursus completus: series Graeca.* Paris, 1857.

Miller, David M. "Ethnicity Comes of Age: An Overview of Twentieth-Century Terms for Ioudaios." *CBR* 10 (2012): 293–311.

———. "Ethnicity, Religion and the Meaning of Ioudaios in Ancient 'Judaism.'" *CBR* 12 (2014): 216–65.

———. "The Meaning of Ioudaios and Its Relationship to Other Group Labels in Ancient 'Judaism.'" *CBR* 9 (2010): 98–126.

Millis, Benjamin W. "The Social and Ethnic Origins of the Colonist in Early Roman Corinth." Pages 13–36 in *Corinth in Context: Comparative Studies on Religion and Society.* Edited by Steven J. Friesen, Daniel N. Schowalter, and James C. Walters. Leiden: Brill, 2010.

Minear, Paul S. "Luke's Use of the Birth Stories." Pages 111–30 in *Studies in Luke-Acts: Essays Presented in Honor of Paul Schubert.* Nashville: Abingdon, 1966.

Moessner, David P. "The Ironic Fulfillment of Israel's Glory." Pages 35–51 in *Luke-Acts and the Jewish People: Eight Critical Perspectives.* Edited by Joseph B. Tyson. Minneapolis: Augsburg, 1988.

Moles, John. "Time and Space Travel in Luke-Acts." Pages 101–22 in *Engaging Early Christian History: Reading Acts in the Second Century.* Edited by Rubén R. Dupertuis and Todd C. Penner. BibleWorld. Durham: Acumen, 2013.

Murphy-O'Connor, J. *St. Paul's Corinth: Texts and Archaeology.* Collegeville, MN: Liturgical Press, 1990.

Nanos, Mark D. "The Question of Conceptualization: Qualifying Paul's Position on Circumcision in Dialogue with Josephus's Advisors to King Izates." Pages 105–52 in *Paul Within Judaism: Restoring the First-Century Context to the Apostle.* Edited by Mark D. Nanos and Magnus Zetterholm. Minneapolis: Fortress, 2015.

Nasrallah, Laura Salah. "The Acts of the Apostles, Greek Cities, and Hadrian's Panhellenion." *JBL* 127 (2008): 533–66.

———. *Christian Responses to Roman Art and Architecture: The Second-Century Church Amid the Spaces of Empire.* Cambridge: Cambridge University Press, 2010.

Nasrallah, Laura Salah, and Elisabeth Schüssler Fiorenza, eds. *Prejudice and Christian Beginnings: Investigating Race, Gender, and Ethnicity in Early Christian Studies.* Minneapolis: Fortress, 2009.

Nestle, Eberhard, Erwin Nestle, Kurt Aland, and Barbara Aland, eds. *Novum Testamentum Graece.* 28th ed. Stuttgart: Deutsche Bibelstiftung, 2012.

Nicklas, Tobias. "Versöhnung mit Israel im Matthäusevangelium?" *Bibel und Liturgie* 88 (2015): 17–24.

Nock, Arthur Darby. *Conversion: The Old and the New in Religion from Alexander the Great to Augustine of Hippo.* Oxford: Oxford University Press, 1933.

Nolland, John. "Uncircumcised Proselytes?" *JSJ* 12 (1981): 173–94.

Novak, David. *The Image of the Non-Jew in Judaism: The Idea of Noahide Law.* Lewiston, NY: Mellen, 1983.

O'Donnell, James J. "The Demise of Paganism." *Traditio* 35 (1979): 45–88.

Oliver, H. H. "The Lucan Birth Stories and the Purpose of Luke-Acts." *NTS* 10 (1964): 202–26.

Oliver, Isaac W. *Torah Praxis after 70 CE: Reading Matthew and Luke-Acts as Jewish Texts.* WUNT 2/355. Tübingen: Mohr Siebeck, 2013.

Oster, Richard E. "Ephesus as a Religious Center Under the Principate, I: Paganism Before Constantine." Pages 1661–1728 in *ANRW* 2.18:3. Berlin: de Gruyter, 1990.

Packard Humanities Institute. "Searchable Greek Inscriptions: A Scholarly Tool in Progress." Last updated November 1, 2017. http://epigraphy.packhum.org/inscriptions/main.

Paden, William. *Religious Worlds: The Comparative Study of Religion.* Boston: Beacon, 1994.

Parsons, Mikeal C., and Richard I. Pervo, eds. *Rethinking the Unity of Luke and Acts.* Minneapolis: Fortress, 1993.

Parsons, Mikeal C. *Acts.* Grand Rapids: Baker Academic, 2008.

Pausanias. *Description of Greece.* Translated by W. H. S. Jones. 4 vols. LCL. Cambridge, MA: Harvard University Press, 1933.

Peirano, Irene. "Hellenized Romans and Barbarized Greeks. Reading the End of Dionysius of Halicarnassus, Antiquitates Romanae." *JRS* 100 (2010): 32–53.

Pervo, Richard I. *Acts: A Commentary.* Hermeneia. Minneapolis: Fortress, 2008.

———. "Acts in the Suburbs of the Apologists." Pages 29–46 in *Contemporary Studies in Acts*. Edited by Thomas E. Phillips. Macon, GA: Mercer University Press, 2009.

———. *Dating Acts: Between the Evangelists and the Apologists*. Santa Rosa, CA: Polebridge, 2006.

Phillips, Thomas E. "Prophets, Priests, and Godfearing Readers: The Priestly and Prophetic Traditions in Luke-Acts." Pages 222–39 in *Contemporary Studies in Acts*. Edited by Thomas E. Phillips. Macon, GA: Mercer University Press, 2009.

Pickett, Raymond. "Luke and Empire: An Introduction." Pages 1–22 in *Luke-Acts and Empire: Essays in Honor of Robert L. Brawley*. Edited by David M. Rhoads, David Esterline, and Jae-won Lee. Princeton Theological Monograph Series 151. Eugene, OR: Wipf & Stock, 2011.

Plunkett, Mark A. "Ethnocentricity and Salvation History in the Cornelius Episode." Pages 465–80 in *Society of Biblical Literature 1985 Seminar Papers*. Edited by Keith H. Richards. SBLSP 24. Atlanta: Scholars Press, 1985.

Powell, Mark Allan. *What Are They Saying About Acts?* New York: Paulist, 1991.

Preston, Rebecca. "Roman Questions, Greek Answers: Plutarch and the Construction of Identity." Pages 86–119 in *Being Greek Under Rome: Cultural Identity, the Second Sophistic and the Development of Empire*. Edited by Simon Goldhill. Cambridge: Cambridge University Press, 2001.

Price, Simon R. F. *Rituals and Power: The Roman Imperial Cult in Asia Minor*. Cambridge: Cambridge University Press, 1984.

Rajak, Tessa. "Friends, Romans, Subjects: Agrippa II's Speech in Josephus's Jewish War." Pages 122–34 in *Images of Empire*. Edited by Loveday Alexander. JSOTSSup 122. Sheffield: JSOT Press, 1991.

———. "Greeks and Barbarians in Josephus." Pages 244–62 in *Hellenism in the Land of Israel*. Edited by John J. Collins and Gregory E. Sterling. South Bend, IN: University of Notre Dame Press, 2001.

———. "Was There a Roman Charter for the Jews?" *JRS* 74 (1984): 107–23.

Rajak, Tessa, and David Noy. "Archisynagogoi: Office, Title and Social Status in the Greco-Jewish Synagogue." *JRS* 83 (1993): 75–93.

Revell, Louise. *Roman Imperialism and Local Identities*. Cambridge: Cambridge University Press, 2009.

Reynolds, Joyce M. *Aphrodisias and Rome: Documents from the Excavation of the Theatre at Aphrodisias Conducted by Professor Kenan T. Erim, Together with Some Related Texts*. London: Society for the Promotion of Roman Studies, 1982.

———. "New Evidence for the Imperial Cult in Julio-Claudian Aphrodisias." *ZPE* 43 (1981): 317–27.

Reynolds, Joyce, Charlotte Roueché, and Gabriel Bodard. *Inscriptions of Aphro-disias*. Last updated October 1, 2017. http://insaph.kcl.ac.uk/iaph2007.

Reynolds, Joyce Marie, and Robert Tannenbaum. *Jews and God-Fearers at Aph-rodisias: Greek Inscriptions with Commentary: Texts from the Excavations at Aphrodisias Conducted by Kenan T. Erim*. Cambridge: Cambridge Phil-ological Society, 1987.

Rives, James B. "Graeco-Roman Religion in the Roman Empire: Old Assump-tions and New Approaches." *CBR* 8 (2010): 240–99.

———. *Religion in the Roman Empire*. Blackwell Ancient Religions. Malden, MA: Blackwell, 2007.

Rogers, Guy MacLean. *The Mysteries of Artemis of Ephesos: Cult, Polis, and Change in the Graeco-Roman World*. New Haven: Yale University Press, 2013.

———. *The Sacred Identity of Ephesos: Foundation Myths of a Roman City*. New York: Routledge, 1991.

Rothschild, Clare K. *Paul in Athens: The Popular Religious Context of Acts 17*. WUNT 341. Tübingen: Mohr Siebeck, 2014.

Rowe, C. Kavin. *World Upside Down: Reading Acts in the Graeco-Roman Age*. Ox-ford: Oxford University Press, 2009.

Runesson, Anders. "Inventing Christian Identity: Paul, Ignatius, and Theodo-sius I." Pages 59–92 in *Exploring Early Christian Identity*. Edited by Bengt Holmberg. WUNT 226. Tübingen: Mohr Siebeck, 2008.

Rutgers, Leonard Victor. *The Hidden Heritage of Diaspora Judaism*. Leuven: Peeters, 1998.

———. *The Jews in Late Ancient Rome: Evidence of Cultural Interaction in the Roman Diaspora*. Religions in the Graeco-Roman World 126. Leiden: Brill, 1995.

Salmon, Marilyn. "Insider or Outsider? Luke's Relationship with Judaism." Pages 76–82 in *Luke-Acts and the Jewish People: Eight Critical Perspectives*. Edited by Joseph B. Tyson. Minneapolis: Augsburg, 1988.

Sanders, E. P. *Jesus and Judaism*. Philadelphia: Fortress, 1985.

Sanders, Jack T. "The Jewish People in Luke-Acts." Pages 51–75 in *Luke-Acts and the Jewish People: Eight Critical Perspectives*. Edited by Joseph B. Tyson. Minneapolis: Augsburg, 1988.

———. *The Jews in Luke-Acts*. Philadelphia: Fortress, 1987.

———. "The Salvation of the Jews in Luke-Acts." Pages 104–28 in *Luke-Acts: New Perspectives from the Society of Biblical Literature*. Edited by Charles H. Talbert. New York: Crossroad, 1988.

———. "Who Is a Jew and Who Is a Gentile in the Book of Acts." *NTS* 37 (1991): 434–55.

Schäfer, Peter. *Judeophobia: Attitudes Toward the Jews in the Ancient World*. Cambridge, MA: Harvard University Press, 1997.

Scheidel, Walter, and Steven J. Friesen. "The Size of the Economy and the Distribution of Income in the Roman Empire." *JRS* 99 (2009): 61–91.

Scherrer, Peter. "The City of Ephesos from the Roman Period to Late Antiquity." Pages 1–25 in *Ephesos: Metropolis of Asia. An Interdisciplinary Approach to Its Archaeology, Religion, and Culture*. Edited by Helmut Koester. Harvard Theological Studies 41. Cambridge, MA: Harvard University Press, 2004.

———, ed. *Ephesus: The New Guide*. Istanbul: Ege Yayınları, 2000.

Schmidt, Ernst A. "The Meaning of Vergil's Aeneid: American and German Approaches." *CW* 94 (2001): 145–71.

Schram, Terry. "The Use of ΙΟΥΔΑΙΟΣ in the Fourth Gospel: An Application of Some Linguistic Insights to a New Testament Problem." PhD diss., Utrecht University, 1974.

Schürer, Emil. *The History of the Jewish People in the Age of Jesus Christ (175 B.C.–A.D. 135)*. Edited by Geza Vermes, Martin Goodman, and Fergus Millar. 3 vols. Rev. ed. Edinburgh: T&T Clark, 1973.

Schwartz, Daniel R. "'Judaean' or 'Jew'? How Should We Translate Ioudaios in Josephus." Pages 3–28 in *Jewish Identity in the Greco-Roman World*. Ancient Judaism and Early Christianity. Leiden: Brill, 2007.

Schwartz, Seth. "How Many Judaisms Were There? A Critique of Neusner and Smith on Definition and Mason and Boyarin on Categorization." *JAJ* 2 (2011): 208–38.

———. "The Rabbi in Aphrodite's Bath: Palestinian Society and Jewish Identity in the High Roman Empire." Pages 335–61 in *Being Greek Under Rome: Cultural Identity, the Second Sophistic and the Development of Empire*. Edited by Simon Goldhill. Cambridge: Cambridge University Press, 2001.

Scott, James M. "Acts 2:9–11 as an Anticipation of the Mission to the Nations." Pages 87–123 in *The Mission of the Early Church to Jews and Gentiles*. Edited by J. Adna and H. Kvalbein. Tübingen: Mohr Siebeck, 2000.

———. "Luke's Geographical Horizon." Pages 483–544 in *The Book of Acts in Its Graeco-Roman Setting*. The Book of Acts in Its First Century Setting 2. Grand Rapids: Eerdmans, 1994.

———. *Paul and the Nations: The Old Testament and Jewish Background of Paul's Mission to the Nations with Special Reference to the Destination of Galatians*. WUNT 84. Tübingen: Mohr Siebeck, 1995.

Segal, Alan F. *Paul the Convert: The Apostolate and Apostasy of Saul the Pharisee*. New Haven: Yale University Press, 1990.

Sforza, Francesco. "The Problem of Virgil." *CR* 49 (1935): 97–108.

Shellberg, Pamela. *Cleansed Lepers, Cleansed Hearts: Purity and Healing in Luke-Acts*. Emerging Scholars. Minneapolis: Fortress, 2015.

Sherwin-White, A. N. *Roman Society and Roman Law in the New Testament*. Oxford: Clarendon, 1963.

Sleeman, Matthew. *Geography and the Ascension Narrative in Acts*. SNTSMS 146. Cambridge: Cambridge University Press, 2009.

Slingerland, H. Dixon. "'The Jews' in the Pauline Portion of Acts." *JAAR* 54 (1986): 305–21.

Smallwood, E. Mary. *The Jews Under Roman Rule: From Pompey to Diocletian: A Study in Political Relations*. 2nd ed. SJLA 20. Leiden: Brill, 1981.

Smith, Anthony D. *The Ethnic Origins of Nations*. Oxford: Blackwell, 1987.

———. *National Identity*. London: Penguin, 1991.

Smith, Daniel Lynwood. *The Rhetoric of Interruption: Speech-Making, Turn-Taking, and Rule-Breaking in Luke-Acts and Ancient Greek Narrative*. Berlin: de Gruyter, 2012.

Smith, Mitzi J. *The Literary Construction of the Other in the Acts of the Apostles: Charismatics, the Jews, and Women*. Eugene, OR: Pickwick, 2011.

Smith, R. R. R. "The Imperial Reliefs from the Sebasteion at Aphrodisias." *JRS* 77 (1987): 88–138.

———. "Myth and Allegory in the Sebasteion." Pages 89–100 in *Aphrodisias Papers: Recent Work on Architecture and Sculpture*. Edited by Charlotte Roueché and Kenan T. Erim. JRASS 1. Ann Arbor, MI: Journal of Roman Archaeology, 1990.

———. "Simulacra Gentium: The Ethne from the Sebasteion at Aphrodisias." *JRS* 78 (1988): 50–77.

Sourvinou-Inwood, Christiane. "What Is Polis Religion?" Pages 295–322 in *The Greek City from Homer to Alexander*. Edited by Simon R. F. Price and Oswyn Murray. Oxford: Clarendon, 1990.

Stavrianopoulou, Eftychia. "The Archaeology of Processions." Pages 349–61 in *A Companion to the Archaeology of Religion in the Ancient World*. Edited by Rubina Raja and Jörg Rüpke. Blackwell Companions to the Ancient World. Oxford: Wiley-Blackwell, 2015.

Stendahl, Krister. "The Apostle Paul and the Introspective Conscience of the West." *HTR* 56 (1963): 199–215.

Stern, Menahem. *Greek and Latin Authors on Jews and Judaism*. Jerusalem: Israel Academy of Sciences and Humanities, 1974.

Stoler, Ann Laura. *Along the Archival Grain: Epistemic Anxieties and Colonial Common Sense*. Princeton: Princeton University Press, 2009.

———. *Carnal Knowledge and Imperial Power: Race and the Intimate in Colonial Rule*. Berkeley: University of California Press, 2002.

———. "Racial Histories and Their Regimes of Truth." *Political Power and Social Theory* 11 (1997): 183–206.

Stowers, Stanley K. "Review of *Why This New Race? Ethnic Reasoning in Early Christianity*." *JAAR* 75 (2007): 727–30.

Strabo. *Geography*. Translated by Horace L. Jones. 8 vols. LCL. Cambridge, MA: Harvard University Press, 1929.

Swain, Simon. *Hellenism and Empire: Language, Classicism, and Power in the Greek World AD 50–250*. Oxford: Clarendon, 1996.

Swanson, Reuben, ed. *New Testament Greek Manuscripts: Variant Readings Arranged in Horizontal Lines Against Codex Vaticanus: Acts*. Sheffield: Sheffield Academic Press, 1998.

Taeuber, Hans. "C. Vibius Salutaris—Wohnungsbesitzer im Hanghaus 2?" Pages 349–53 in *Synergia: Festschrift für Friedrich Krinzinger*. Edited by Barbara Brandt, Verena Gassner, and Sabine Ladstätter. Vienna: Phoibos, 2005.

Tajra, H. W. *The Trial of St. Paul: A Juridical Exegesis of the Second Half of the Acts of the Apostles*. Tübingen: Mohr Siebeck, 1989.

Talbert, Charles H. *Luke and the Gnostics: An Examination of the Lucan Purpose*. Nashville: Abingdon, 1966.

Tannehill, Robert C. "Israel in Luke-Acts: A Tragic Story." *JBL* 104 (1985): 69–85.

———. *The Narrative Unity of Luke-Acts: A Literary Interpretation*. 2 vols. Philadelphia: Fortress, 1991.

———. "Rejection by Jews and Turning to Gentiles: The Pattern of Paul's Mission in Acts." Pages 83–101 in *Luke-Acts and the Jewish People: Eight Critical Perspectives*. Edited by Joseph B. Tyson. Minneapolis: Augsburg, 1988.

Taussig, Hal. "Melancholy, Colonialism, and Complicity: Complicating Counterimperial Readings of Aphrodisias' Sebasteion." Pages 280–95 in *Text, Image, and Christians in the Graeco-Roman World: A Festschrift in Honor of David Lee Balch*. Edited by Aliou Cissé Niang and Caroline E. Osiek. Princeton Theological Monograph Series. Eugene, OR: Pickwick, 2012.

Taylor, Justin. "The Jerusalem Decrees (Acts 15.20, 29 and 21.25) and the Incident at Antioch (Gal 2.11–14)." *NTS* 47 (2001): 372–80.

Taylor, Lily Ross. *The Voting Districts of the Roman Republic: The Thirty-Five Urban and Rural Tribes*. Papers and Monographs of the American Academy in Rome 20. Rome: American Academy in Rome, 1960.

Thiessen, Matthew. *Contesting Conversion: Genealogy, Circumcision, and Identity in Ancient Judaism and Christianity*. Oxford: Oxford University Press, 2011.

———. "Revisiting the προσήλυτος in 'the LXX.'" *JBL* 132 (2013): 333–50.

Thomas, Christine M. "Greek Heritage in Roman Corinth and Ephesos: Hybrid Identities and Strategies of Display in the Material Record of Traditional Mediterranean Religions." Pages 117–47 in *Corinth in Context: Comparative Studies on Religion and Society.* Edited by Steven J. Friesen, Daniel N. Schowalter, and James C. Walters. Leiden: Brill, 2010.

Thür, Hilke. "The Processional Way in Ephesos as a Place of Cult and Burial." Pages 157–87 in *Ephesos: Metropolis of Asia: An Interdisciplinary Approach to Its Archaeology, Religion, and Culture.* Edited by Helmut Koester. Harvard Theological Studies 41. Cambridge, MA: Harvard University Press, 2004.

Tiede, David L. "'Glory to Thy People Israel': Luke-Acts and the Jews." Pages 21–34 in *Luke-Acts and the Jewish People: Eight Critical Perspectives.* Edited by Joseph B. Tyson. Minneapolis: Augsburg, 1988.

Tilborg, Sjef Van. *Reading John in Ephesus.* Leiden: Brill, 1996.

Townsend, John T. "The Date of Luke-Acts." Pages 47–62 in *Luke-Acts: New Perspectives from the Society of Biblical Literature Seminar.* Edited by Charles H. Talbert. New York: Crossroad, 1986.

Trebilco, Paul R. "The Province of Asia." Pages 292–362 in *The Book of Acts in Its Graeco-Roman Setting.* Edited by David W. J. Gill and Conrad H. Gempf. The Book of Acts in Its First Century Setting 2. Grand Rapids: Eerdmans, 1994.

———. "Why Did the Early Christians Call Themselves ἡ ἐκκλησία?" *NTS* 57 (2011): 440–60.

Tyson, Joseph B. *Images of Judaism in Luke-Acts.* Columbia: University of South Carolina Press, 1992.

———. "The Jewish Public in Luke-Acts." *NTS* 30 (1984): 574–83.

———. "Jews and Judaism in Luke-Acts: Reading as a Godfearer." *NTS* 41 (1995): 19–38.

———, ed. *Luke-Acts and the Jewish People: Eight Critical Perspectives.* Minneapolis: Augsburg, 1988.

———. *Luke, Judaism, and the Scholars: Critical Approaches to Luke-Acts.* Columbia: University of South Carolina Press, 1999.

———. *Marcion and Luke-Acts: A Defining Struggle.* Columbia: University of South Carolina Press, 2006.

———. "The Problem of Jewish Rejection in Acts." Pages 124–37 in *Luke-Acts and the Jewish People: Eight Critical Perspectives.* Edited by Joseph B. Tyson. Minneapolis: Augsburg, 1988.

Walaskay, Paul W. *And So We Came to Rome: The Political Perspective of St. Luke.* Cambridge: Cambridge University Press, 2005.

Walbank, Mary E. Hoskins. "Review of the Sacred Identity of Ephesos." *Phoenix* 48 (1994): 89–91.

Wallace-Hadrill, Andrew. *Rome's Cultural Revolution*. Cambridge: Cambridge University Press, 2008.

Walters, Patricia. *The Assumed Authorial Unity of Luke and Acts: A Reassessment of the Evidence*. Cambridge: Cambridge University Press, 2009.

Walton, Steve. "Trying Paul or Trying Rome? Judges and Accused in the Roman Trials of Paul in Acts." Pages 122–41 in *Luke-Acts and Empire: Essays in Honor of Robert L. Brawley*. Edited by David M. Rhoads, David Esterline, and Jae-won Lee. Princeton Theological Monograph Series 151. Eugene, OR: Wipf & Stock, 2011.

Wander, Bernd. *Gottesfürchtige und Sympathisanten: Studien zum heidnischen Umfeld von Diasporasynagogen*. Tübingen: Mohr Siebeck, 1998.

Weatherly, Jon A. *Jewish Responsibility for the Death of Jesus in Luke-Acts.* JSNTS 106. Sheffield: Sheffield Academic Press, 1994.

Wedderburn, A. J. M. "The 'Apostolic Decree': Tradition and Redaction." *NT* 35 (1993): 362–89.

———. "Traditions and Redaction in Acts 2:1–13." *JSNT* 55 (1994): 27–54.

Weinstock, Stefan. "The Geographical Catalogue in Acts II, 9–11." *JRS* 38 (1948): 43–46.

White, L. Michael. "Urban Development and Social Change in Imperial Ephesos." Pages 27–65 in *Ephesos: Metropolis of Asia: An Interdisciplinary Approach to Its Archaeology, Religion, and Culture*. Edited by Helmut Koester. Harvard Theological Studies 41. Cambridge, MA: Harvard University Press, 2004.

Whitmarsh, Tim. *Greek Literature and the Roman Empire: The Politics of Imitation*. Oxford: Oxford University Press, 2001.

———. *Narrative and Identity in the Ancient Greek Novel: Returning Romance*. Cambridge: Cambridge University Press, 2011.

———. "Reading Power in Roman Greece: The Paideia of Dio Chrysostom." Pages 192–213 in *Pedagogy and Power: Rhetorics of Classical Learning*. Edited by Yun Lee Too and Niall Livingstone. Ideas in Context 50. Cambridge: Cambridge University Press, 1998.

———. *The Second Sophistic*. Greece & Rome 35. Oxford: Oxford University Press, 2005.

Williams, Margaret. *The Jews Among the Greeks and Romans: A Diasporan Sourcebook*. Baltimore: Johns Hopkins University Press, 1998.

Wills, Lawrence M. "The Depiction of the Jews in Acts." *JBL* 110 (1991): 631–54.

———. "Jewish Novellas in a Greek and Roman Age: Fiction and Identity." *JSJ* 42 (2011): 141–65.

———. *Not God's People: Insiders and Outsiders in the Biblical World.* Lanham, MD: Rowman & Littlefield, 2008.

Wilson, Stephen G. *The Gentiles and the Gentile Mission in Luke-Acts.* Cambridge: Cambridge University Press, 2005.

———. *Luke and the Law.* SNTSMS 50. Cambridge: Cambridge University Press, 1983.

Winter, Bruce W. "Gallio's Ruling on the Legal Status of Early Christianity (Acts 18:14–15)." *TynBul* 50 (1999): 213–24.

Witherington, Ben. *The Acts of the Apostles: A Socio-Rhetorical Commentary.* Grand Rapids: Eerdmans, 1998.

Wood, John Turtle. *Discoveries at Ephesus: Including the Sites and Remains of the Great Temple of Diana.* London: Longmans, Green, 1877.

Woolf, Greg. *Becoming Roman: The Origins of Provincial Civilization in Gaul.* Cambridge: Cambridge University Press, 2000.

———. "Monumental Writing and the Expansion of Roman Society in the Early Empire." *JRS* 86 (1996): 22–39.

———. "Polis-Religion and Its Alternatives in the Roman Provinces." Pages 71–84 in *Römische Reichsreligion und Provinzialreligion.* Edited by Hubert Cancik and Jörg Rüpke. Tübingen: Mohr Siebeck, 1997.

Zanker, Paul. *The Power of Images in the Age of Augustus.* Ann Arbor: University of Michigan Press, 1990.

Ziegler, Joseph, ed. *Duodecim prophetae.* 2nd ed. Septuagint 12. Göttingen: Vandenhoeck & Ruprecht, 1967.

Index of Subjects

Acts: dating of, 19–20; urban context of, 1–3, 9, 20–23, 33–34, 71, 103, 125, 132–33

Aeneas, 43–44, 48, 51, 67–68, 129, 155n31; shield of, 47, 50, 62, 159n71. *See also* Virgil

Antioch, 83–84, 86–87, 90, 108, 118, 126, 168n54, 169n61

Aphrodisian identity, 15, 48–52, 64, 68

Aphrodisias, city of, ix–xi, 48–52; Sebasteion, 11, 14–15, 41–42, 48–52, 57, 61–63, 67–69, 129, 139n50, 154nn16,17. *See also* Aphrodisian identity; Caria

Aphrodite, 15, 42–44, 48–49, 51, 58, 67–68, 129

Artemis, 72–76, 106, 126–27, 165n33, 167n45, 174nn7,8; annual procession of, 97–102, 112; narrative of Acts and 9, 36–37, 80, 83, 103, 139n42; Salutaris Foundation and, 79–80, 82, 91, 103

Artemision, 72–75, 103, 163nn7,19, 164n22, 175n9; procession from, 98–99, 100–102, 112

Athens, 37–38, 104, 114, 117, 127, 132, 166n39, 181nn54,55

Augustus, 42–44, 47–48, 50–51, 67–68, 154nn7,8

benefaction, 1, 16, 22, 42, 52, 72–73, 75, 77–79, 96, 128–29, 173n3, 181n62; Acts and, 114–15, 121–23, 125–26

Caria, 44, 50–52, 57–58, 68, 73, 129, 131, 163n16

Christian identity, 14, 18, 22–23, 34, 58, 64, 80–81, 107–8, 119; the *polis* and, 1–3, 8, 20, 22–23, 104–5, 112–13, 131

Christian Pharisees, 84, 86–87, 90, 92, 94, 109, 111. *See also* Christian identity; Jerusalem council

circumcision, 67, 80–87, 93–94, 107–11, 123, 128–30, 141n70, 161n87, 169nn60,63, 66,67,68, 172n105, 179n39. *See also* Jerusalem council; Timothy, as symbol of Christian Jewishness

civic association, 21, 70, 173n3; Jewish, 16, 104, 122, 133, 144n22, 186n96

civic authority, 117, 144n21

civic identity, 3–4, 6–8, 10–11, 23, 35, 41, 70–71, 94, 122, 128–29, 132, 184n82

civic space, 16, 73, 96, 101, 103, 107, 116–17, 129; sculptures and, 1, 41–43, 47–48, 72–73, 75–77, 83, 95, 98, 100–102, 165n33, 174n8

Corinth, 36, 45 97, 107; Lukan Jewish association and 117–19, 120 123–27

Cornelius, 56, 81–83, 87, 157n49, 168nn58,60, 169n66

Crispus, 118, 121–23, 126, 184n80

diaspora, 7, 19, 21, 26, 44–45, 55, 61, 144n22

Ephesian identity, 16, 72, 76–81, 93, 97–99, 101–2, 105–6, 108–9, 112, 121–22, 126

209

Ephesus, 36, 71–77, 96–97, 98–103, 106,
112; agoras, 74, 99–101, 116; composition of Acts and, 20–21; council of,
77–80; Embolos, 100–101, 165n30,
175nn13,14; Prytaneion, 74, 100,
102–3, 164n22, 175n13, 176nn16,20;
Stoa Basilica, 74, 100, 175n13; theater
of, 9–10, 72, 75–76, 99, 191–202.
See also Artemis; Artemision;
Salutaris Foundation
ethnic difference, 4, 42, 48, 50–51, 54,
64, 104, 110
ethnic identity, 2, 4–5; ancestral customs
and, 15, 22, 36, 39, 41, 46, 55, 67–68,
70, 85, 106, 170n77; ancestral deities
and, 3, 15, 21, 25, 35, 38–39, 46–47,
58, 70–71, 80–81, 84, 94, 126;
flexibility of, 71, 86, 94, 96, 103;
mythic past and, 15, 22, 49, 71, 73–76,
80–81, 90, 93–94, 96, 107. *See also*
civic identity; hybridity
ethnic reasoning, definition of, 5–9, 11,
14–16; civic identity and, 42, 50–51,
129–31; empire and, 42–44, 46,
50–52, 58, 61, 64; Jerusalem council
and, 92–95; Lukan use of, 18, 35–40,
55–58, 66, 68–69, 71, 73, 80;
movement and, 96–98, 104–7,
117–19, 126–27; Roman use of, 50,
61–64, 100
ethnic rhetoric, 3, 5–6, 10, 18, 23, 41–42,
61–64

Godfearers, 115, 118, 121, 141n70, 161n88,
180nn49,51. *See also* proselytes
Greekness, 21–22, 145n26

hybridity, 2–3, 6, 8, 14, 18, 41, 45, 51–52,
57, 110–11, 118, 123, 135n3

Irenaeus, 20, 29, 140n63, 142n5, 150n81
Izates, 85–86, 170n73

Jerusalem, 36, 41, 44–47, 52–55, 57–58,
62, 65–66, 109–10, 112, 118, 126–27,
131, 144n19, 160n84, 168n59, 170n71,
179–80n43. *See also* Jerusalem
council
Jerusalem council, 15, 70–71, 80–81,
83–84, 87–94, 96–97, 104, 107–12,
129–30, 167n53, 169n66
Jewish identity, 41, 51–52, 57, 63–68,
80, 110–11, 117–18, 122–23, 129–31;
Acts and, 2–3, 8, 10–11, 14, 52–54,
63–68. *See also* Jewishness,
narrative construction of;
proselytes
Jewishness, narrative construction of,
17–19, 23, 28–30, 37, 41, 97–98, 106,
124–25
Josephus, 44, 46–48, 53, 61, 63, 85–86,
143n11, 144n17, 158n60, 170n77,
177n29
Judean, translation of 12–14, 66, 151n95
Justin Martyr, 13, 40, 140n63, 140–41n64,
150n81

Kouretes, 73–74, 98–100, 102–3, 106, 108,
113, 164n22

Lystra, 83, 97, 104, 107, 109, 111–13, 127,
173n2

Marcion, 20, 29–30, 150n76

Ortygia, grove of, 73, 98–101, 102–3,
174n6

Philippi, 36, 104, 113, 127
Philo of Alexandria, 44–49, 52–53,
63–66
population lists, 42–44, 47, 68; as
collection, 41–42, 46, 49–53, 58–62;
contested population, 42, 71–72, 94,
108, 112

Index of Modern Authors

Index of Ancient Sources